THE WHITE MAN'S PEACE

AN ORIENTAL VIEW OF OUR ATTEMPS AT MAKING WORLD PEACE

By NO-YONG PARK, PH.D. (Harvard)

Author of *Retreat of the West, An Oriental View of American Civilization, Making a New China, Chinaman's Chance: An Autobiography,* etc.

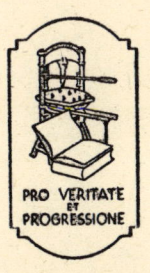

Foreword by Arthur N. Holcombe,
Professor of Government, Harvard University

BOSTON
MEADOR PUBLISHING COMPANY
PUBLISHERS

Copyright 1948, by No-Yong Park

172.4
P219w

Mar. 4, 1949
Gift

Printed in the United States of America

Dedicated
To the Success of the UN

FOREWORD

It gives me a distinct pleasure to introduce to the American public a timely volume on a vital subject written by Dr. No-Yong Park, one of my former students at Harvard University.

Born and reared in Manchuria, he came to the United States for the purpose of acquiring a Western education. He was graduated from the University of Minnesota in 1927 and did his post-graduate work at Harvard, where he received the degrees of A.M. and Ph.D. He specialized in the field of international relations, and wrote his doctoral dissertation on *China and the League of Nations*. Following his graduation from Harvard in 1932, he lectured on Far Eastern international relations at the New School of Social Research, New York; The Western Reserve University; the University of Minnesota, and the University of Kansas City. For the past six years he has been engaged by the Northeast Missouri State Teachers College in developing a new college course on How to Teach World Peace. At present he is a visiting professor of Far Eastern affairs at the University of Kentucky and a special lecturer on Asiatic problems at the Institutes of International Understanding under the auspices of Rotary International.

In his *An Oriental View of American Civilization* and his interesting autobiography entitled *Chinaman's Chance*, the author gave his views on Western civilization in general. In his *Retreat of the West*, he reviewed the policies and the practices of the Occidental nations in Eastern Asia. In his latest book, *The White Man's Peace*, he discusses the attempts of the Western powers to make peace in Asia and the rest of the world.

The White Man's Peace is provocative and stimulating as well as intensely interesting. He discusses this serious subject in such a delightful way that the reader will not want to stop until he has finished reading the entire volume. I hope that this challenging book will strengthen American determination to build a lasting peace on earth.

Arthur N. Holcombe,
Professor of Government

Harvard University,
Cambridge, Mass.

PREFACE

The White Man's Peace is an Eastern appraisal of the Western attempt to create peace, freedom, and democracy. It analyzes and evaluates the rôle played by the Western nations, past and present, in the making of world peace and inquiries into the question whether the great Western powers can create a perpetual peace.

The first part is devoted to the white man's contribution to the making of peace among the primitive peoples. The second part is given to his attempts at banishing war among the civilized men in general. The third part deals with his efforts of making peace among the Asiatics in particular.

I wish to express my appreciation to the students and faculty of the Northeast Missouri State Teachers College for all their encouragement given me during the past six years when I was engaged in developing a college study course on world peace, to my knowledge the first of its kind. I also acknowledge my indebtedness to the members of the faculty of the University of Chicago for their kindness in making many valuable suggestions in my experimental teaching as well as in preparing this volume. I likewise wish to thank Rotary International for helping me in presenting some of the ideas and materials contained in this volume through their Institutes of International Understanding held in various countries. Finally, I wish to express my gratitude to the editors of *Asia and the Americas, Current History,* and *The Journal of the National Education Association* for their permission to reprint my articles which appeared in their magazines.

No-Yong Park

University of Kentucky
June, 1947

CONTENTS

FOREWORD vii
PREFACE ix
INTRODUCTION 1

PART ONE
THE MAKING OF PEACE AMONG PRIMITIVE MEN

I. THE MAKING OF PEACE BY THE
   PRIMITIVE MEN 11
II. THE MAKING OF PEACE BY WHITE MAN   20

PART TWO
THE MAKING OF PEACE AMONG CIVILIZED MEN

III. THE TREND OF WAR AND PEACE
     AMONG CIVILIZED MEN 31
IV. THE ANATOMY OF WAR AND PEACE 44
V. THE EARLY WESTERN CONTRIBUTION
   TO PEACE 53
   1. Peace through Regulating War 53
   2. Peace through Pacifism 57
   3. Peace through Disarmament 69
   4. Peace through Gentlemen's
      Agreements 72
   5. Peace through Universal Religion 74
   6. Peace through Universal Education 80
   7. Peace through Economic Reforms
      and Communism 84
   8. Peace through Democracy 92
   9. Peace through Conquest and Domination 96
   10. Peace through the Balance of Power 103

CONTENTS

       11. Peace through the Spheres of Influence   106
       12. Peace through Isolation, Neutrality
           and Preparedness 108
       13. Peace through the Oriental way 109

VI.   THE FIRST STEP TOWARD WORLD PEACE   114

VII. THE GREAT EXPERIMENT 124

       1. Prelude to the Great Experiment 124
       2. The Great Experiment 127
       3. The Collapse of the Experiment 136
          A. The Alleged Cause of its Collapse .. 136
          B. The Retrial of the Alleged
             Saboteurs of Peace 143
          C. The Final Verdict on the Collapse
             of the League 152

VIII. THE PROPOSED ROAD TO ETERNAL
      PEACE 157

       1. The Promise of the United Nations 157
       2. The Future of the UN World Peace 164

PART THREE
THE MAKING OF PEACE IN ASIA

IX.   AMERICA AND RUSSIA IN ASIA 183

X.   THE REMAKING OF MODERN JAPAN 194

XI.   SOVIET-AMERICAN RIVALRY IN KOREA   201

XII. THE MAKING OF UNITED CHINA 213

XIII. THE FUTURE OF THE WHITE
      MAN'S BURDEN 230

XIV. A SOLUTION FOR ASIA 240

INTRODUCTION

The methods and principles applied in *The White Man's Peace* are radically different from the traditional methods and principles of examining international relations. The assumptions and conclusions of this thesis likewise challenge the soundness of the popular ideas and notions entertained by many Occidental and Oriental students of history and international relations.

The new thesis expounded in this volume contradicts the common notion that wars are created by imperialism, militarism, nationalism, patriotism and sovereignty; it repudiates the contention that conflicts are caused by economic, psychological, cultural, moral and religious forces, or by human nature and man's struggle for wealth, power, glory, honor and the like.

It scoffs at the whole contention that a lasting peace among nations can be created only through the changing of human nature, through disarmament, pacifism, education, religion, economic reforms and moral and spiritual regeneration, or through the frontal attacks on imperialism, militarism, nationalism, patriotism and sovereignty. It debunks all the loose talk that humanity cannot be organized for peace until all men will have learned to live like brothers, or until all nations will have abandoned power politics and laid down their arms, or until a uniform brand of creeds or ideas, be it communism, socialism, democracy or dictatorship, prevails throughout the entire world.

The so-called causes of wars which have been accepted as such by most scholars are treated in this volume as the products of wars instead of being fundamental causes of conflict. The traditional ideas of combating war and of creating peace among nations have also been turned around completely in this treatise. For example, instead of holding that there can be no peace until men change their militant nature, cultures and institutions, it maintains that men cannot, and will not, change any of these until the world is organized for peace and security. Instead of contending that there can be no peace until the nations beat their swords into ploughshares, or until they learn to live with their neighbors like brothers, it maintains that they will not beat their swords into ploughshares until peace on earth is established; nor will they live like brothers until society is so organized as to enable them to do so. Instead of holding that war cannot be banished until the nations abandon their power politics and their ideas of conquest and domination, it contends that the nations cannot, and will not, abandon these policies until the establishment of a new world order in which these policies are no longer necessary for their survival. Instead of holding that no peace can be created until the economic problems of the world are solved, it maintains that no economic problems can be solved satisfactorily without organizing the world for peace and security. Contrary to the popular contention that no permanent peace is possible until all states are converted into democracies, this thesis maintains that no true democracy can prevail over dictatorships without creating a peaceful political climate favorable for the growth of democratic ideals. These and many other conclusions which upset the old views are based on several important basic assumptions.

One of the basic assumptions of this thesis is that all warlike cultures and ideas like militarism, nationalism, imperialism, Nazism, Fascism and Shintoism and all militant institutions like those of Hitler's Germany, Tojo's Japan and other similar empires are the products of international anarchy in which few peoples can survive without developing militant cultures and institutions.

What it maintains is that the character of men, cultures, and institutions are determined by the international political atmosphere in the same way that the kinds of plants in various areas are determined by climatic conditions. For example, the modern white man has developed a very militant and materialistic civilization whereas the old Chinese created a peaceful "spiritual" civilization which worshipped scholars instead of warriors because the white man has suffered, thanks to his

INTRODUCTION

balance of power system, the state of international anarchy longer than the old Chinese who enjoyed a prolonged period of comparative peace and security brought about through the unification of their warring states under a central political authority.

It is not difficult to understand how order and disorder in a given society affect the cultural patterns of the people, if we know what men would do in case all organized authority should collapse and all of them should become the defenders of their own persons and their own homes. They would then not spend their time and energy in beautifying their homes, in painting their walls, or in planting flowers in their gardens. On the contrary, they would waste their energies and resources in erecting impenetrable walls and in manufacturing the strongest armor and the most powerful shotguns, for the failure to do so would mean their defeat and annihilation.

The second main contention of this volume, therefore, is that the state of anarchy, intertribal or international, is the sole cause of war—the ultimate breeder of all warlike cultures and institutions. Proceeding from this point, it further maintains that world peace cannot be created by merely attempting to destroy or remove these warlike cultures and institutions, be they Eastern or Western. For such attempts to create peace are very much like trying to combat mosquitoes without draining the swamps. As the swatting of several individual mosquitoes will not improve the health situation, so the removal of Hitler or Tojo, or the destruction of the German and Japanese empires, or the dissolution of the British, French and Russian empires will not make the world one whit the better, unless the state of international anarchy is totally banished through the creation of an effective world authority. In other words, since all warlike cultures and civilizations, Eastern or Western, have planted their roots in the state of chaos, the only sound way to lasting peace is through the creation of a world organization to preserve justice among nations so that no nation will be forced to develop militant cultures and civilizations for the sake of survival.

The third main contention is that civilized men can, and

probably will, succeed in constructing a peaceful world order despite their cultural differences and national and racial antipathies because, thanks to the white man's scientific contribution, the world has grown so small and warfare has become so destructive that no nation can survive in peace and security without a universal authority to preserve justice among nations.

Many Oriental students of human relations do not think that the human race can ever unite for peace under the leadership and domination of the militant white men who have waged more wars than any other race in modern history. It is a fact that the Western nations have cursed mankind with their fratricidal wars more than any other race. It is also a fact that their present policies of conquest and domination constitute a great threat, not only to world peace, but also to the very survival of the entire human race. Nevertheless, one cannot deny that the white men, with their modern science and their genius and ability to organize, have made a great contribution toward the building of world peace. As shall be pointed out presently, they have already banished most of the ferocious warfare among the primitive peoples. They might surprise the entire world one of these days by eradicating not only their own eternal "Christian" wars, but also the "pagan" wars, which have tortured mankind from time immemorial.

The fourth contention of this book is that the United Nations Organization which is largely a product of Western statesmen, points in the right direction toward world peace under an organized authority based on law. Contrary to the opinions of Emery Reves, author of *The Anatomy of Peace,* and the hasty conclusions of the signers of the Dublin Declaration, the UN is not foredoomed to failure: The success or failure of the new organization, like that of all other institutions of men, will depend, not so much on a perfect instrument of co-operation, as on the degree of willingness with which men will co-operate for the attainment of their objectives. And the degree of willingness to co-operate will depend, not so much on cultural or racial similarities, as on the growth of men's understanding or conviction that their welfare and their very survival depend on mutual co-operation for their common destiny.

INTRODUCTION

If the civilized nations of the world, especially the powerful Western nations, still believe that they can find peace and prosperity through military might, power politics or geographical advantages, they will not have an earnest desire to co-operate for their common security and, therefore, even if they should start with a perfect government of an indissoluble union, they will not succeed. On the other hand, if they have learned at heart that no nation, however powerful and fortunate, can survive free and independent in a world of anarchy without a universal authority to preserve justice among nations, then they will have an unconquerable will to work together and, therefore, they will probably succeed even if they start with a poor, imperfect instrument of peace like the UN.

Where the question of survival is at stake, even the nonhuman animals learn to develop a sort of animal order, animal culture and civilization. Therefore, if civilized men understand the survival value of this international organization, nothing will prevent them from making it a success. If this assumption is sound, one can say without irony that the white man's greatest contribution to world peace is his atomic bomb, for it has taught men the value of mutual co-operation better than a million years of schooling will.

It is a fact that the associations of sovereign states, like all other forms of political institutions, have not always been a success, but on some occasions they have. For instance, the Boeotian League of ancient Greece, the Iroquois League of the five Indian nations and the confederation of the Swiss cantons survived from three to six centuries. The present day British Commonwealth of Nations, though more loosely organized than any confederation known in history, has successfully survived all kinds of staggering crises, including two of the greatest world wars in history. It is, therefore, an inexcusable distortion of historical facts to contend that all associations of sovereign political units have failed and therefore the UN is foredoomed to failure.

The fifth main contention is that if the nations of the world should fail to unite by voluntary co-operation through the UN, or a similar world organization, they will be forced to unite under a universal authority by war and conquest, not in the distant future, but probably in our times, before the end of this century.

A close look at the histories of nations shows that in all ages and in all regions where the people were either too stupid and shortsighted, or too obsessed with hatred and jealously to work together for their common destiny, they were forced to unite by war, provided that there were no insurmountable geographical barriers which could prevent them from attacking one another. The main reason for it was that when hostile groups were settled within a striking distance from one another, no people could feel safe, because there was nothing that could protect them against each other. So they all sought to conquer or annihilate their neighbors who were not within their own cooperative circle. As a result, one state after another was conquered or absorbed by more powerful ones, and thousands of states which at one time covered the earth like the stars in heaven were reduced to sixty-odd countries. These in turn are now divided into two rival spheres between two great Western power blocs: Russia on the one hand and Great Britain and the United States on the other. Unfortunately for all mankind, both spheres remain within striking distance from one another without any insurmountable barriers which can protect them from each other. Therefore, neither side can feel safe from the other until both are united under one authority. If peaceful means should fail to unite them, nothing will prevent them from seeking to achieve their objectives by war and conquest. And in this age of science it should not be any more difficult to unite the world by force than it was for the Romans to conquer the Mediterranean rimlands.

Looking back through the centuries of history, men have travelled a long way from the jungles of intertribal warfare toward the promised land of universal peace. They have overcome countless obstacles in their struggle for peace and security. Now they stand before the very last obstacle to world peace—the gulf between the Soviet Union and the United States of

INTRODUCTION

America. As soon as they cross that gulf, they will find the promised land of universal peace which men have dreamed of and prayed for from time immemorial.

With the promised land of peace in sight, and with the mortal fear of total destruction in atomic warfare haunting them like an endless nightmare, civilized men will not, and cannot, give up their fight for a united world of universal peace. They may build a golden bridge of peace, like the UN, and cross it, arm in arm, like brothers of common fate. Or, they will fly over it in bombing planes, or sail across on battleships. By whatever means and whatever the cost, they will, and must, cross it, sooner or later. In the hope that they will bridge the gulf without unnecessary bloodshed, I have presented in this volume a brief account of the valuable experiences in making peace by various nations and races, especially the white race.

PART ONE

THE MAKING OF PEACE AMONG PRIMITIVE MEN

Chapter 1

THE MAKING OF PEACE BY THE PRIMITIVE MEN

The savages, like us moderns, enjoyed internal peace with their in-group, but suffered external war with out-groups constantly. So the study of war and peace among the primitives, why they fought and how they gained peace, will enable us to see more clearly than ever how the civilized men can build lasting peace among nations.

Primitive man in the lowest stage of development was probably one of the most helpless among the animals. So he soon found out that he could not survive without co-operation with his fellowmen for mutual aid against other powerful animals and harsh nature. As a result, he probably began the struggle for survival through mutual co-operation when he was not very different from other animals, many of which have learned the advantages of mutual aid. Once the process began, the circles of co-operation and mutual aid grew bigger and bigger until some of them became formidable states with well-trained standing armies. The Zulu kingdom, the Peruvian kingdom, the kingdoms of Benin, of Dahomey and of the Aztecs were some of the great military states created by the primitives through war and conquest, states which were not very different from the modern military states. But most primitive men have never gone beyond the tribal stage of development.

Within their tribal limits, they had a government, however rudimentary, to serve as an instrument of co-operation for the maintenance of tribal welfare; they had tribal customs and laws, defining rights and wrongs, providing for the punishment of thieves, robbers, murderers, and reward for the good, brave, courageous and unselfish. All members of the tribe learned to behave, or were induced or forced to behave, like decent human beings, helping one another like brothers, sharing with one another both happiness and sorrow. As a result, the primitive peoples enjoyed a high degree of law and order, moral integrity and mutual aid and co-operation seldom found even among civilized men.

Among some tribes, for instance, the practice of mutual aid was carried out so far that when there was scarcity of food, the old people committed suicide so that the young might live.

P. Kolben states in *The Present State of the Cape of Good Hope,* that back in the eighteenth century the Hottentots knew nothing of the corrupt and faithless arts of Europe. They were strictly honest and their word was sacred. They showed nothing but kindness and good will to one another. Their integrity, their chastity and their strictness in the exercise of justice were things in which they excelled all or most other nations in the world. Mrs. Helen Hunt Jackson, author of *A Century of Dishonor,* tells the story of how a costly volume of the Holy Bible, studded with jewels, remained in a Greek Church in Alaska for seventy years without any guard when the territory was Indian. The day after it became American, the Bible was stolen! Elbridge S. Brooks explains in *The Story of the American Indian* that theft, dissimulation, cowardice and drunkenness were unknown among the Indian tribes before the coming of the white men.

Most primitive men were much more law-abiding within the tribal limits than the civilized men in their own communities. Prince Kropotkin quotes in his *Mutual Aid* the report of a missionary to the effect that among 1,800 Aleuts not a single common law offense was known in forty years and that among another group of Aleuts composed of 60,000 people there was only one murder in one hundred years.

Perhaps one of the most striking examples of blind obedience to tribal law and custom was cited by **Gerland and Waitz** in *Anthropologies.* The story is that of a young woman who was to be immolated in her husband's grave, according to her tribal custom. On the day before the funeral ceremony the young widow was rescued by a missionary and taken to an island and placed under the care of the church. She escaped in the dark of the night, swam across a broad sea-arm, and rejoined her tribe to be buried alive in her husband's grave!

Because of the fact that all the members of the primitive community lived under their tribal authority, observing their tribal customs and mores and acted like honest, decent and law-abiding human beings, peace and order naturally prevailed within their tribal limits. Where several tribes formed a federation, peace and order likewise prevailed within the federal limits. But beyond that there was no peace, no order, no security, nothing but eternal chaos. The reason for this is very simple: most organized authority and social regulations stopped on the border, and in the realm of intertribal or interfederal affairs there was no government, no authority, no effective organization to preserve peace and justice among the several tribes or federations. Since there was no authority which could decree what was good and what was bad, there were no laws, no rules, defining what was right and what was wrong. Since there were no rules and no law, there were no ethics and no morals. Since there were no ethics and morals, men could cheat, steal, rob, and murder, not only without shame, but with much pride. No one expects that there could be peace in a world of robbers and murderers, who recognize no authority except their might, who respect no law except that of force. Eternal war was the logical result of a world without an authority to serve as a guardian of justice and peace.

Living in a world of anarchy and chaos, the primitive men, like the civilized beings, were forced to develop all sorts of warlike ideas and institutions for the sake of survival. For the purpose of fortifying the contention that all warlike men and cultures are born of anarchy, intertribal or international, I shall state briefly how the savages came to develop their militant social, political, moral and religious ideas and institutions.

The primitives who settled in comparatively isolated regions where they did not encounter the necessity of warring ceaselessly had very little or no government in time of peace. What little government they had was a rudimentary form of democracy. But those who were obliged to fight constantly had compact and well-organized governments. Even those who enjoyed primitive democracy, with little or no government, set up in time of war a temporary dictatorship under a chosen war chief, as have modern democracies. These interesting facts seem to support the thesis that warlike governments, primitive or modern, were born of the state of chaos.

The same is true of militant religion. Living in a world of strife and turmoil, the primitive men as well as the ancient peoples conceived of God as a god of war who was believed to be mighty in battle. For the gods, states A. E. Haydon, professor of religion at the University of Chicago and author of *Biography of the Gods,* were born according to the needs and aspirations of the people. To the pastoral people, he was a shepherd. To the farmer, he was the giver of rain and good harvest. So to the savages who suffered endless wars, God was a warrior who could smite the foe and bring victories. Even Jehovah was originally conceived of as a god of war and has often been regarded as such till this day when the children of God can sing without embarrassment "Praise the Lord and Pass the Ammunition." Thus we see all the militant religious cults, either primitive or modern, were likewise born of the state of anarchy and chaos.

Living like little frogs in a deep, impenetrable well, the savages came to identify themselves as a chosen people, a sort of salt of the earth and a flower of the human race, and to regard others as beasts of prey, enemies of mankind, who were to be killed and eaten without mercy and concern.

Davie gives a long list of tribal names in *The Evolution of War.* It is interesting to note that most of the tribal names meant man, people, brave warrior and the like, implying that other tribes were not human beings. The word Bantu means men. The Hottentots call themselves "men of men," and the Indian tribal names Illinois and Delaware mean men and original and principal men respectively. The word Inuit, applied by the Eskimos to themselves, means man or people. Incidentally, the Eskimos believed that God's first creation, the white man, was a failure, and that his best creation was the Eskimo.

However abnoxious they may sound, such ideas of superiority, tribal or racial, are an indispensable asset for survival in the state of anarchy because, if you do not believe that your own people and your own ideas and cultures are superior to those of others, you will not fight for your own group. If you do not stand up for your own, you will not survive the impact of external attack.

Right or wrong, the savages laid the foundations of the modern racial theory of superiority, the theory which was believed as a gospel truth by all peoples from the ancient Hebrews, Greeks and Chinese down to the present-day Germans and Japanese.

Living in the state of anarchy, the primitives measured all human values in terms of military prowess. It was necessary for them to do so for the simple reason that in the state of anarchy only the strongest can survive. The most honorable man was the bravest and strongest one whom the savages made their chief during his life and their god after his death. The most popular figures who were sought by women and girls, as are the football and movie stars in our society, were those who possessed the largest number of skulls. In Dutch New Guinea, as in many other places, no youth was considered an adult until he had taken a head, and no girl would have him for her husband. Heads and skulls were considered so valuable that they were used as bridal gifts, so that the fiancees of the head-hunters could wear or display them, as our modern co-eds do fraternity pins.

As bravery and physical strength were regarded the highest virtues, the primitives did almost everything to show these virtues. One celebrated Fijian chief erected with pride nine hundred commemorating stones around his house, boasting that he had eaten that many men. What a relief that he is now dead!

In the art museum of Santa Fe, New Mexico, there is hung a picture of a Crow Indian chief by J. H. Sharp. It shows in a most vivid color how, following the death of his beloved son, the chief cut off the heads of his son's favored ponies, how he drove the buckskin thongs through their noses, and tied them on the skin of his mutilated back, which he cut up for that purpose, and then how he dragged the horses' heads uphill by the force of his lacerated skin still clinging to his bare and bleeding back—all for the purpose of proving that he was a brave man!

Bravery is such a great honor among the Ponape savages that they cut their arms and burn holes in their chests to prove that they are brave.

Among the savages of British Central Africa one mark of cowardice was the failure of men to dominate their wives. To prove their bravery, therefore, they must beat their wives without mercy. What a strange proof of bravery! According to their sense of values, we moderns are hopeless cowards!

The primitive social values, like those of our civilized society, had religious sanctification. The Tankhuls of Manipur, states Hodson, believe that the souls of courageous men were welcomed in the after-world but those of cowards were met with groans and jeers. The Hervey Islanders were of the belief that the souls of the cowards were caught in a net, then cooked and eaten by the nether-world inhabitants, whereas the spirits of the brave warriors would reside in their paradise where they were honored and glorified. Many American Indians, the Aztecs and the Peruvians believed that only war heroes went to the sun, the rest going to the underworld.

The Tupi-nambas of Brazil, according to Tylor, thought that only those who had eaten many enemies could ascend to the place of the blessed. The natives of Savage Island believed that the more crimes, be they murder, robbery or theft, they would perpetrate on their enemy, the better off they would be in the next world. The Fiji Islanders were taught that they could rejoin their worthy gods in the next world only by killing many people and destroying many villages, for their gods were the incarnations of atrocities known as the Adulterer, the Nocturnal Ravisher of Rich Women, the Quarreller, the Bully, the Murderer, etc.

However crude and vulgar, considering the circumstances in

which the primitives struggled for life and security, their sense of honor and glory was no more revolting than that of our moderns. It was probably as honorable and glorious for them to slay their enemies, chop their heads off, cure them in smoke and fasten them over the doorway of their cabins as a symbol of honor as for us civilized beings to wear or display flying crosses or Victoria Crosses. It was perhaps as glorious and honorable for them to build mounds, pagodas and pyramids of ears, noses and skulls as for us moderns to build monuments and parks commemorating victory over our enemies. It was perhaps as glorious and honorable for the savages to capture enemies, fatten them in a pen, bathe them and place them on the altar, slash open their breasts, wring their still beating hearts and offer them to their gods as for the inquisitors to burn the heretics at the stake, tear their tongues out by the roots, pull their horrified eyes out with sizzling red hot pokers, all in the name and to the honor of the ever-benevolent and merciful God. It was perhaps as honorable and glorious for the savages to attack their neighboring tribes, destroy their dwellings, slaughter their inhabitants, cut up their flesh and bones with oyster shells and boil or roast them and devour them in gusto, in the belief that they had created by magic or witchcraft some disease or misfortune, as for civilized men to rain deadly blockbusters on our neighbors, burn their cities, slaughter their men, women and children, all in the glorious name of national honor and prestige.

Because of these barbarous, egotistic, chauvinistic and militaristic ideas and cultures, together with their ignorance and stupidity, and fear and hatred for strange tribes, no ordinary methods of building peace could eradicate the age-old horrors of intertribal warfare. However, it is interesting to note here that the primitive men tried practically all the principles and methods of building peace which are known to civilized men. They introduced the spirit of chivalry and fairness into battles; they made the rules of declaring wars and executing them; they had the custom of respecting the rights of asylum and of neutrality; they had the rules outlawing the use of poisoned weapons; they practiced the method of settling disputes through arbitration, diplomacy, or single combats to avoid unnecessary bloodshed; they made treaties of peace and friendship with their neighboring tribes and promoted intertribal friendship through commerce, fraternal associations, intertribal marriages, religious fellowship and the making of blood brotherhood whereby men of different tribes could become brothers. Although primitive men observed these customs and regulations and treaties far more faithfully than civilized men, none of these measures succeeded in creating lasting peace among them.

The most effective methods of establishing intertribal peace tried by the primitive peoples was that of unification of several tribes either through the formation of federations, or by outright conquest. Because of their intense fear and hatred for other peoples, together with their ignorance and stupidity, not many primitive peoples were willing to form federations through voluntary co-operation. Forcible conquest, therefore, was about the only practical method of uniting the hostile tribes. There were, however, a few successful federations which were formed by peaceful means. The Iroquois League of the Five Nations was one of such federations, which left behind a more brilliant record than most other similar political combinations.

According to legend, Hiawatha, a sort of Woodrow Wilson of his day, conceived the idea of forming a league to preserve peace among the warring states. But his plan was opposed by Atotarho, a miniature Hitler of that time and a warlike chief of the powerful Onondagas. Consequently, Hiawatha, like Woodrow Wilson, failed to gain the support of his people. Defeated and rejected, he left his state in sorrow, never abandoning hope, however, for the fulfilment of his cherished dreams. He wandered about among other nations and gained their support for the cause of peace. But his own nation, the Onondagas, still refused to co-operate. At last the warlike chief Atotarho was promised that he would be made a leading chief and the Onondagas a dominant nation of the confederacy. That proposal finally won the support of Atotarho and the Onondagas.

The capital of the Onondagas was made the capital of the

confederacy. Atotarho was given the exclusive right to summon the meeting of the league's council. He was likewise given the power to veto any act of the council. But as all decisions required unanimity, the other chiefs likewise enjoyed the same veto power. The Onondagas were given the right to send fourteen delegates to the council, whereas other nations could not send more than ten each. But the vote of the Onondagas did not count for more than that of other nations, as each nation could cast only one vote. All these face-saving devices seem to indicate that the Indians were possessed of much sagacity and wisdom seldom exhibited by the statesmen of even our times.

What is worth recalling is that the man who has been glorified as an immortal hero through legend and fable is not Atotarho who sought after power and prestige, but Hiawatha, who loved peace so much as to place it above his personal or tribal honor and prestige.

The Iroquois League thus formed stopped feuds, banished internecine wars, and sent its emissaries to the neighboring tribes with the offer of peace and security, if they would join the league as younger brothers and would speak the Iroquois language. But most primitives, like our modern nations, refused to subordinate themselves to a higher authority. So the league conquered them and absorbed them by force. Largely through this method of conquest, the league extended its control over a wide area and preserved law and order within its sphere of control. At one time it had the possibility of uniting the whole continent. But like the Greeks of old, the Indians probably started federating themselves too late to survive the impact of external attack.

Chapter II

THE MAKING OF PEACE BY WHITE MAN

It is most interesting to note how the white men, who have failed to make peace with their own white brethren, succeeded in making peace among the countless savage tribes throughout the world. Let us see how they did it.

In the year 1492 the white man controlled only about nine per cent of the earth's land surface. By the end of the nineteenth century he controlled eighty-five per cent of the entire globe. From Greenland's icy mountain's to India's coral strands, everywhere he went, he carried with him his guns and gunpowder, his system of government backed by physical sanctions and his religion, science and commerce. With his guns and gunpowder he conquered the loosely organized peoples outright; with his system of government, he maintained peace and order; with his commerce, religion and science he impressed on the natives to welcome the blessings of western civilization. As a result, he has helped banish countless feuds and internecine wars among thousands of independent and separate tribes scattered in all continents.

Within the limits of the continental United States, not including Alaska, there were some 300 tribes, according to Helen Hunt Jackson, and their total population figured at 300,000 when the white man began his conquest of this new world. Although some of these tribes were peaceful, warfare among many of them was more than frequent. Today there are probably more Indians then ever before but we never hear of wars among them, except in the movies or in fiestas. Of course, some Indians have fought with the white man in Europe and have killed off some other white men, as most civilized white men have done. But they no longer scalp each other's heads or burn each other's villages. Peace and order prevail from ocean to

THE MAKING OF PEACE BY WHITE MAN 21

ocean except in some dark, spooky street corners of some semi-civilized cities where the crooks rule with the Republicans and the Democrats.

Until some 500 years ago the Empire of the Aztecs in Mexico slaughtered annually thousands of human beings to propitiate their evil gods. To secure the victims for human sacrifice numerous raids into the border tribes were undertaken and bloody battles were fought year after year. But after their arrival, the Spaniards stopped that barbaric practice through persuasion and coercion. When the natives failed to respond to the message of Christian love and charity, the Spanish authorities removed the chiefs who were responsible and replaced them with converted Christians. Had it not been for the white men, such cruel and inhuman practices, with all their accompanying wars and bloodshed, might still be in vogue in the land of romantic Mexico.

Following the Spanish-American War, Uncle Sam suddenly inherited some of the head-hunters in the Philippine Islands as a gift from old Spain. Professor Fay-Cooper Cole, of the University of Chicago, who had spent many years as an anthropologist among the head-hunters in northwestern Luzon, told me how the United States of America talked them out of seeking for those useless curios. The Americans first tried to understand them and then explained to them that head-hunting was an undesirable practice. They finally introduced some western games, such as baseball and tennis, through which the natives could release their combative instincts and their urge for glory and honor. But many tribes still persisted in carrying out their old custom and undertook head-hunting expeditions into the neighboring territories. The American forces, at last, attacked these tribes, burned their villages, executed or threatened to execute the ringleaders in the event of repeating the barbarous practice. At last head-hunting disappeared from that part of the world.

Another practice which often disturbed peace and order in some sections of the Philippine Islands was that of running amuck. A perfectly sane man, suddenly seized upon by spirits, ran through the villages, murdering everyone falling into his path. The datos of the tribes were asked to co-operate with the American authorities to stop that carnage. They explained that they could do nothing about it because it was the work of the "spirits" which were beyond their control. And so one day an American gunboat zigzagged around the bay and fired shells indiscriminately into the villages where running amuck occurred frequently. The datos immediately protested to the American authorities against that shelling. Whereupon the Americans replied that they were very sorry but that they could do nothing about it because one of their gunboats "ran amuck." After this incident, there was no more running amuck. Thus the resourceful Yankees stopped the age-old evil practices with their wits.

The American crusade against the savage warfare has not always met with success. On the Gulf of Davao, according to Professor Cole again, there were tribes which practiced human sacrifices, not very different from those of the Aztecs in Mexico. They captured neighboring tribesmen, killed them, and after offering them to their evil spirits, they ate the heart and liver to inherit courage, while wasting all other parts, including the head. They, however, decorated their costumes according to the number of enemies they captured.

After a long and painful attempt, most of the datos, or chiefs, were persuaded to substitute the animal sacrifice for the human sacrifice. But alas, nature had a hand in this crusade. More than half of the datos who had used pigs in place of human beings died, and a plague of locusts added misery to the region. All American cajolery, threat and persuasion failed to prevent the return of human sacrifices. Then came a large number of Japanese immigrants to Davao and pushed the natives farther and farther into the hills. The savages replied to this external pressure by killing off two thousand Japanese before the Philippine Islands were invaded in the Second World War.

Most primitive peoples regarded hunting, robbing and warring as the only honorable professions for man. When the white men came and outlawed the warring against one another, it created one of the biggest unemployment problems in the world. Dr. Letourneau relates that the chief grievance of the New

Caledonians against the French and their missionaries was the prohibition of tribal warfare. "Since we do not fight," they said, "we are no longer men." The New Zealanders, who looked to fighting as their sole occupation, with their women and children cultivating the fields, were no longer able to practice their warrior profession under the white man's domination. The primitive tribes of British East Africa had the added duty of guarding the women working in the field, when they were not in active warfare. Since Pax Brittanica abolished tribal wars, the warriors lost their jobs as guards or fighters. Such stories as these can easily be multiplied many fold from Africa to Australia.

But many students of anthropology maintain that instead of creating peace by making the primitives more peaceful, the white man has made the savages much more warlike than before by introducing to them deadly firearms and the militant Christian religion and by stirring up the hatred and resentment of the natives against his ruthless conquest and exploitation.

Clark Wissler, for instance, maintains in *The Influence of the Horses in the Development of Plains Culture* that the introduction of horses and firearms by the white man made the Indians much more warlike. The animals enabled the Indians to cover a great distance, and mobility and contact with other tribes often resulted in conflict, which was made more destructive by firearms. Davie, however, does not believe the introduction of firearms has had much effect on their warlike dispositions. For one thing, the firearms were so expensive that few tribes could afford them, and for another, most savages were unskilled in the use of modern weapons of destruction. In one case two hundred Congo savages fought thirty-two enemies for two and a half days with firearms. In that grand battle, only one man was struck on the ankle by a spent plug, which penetrated the flesh so slightly that it was removed with a pen-knife. But many savages, says Davie, liked firearms for the great deafening and terrifying noise they made!

The better view on this subject appears to be that the introduction of firearms made some savages more sanguinary, while making no apparent difference to some others.

Undoubtedly, some missionaries made some savages more warlike than before by spreading religious bigotry and intolerance. According to Elbridge Brooks, back in the seventeenth century the French "black robes" told the American Indians that the war between the English and the French was Christ's quarrel. The Saviour was a Frenchman and was murdered by the English. He rose from death and went to heaven to prepare the "Happy Hunting Grounds" for the French allies. And all those who wished to enter the Happy Hunting Grounds must fight for the French.

While many missionaries were free from propagating this kind of satanic messages, they often promoted religious intolerance for the simple reason that they believed in one God, that is the God the white men understood or misunderstood. Their appearances in most places, therefore, were followed by an unprecedented religious strife.

Furthermore, Felix M. Keesing points out in *The South Seas in the Modern World* that Christianity made some tribes in that area more warlike because it gave them the belief that a powerful Christian God was on their side of the battle.

If Christianity made some primitives more belligerent, it has probably made many others more peaceful. The idea that all men are the children of the same God has brought many primitives into a wholesome contact which has had a salutary effect on the preservation of peace. For instance, the various tribes in Nigeria were brought together for the first time in their history through a religious conference sponsored by the Christian missionaries. Similar stories are found in many other sections of the world where the messengers of Christ have blazed unbeaten trails to tell the love of God.

When all things are considered, it is not easy to jump into sweeping conclusions one way or the other. But the present verdict of history appears to be that, for a short period of time, the white man made most savages very much more sanguinary by breaking down their institutions and by stirring up their hatred and vengeance against his cold and cruel attacks. But in the end he has tamed or annihilated them and has established a reign of law and order in many of the open plains of the world where intertribal wars had raged for centuries.

Had the white men who explored and conquered the world been real Christian men of peace and love, the primitives might have been given the blessings of Western civilization without undue bloodshed and suffering. But unfortunately, most of the white adventurers of those days knew little or no Christian ways of meeting their fellow beings.

What St. Bernard said about the crusaders, who may be regarded as the forerunners of the white man's overseas invasion forces, may be a fitting description of the various hordes of European invaders who ultimately overran the entire world. St. Bernard spoke of the character of his followers who participated in the Second Crusade:

> "In that countless multitude you will find few except the utterly wicked and impious, the sacrilegious, homicides, and perjurers, whose departure is a double gain. Europe rejoices to lose them and Palestine to gain them; they are useful in both ways, in their absence from here and their presence there."

The first gift of the Old World to the New World was two shiploads of English convicts who were sent in 1494 to colonize the New World. The settlement of Australia was also initiated by the English convicts. The vanguard of the Russian invasion forces which captured all of Siberia were the notorious Cossacks and the Czarist convicts. Most of the white men who disturbed the tranquillity in the Pacific, and who stirred up trouble in the four corners of the world, were the unscrupulous fortune-hunters, beachcombers, convicts, pirates, and some honest and yet sadly mistaken religious bigots who went to spread the love of God without even understanding the meaning of that message. And there is little doubt that the scum of the white trash, arrogant, overbearing and contemptible, representing the base elements of Christian civilization, cheated, insulted, robbed and murdered these simple and yet unspoiled savages, the Indians, Negroes, Maoris and what not, so cruelly and so shamefully as to drive them into open revolt against the intrusion of the white man's civilization—rather barbarism.

Overwhelmed by the white tide which kept on coming with the power of the earth, some perished without any pretense of defense, but others mustered their power, the only one which they or the foreign invaders understood, the power of the sword. But in the contest of arms few could excel the white man with his superior guns and training. As a result, all were annihilated or conquered and were given the white man's peace.

It is a tragedy in history that peace had to come to the primitives in such a hard and bloody war. But the peoples who are too stupid and ignorant, or too much obsessed with hatred and jealousy to banish wars through voluntary co-operation perhaps do not deserve peace delivered to them on a silver platter free of charge. The price of peace the primitives paid was very high, but it was not as high as the cost of eternal war, which would probably have continued raging but for the white man's peace. So whatever sins and crimes he has committed against the helpless natives, one cannot deny that the white man, after all, has been a very capable peacemaker. The only wars which he has failed to prevent are those between him and his own brethren.

The final verdict on the white man's contribution to the maintenance of peace among the savages, however, cannot be written at this time. He has ruled these so-called backward peoples of the world for only two hundred years, more or less. The time is too short to give a conclusive judgment on his contribution.

Though some tribes were totally annihilated by the white men, the surviving tribes are reported to number more than a thousand, and their combined population probably constitutes about five per cent of the world's two billion human beings. Instead of dying out, many of these primitive peoples are growing in number under the white man's reign of law and order, sanitation and better livelihood. No one can tell what these peoples will be like in the years to come. If they continue to receive Western influence, they too may learn to wage bigger and better "Christian" wars and cease altogether to be savages who used to wage only smaller and less destructive wars.

For the better or worse, the warfare among the primitives has been arrested for the present. Now let us see what the white men will do with the modern wars which are largely their own private wars fought in the four corners of the earth. Will they, or can they, banish their fratricidal wars? By what means will they banish them, by peaceful means or with the atomic bombs? But before taking up these questions, let us see first what the modern trend of war and peace is, what the nature of the white man's understanding of war and peace is, and by what means they have attempted to cure war and to create peace.

PART TWO

THE MAKING OF PEACE AMONG CIVILIZED MEN

Chapter III

THE TREND OF WAR AND PEACE AMONG CIVILIZED MEN

The study of the primitive men shows that the warlikeness of the savage tribes increased rather than decreased with the progress of civilization. The most primitive primary groups, living under a clan or family, were the most peaceful; the secondary groups, living in village communities, were the next most peaceful; the tertiary groups, living under tribal units composed of several villages, were more warlike than the primary or secondary groups; the quaternary groups which formed federations of tribes were the most warlike.

The progressive growth of warlikeness among the savages was due to the fact that in the state of anarchy only the most skilled in war could survive against their hostile neighbors and, therefore, all strove to excel others in warlikeness.

Is the trend of war among the civilized men the same as it was among the savages? Are we civilized men growing more warlike or more peaceful? Is our boasted civilization growing more militant or more pacific?

Some students of history inform us that there have been only 268 years of peace out of the 3,521 years of recorded history of the world, or about eight peace years out of every hundred. Assuming that this statement is partly correct, is the ratio between the peace and war years growing more or less discrepant than before?

That noted Yale anthropologist, the late Dr. Bronislaw Malinowski, stated that the cave men crouched in rock shelters in prehistoric times while the modern city dwellers crouch in caves of steel and concrete, and the "progress" of civilization, therefore, has apparently led men from one cave to another.

Quincy Wright points out in his *A Study of War* that civilizations grew more warlike as they progressed. The primary civilizations—the Egyptian, Mesopotamian, Minoan, Indian, and Mayan—were more peaceful than their immediate offspring, the secondary civilizations—Babylonic, Syriac, Classic, Hindu and Mexican. The tertiary civilizations—the Western, Arabian, Iranian and Russian, all of which sprang from the secondary civilizations—were most warlike.

Professor Pitirim A. Sorokin, of Harvard University, presents in his *Social and Cultural Dynamics* a war index for Europe, showing the progressive growth of militancy in that continent. After comparing by centuries the number of major wars, the duration of conflicts, the size of the fighting forces, the number of casualties, the number of participating countries, and the proportion of combatants to the total population, he has arrived at the conclusion that the intensity of war has steadily increased in the past nine centuries, as shown in the following index:

12th	13th	14th	15th	16th	17th	18th	19th	20th
18	24	60	100	180	500	370	120	3080

A closer examination of major European wars reveals, according to Wright, the following general trends: the number of major wars has decreased in the past four hundred years, but the number of battles has sharply increased from 106 in the sixteenth century to 882 in the first forty years of this century. The length of the wars has been reduced from 4.4 years between 1450 and 1930 to 2.6 years in the first forty years of this century, but the number of the participating nations has increased from 2.4 in the sixteenth century to 5.6 in this century. Thirty-three nations participated in the First World War, but practically every country under the sun took part in the last war.

In the sixteenth and seventeenth centuries the major European states were "formally" at recognized war, excluding the revolutions, insurrections, interventions, and expeditions, sixty-five per cent of the time, and now eighteen per cent. But as the modern wars take more time to prepare, the decrease of the actual fighting time does not indicate the decrease of militancy.

THE TREND OF WAR AND PEACE AMONG CIVILIZED MEN   33

The percentage of casualties resulting from combat and disease has dropped sharply, but as the number of combatants became larger, the total casualties grew much bigger. The First World War alone accounted for ten million direct casualties and thirty million indirect.

The size of the combat forces increased, not only in number but in proportion to population. Rome had three soldiers for every thousand inhabitants, but France in 1937 had nineteen soldiers for every thousand.

At the dawn of our civilization the size of the army was limited by the size of the states, most of which were small. Besides, free men in ancient Greece and Rome who were subject to military duties constituted only twenty-five per cent of the total population, the other seventy-five per cent being slaves. The armies of Alexander, therefore, rarely exceeded 30,000 men. The reports that Xerxes invaded Greece with 1,700,000 men and Attila massed one million men against Rome were probably exaggerated out of proportion.

The size of the medieval European army was likewise limited by several factors. First, the medieval suit of armor cost a whole year's rent of a farm, and this exorbitant cost of armor limited the number of participating men. Second, the feudal lords could order their vassals to fight for them, and the vassals were bound by their oaths of allegiance to fight for their lords only forty days a year and beyond that their services must be paid for by their lords. The lords could not raise money to pay for wars because the custom forbade the taxing of the people beyond ordinary expenses. They could not borrow, either, because the Church forbade interest on loans made for unproductive purposes, such as fighting. The biggest army medieval Europe recruited was that of the First Crusade, numbering some 300,000 men. The Battle of Hastings, which ended in the Norman conquest of England, was fought by some seven thousand Normans against about an equal number of Anglo-Saxons. The famous Hussite armies of fifteenth century Europe rarely numbered more than five thousand men. The American army at Bunker Hill numbered sixteen thousand men, and the first American peace-time standing army consisted of eighty men.

But since the beginning of modern history, the armies have been composed of millions of men. Napoleon was said to have had about a million men under arms. In the First World War well over 66,000,000 men were mobilized, and in the Second World War, probably twice more than that number were mobilized.

The destructiveness of modern wars has grown many times greater than the size of the fighting forces. This is due to the fact that science can multiply its destructiveness, or constructiveness, many times faster than human beings can multiply cannon fodder.

Arthur H. Compton tells us that an aircraft carrier the size of the *Lexington* produces power equivalent to that produced by all the able-bodied citizens of the United States in Thomas Jefferson's day. The engines of the *Queen Mary* generate as much power as eight million galley slaves could. In other words, a few hundred men armed with science can destroy in one day more than many millions can with bows and arrows in years.

One robot bomb was reported to have demolished four square blocks of London, damaging one hundred buildings of steel structure. A similar feat could not have been accomplished by an army of two billion men armed with David's slingshots that knocked down Goliath. The great San Francisco earthquake of 1906 was reported to have destroyed only four square miles of that city. But a single atomic bomb dropped at Hiroshima was reported to have obliterated more than four square miles of that city.

The amazing speed with which civilized men have developed the power of destruction surpasses the imaginations of all men. In the First World War all the bombs dropped on England did not exceed 300 tons. But in the last war one atomic bomb dropped on Japan is said to have equaled the destructive power of 20,000 tons of TNT, or 666 times as much as all of the bombs dropped on England in the First World War. At such a rate of development, it may not be long before men will discover an instrument which could destroy the whole earth.

The cost of war has closely trailed the sky-rocketing progress of destructive weapons. The annual tribute which the Athenian Empire collected from its allies, the tribute with which Athenian imperialism financed its domination of the Hellenic world, amounted to no more than five hundred talents, or about $600,000, not enough to build one super bomber. The cost of killing one man at Caesar's time was estimated at 75 cents; the cost of killing one in the Napoleonic War, $3,000; in the American Civil War, $5,000; in the First World War, $21,000; in the Second World War, $50,000 or more. The direct cost of the First World War to the United States was about $22,000,000,000, which is about equal to all the money appropriated by the American Congress from the first Continental Congress to the American entry in the First World War. The total cost of the First World War was put at $400,000,000,000; in the Second World War, the United States alone probably spent well over this amount, as she was spending at the rate of about $100,000,000,000, annually.

The sum is so vast that it staggers the imagination of the average man, who seldom carries more than a few dollars in his pocket. If a man had spent one dollar every minute since the birth of Christ, he would have spent about one billion dollars. And the so-called civilized nations of our times spent in four years of the First World War four hundred billion dollars in mutual slaughter. The sum could provide, according to *World Peaceways,* every family in the United States, Canada, Australia, Great Britain, Ireland, France, Belgium, Germany and Russia with a $2500 house, $1,000 worth of furniture, $500 worth of land. Every town of 20,000 inhabitants or over in all these countries could have been provided with a $5,000,000 library, a $10,000,000 endowed university. After all this, it could buy the whole of France and Belgium—that is, all the land, houses, factories, railways, churches, roads, harbors, et cetera.

Add to the foregoing staggering figures the indirect cost of war: the disease, hunger, poverty, economic breakdown, financial collapse, industrial paralysis, moral bankruptcy, social disintegration, and political chaos that inevitably has led to revolution, dictatorship, terrorism and bigger and better wars.

In spite of all the efforts to restrain the horrors of war, the cruelties, lawlessness and treachery, and all the barbarous and inhuman savagery of war have kept pace with the progress of the science of destruction.

We think it cruel and unjust when we look back and examine the flimsy pretexts under which the primitive and ancient peoples waged wars: how the savages attacked their neighbors with the charge that they had caused drought, flood or disease through witchcraft; how the imperialistic Athenians attacked the innocent Melians with a frank declaration of naked aggression in which they said: "We know that in the discussion of human affairs the question of justice enters only where there is equal power to enforce it, and that the powerful exact what they can, and the weak grant what they must . . . and we know that you and all mankind, if you were as strong as we are, would do as we do."

But nowadays the aggressors do not have to undergo all the trouble of explaining why they must wage wars. All they have to do is just to go out and murder their neighbors and then use, if necessary, the ready-made excuses in the name of self-defense, national honor and national interest. That is precisely what Hitler, Mussolini and Hirohito did in their attacks on their neighbors.

Until the very recent past, nations waged wars or carried out plunders according to certain rules of war. With a few exceptions, all of them gave their enemies due warning through the declaration of war. But the civilized nations of our times are too clever to do anything so foolish and stupid. When they want to attack their neighboring states, they profess their undying friendship for their would-be victims; they make treaties of peace, amity and mutual aid with them, and when their enemies fall asleep like babies on their laps they then stab them in the back without giving them the slightest chance of defense.

The prosecution of war itself was carried out in accordance with certain principles of decency and fairness until the very recent past. There were international laws and customs in ancient China, India and Greece; there were church regulations and chivalry in medieval Europe, all of which played an important part in reducing the horrors of warfare. Hugo Grotius published in the seventeenth century a formidable collection of the so-called rules of war and peace. Until a few years ago there was a good deal of talk on the subject of international law, its codification, administration and enforcement. I myself wasted many a good year in the study of it with George Grafton Wilson when I was at Harvard.

But our civilization has reached the stage where there is no room for such things as international law, chivalry, kindness and justice in warfare. You shoot down those drowning seamen like ducks and those pilots clinging to their parachutes like birds; machine-gun the civilians, demolish the hospitals, raze to the ground with pride the sacred objects of art and worship and reduce countless cities and towns to ashes in the name of military necessity. The only law of war recognized by all belligerents is the law to kill, destroy and exterminate.

At one time it was thought horrible for Hannibal's troops to throw upon their enemies poisonous snakes and beehives swarming with lively bees. But nowadays we civilized men throw upon our enemies blockbusters, robot bombs and atomic bombs, and demolish their homes, schools and hospitals without discrimination and blast countless men, women and children into shreds without even a feeling of shame or discomfort.

In 1911 Sir Arthur Conan Doyle wrote an article entitled "Danger! A Story of England's Peril," urging England to be prepared to meet the menace of enemy submarines which might starve the island to submission by cutting off its food supply. Admiral Fitzgerald of the British Navy declared in reply that he did not think it necessary to prepare for such an eventuality, as no civilized nation would torpedo unarmed, defenseless trading ships, carrying noncontrabands. Since then literally thousands of helpless merchant ships have been sunk beneath the blue seas. At one time the sinking of commercial ships like the *Lusitania* incensed the American people to cry for war. But in the Second World War it was such an ordinary daily occurrence that no one even wrinkled his eyebrows when reading about such atrocities.

When the Turks weaned away the healthiest Christian children from their parents, put them through years of training and indoctrination and used those Christian troops whom they called Jannissaries as vanguards of the Turkish Army and forced those boys to kill their own Christian brethren for the glory of the Turks, the whole Christian world rebelled against that revolting practice. Today we find an even more revolting practice than the use of Jannissaries in the so-called superior Nordic Nazis. Witness the use of the German boys who had been rescued and fed after the First World War by the Danes, Dutch, and Norwegians in the attack on these same people, who had rescued them from starvation and death!

We weep over the fate of Carthage which suffered seventeen days of merciless slaughter, during which all of its half million inhabitants were reduced to a ghastly mess of human debris, save 50,000 who were spared for Roman slavery. We mourn over the fall of Constantinople, where a handful of valiant Roman defenders held out against an overwhelming force of the Turks only to be slain and buried beneath the crumbling walls that had withstood the tide of Asiatic invasion for centuries, and where a naked crowd of pitiful Christians of both sexes and of all ages, of priests and monks, of matrons and virgins, was whipped and dragged into the public market and sold to the caprice of the Turks.

But from neither of these lands does injustice cry more loudly than from Nanking, Warsaw and hundreds of other cities which have endured years of hell-fire in this civilized world. Just think of the fate of those innocent and helpless Chinese who were butchered like sheep, and their towns and villages reduced to dust and ashes simply because they happened to live near the place where some of Doolittle's planes landed or crashed from their raid on Tokyo. Remember also the fate of hundreds of

THE TREND OF WAR AND PEACE AMONG CIVILIZED MEN

other towns and villages which met the same fate at the hands of the Japanese for the simple reason that they were situated near where guerrilla forces attacked the Japanese garrison. Consider, too, the lives of the millions and millions of unfortunate men, women and children who were driven to poverty, disease, hunger, starvation and death not only by their enemies but by their own troops who applied a scorched earth policy, destroying everything that might be of some value. When compared to the plight of our modern world, the tales of Carthage and Constantinople sound like kindergarten stories.

Whenever we hear of the Mongols we think of them as bloodthirsty savages and maniacs. They must have been, for they appear to have delighted in the gruesome practice of slaughtering all men, women and children indiscriminately. When they invaded China, they planned to exterminate all the Chinese, then numbering only 100,000,000, so that they could convert the cultivated farms into pastures to graze their horses. But Yelu Chu-Tsai, a descendant of Kitan, who had faithfully served the Mongols since his capture by them, persuaded Jenghiz Khan to spare them with the argument that their existence would enrich the Mongols. So the Chinese were not so much butchered as they were taxed. And yet an estimated 50,000,000 Chinese were reported to have perished under the scourge of the Mongols.

Today we scorn the Mongols as savages, but we revert to the practice of the Mongols, as our flying bombs and long range artillery make no more distinction between men and women, combatants and noncombatants, than did the Mongols. We kill them by the millions without mercy, without discrimination, only with the hypocrisy that we are more civilized.

We are indignant when we hear how Sapor, the Persian emperor, used the neck of the Roman Emperor Valerian as a footstool for mounting his horses. But we only laugh when we hear how a Kentucky rifleman skinned the famed Indian chief, Tecumseh, and made razor strops out of his skin, or when we read how the American soldiers made letter openers and other souvenirs out of the bones of the Japanese and sent them to their friends and even to President Roosevelt as a gift.

Our eyes burn with rage when we read how the Romans forced their gladiators to stab and kill each other off for their sheer amusement; how Emperor Tiberius delighted in watching the victims of his displeasure being hurled over a thousand-foot cliff to their death; how Caligula drove a whole line of prisoners to the arena and fed them to the beasts; how Nero burned Christians alive like living candles; how Charles II of Spain celebrated his marriage feast by burning in public and in the presence of his lovely bride the religious heretics, including children who were condemned for a religion which they had sucked in with their mothers' milk. But in our civilized age we burn not only the heretics and infidels but also the faithful Christian men, women and children; we stage gladiatorial combats all over the world, whereas the Romans had them only in their arena, and feed the vultures, not lions, with the flesh and blood of our beloved as well as those of our enemies.

Our hearts ache when we read how the Carthaginians sacrificed their children to the altar of their god. Bathed and clad as if they were to be sent to a Sunday school, the children were placed in the arms of a brazen image of Moloch, inside of which a furnace raged. They were then slowly slipped into the flames, one by one, while the crowd of worshippers, including their own parents, gathered around and applauded. But those children perhaps experienced nothing more cruel and inhuman than those of Leningrad under 515 days of German terror. When they were relieved from the siege, this was what the half-starved children of Russia looked like: they did not smile; they did not laugh. They cried when they saw trinkets such as earrings, because they were reminded of their parents who wore such things, and whom they had seen die of agony and exhaustion. When given good food, they did not eat but hoarded for later consumption. Consider, furthermore, the fate of millions of motherless and fatherless and homeless children from the Yellow Sea to the North Sea, who have seen and experienced the kind of horror and misery which no tongue can recount.

THE TREND OF WAR AND PEACE AMONG CIVILIZED MEN 41

Today we don't see much of Christianity in the act of the Crusaders who, after storming Jerusalem, enacted an orgy of bloody drama for weeks, massacring and burning alive all Jews and Mohammedans, numbering 70,000, then waded through the blood, and put their blood-stained hands together in prayer to the glory of the Merciful Saviour. Today we denounce, in harshest language, the cruel institution of the Inquisition which rounded up heretics with the aid of medieval Gestapo and burned them at the stake, cut off their flesh with oyster shells, put their eyes out with hot pokers or tore out their tongues by the roots. Today we are horrified to recall how the Aztecs of Mexico sacrificed annually some twenty thousand prisoners of war in a most revolting manner imaginable. The bodies of the victims were bent like a bow over a curved stone. Their breasts were slashed open with a knife of obsidian. Their beating hearts were torn out by dignified priests and were offered to their evil god. But all the barbarities and cruelties suffered by the victims of injustice in the past cannot surpass the horror and misery suffered by our civilized men, women and children at the cruel hands of the Nazi terrorists and Japanese militarists, who improved and executed cold, calculating scientific methods of torture and slaughter beyond the imagination of civilized men.

Tamerlane, that blood-curdling Mongol degenerate, built in the fourteenth century a repulsive skull pyramid with 70,000 skulls after storming Ispahan, Persia. During the seven bloody years of war between China and Japan in Korea in the sixteenth century, the Japanese invaders cut off some 30,000 pairs of ears and noses of the Chinese and Korean soldiers, carried them back to Japan as an evidence of their glorious exploit and built an "Ear Mound" which stands to this day in the ancient capital of Kyoto. But neither Tamerlane's Skull Pyramid nor Japan's Ear Mound reaches anywhere near Vernichtungslager, Hitler's extermination camp in Maidanek, Poland. According to the eyewitness description of Roman Karmen, a Soviet war correspondent, and numerous other correspondents from America and elsewhere, in the center of the camp there stands a gigantic crematorium with a daily burning capacity of 1,400 persons. The victims of Nazi terror from different parts of Europe were herded into groups of one hundred or more; they were led like sheep in the stockyards into the gas chamber where they were suffocated to death. The corpses then were dumped into a roaring furnace, heated to 1,500 degrees centigrade. The charred bones and ashes were pulverized, packed in large tin cans and shipped out to fertilize the fields. An estimated number of one and a half million men, women and children was reported to have been massacred in this manner. I wonder if it could be true? In the First World War I heard about a German corpse factory where the Germans extracted oil from the corpses and fried pancakes with it. It turned out to be only propaganda. I hope this one is, too, but if it is true, down all the caverns of hell to their last gulf, there could be found no more revolting monument than this.

Thus a brief survey of the trend of warfare since the dawn of history shows that men have grown progressively more cruel, militant and destructive. It appears that this tragic tendency in civilization is due to the simple fact that civilized men have been forced to struggle for survival in the state of international anarchy in which only the strongest in arms and the most skilled in the science of murder can survive.

G. Lowes Dickinson, author of *War, Its Nature, Cause and Cure,* points out why and how men have grown and will continue to grow in brutality, unless the present tendency toward more destructive war stops. If it is necessary to destroy an enemy, they reason, is it not better to stab him in the back and kill him cheaply and instantly, instead of causing an unnecessary and costly struggle by giving him advance warning? If it is permissible to kill the enemies when they were not wounded, why is it not permissible to kill them after they are wounded? If we do not kill them, our doctors and nurses must work for them and we must feed them with our scanty food! Why not burn them, drown them, or just starve them to death? As doctors and nurses cure wounded men to return to the fighting line, why spare them and their hospitals and the Red Cross?

Why not follow the example of some savages who killed all their enemies, including the babies, to prevent a possible revenge should they be allowed to grow up?

Another reason for the excessive growth of militancy and barbarism among modern men appears to be the lack of the moral and ethical values of life. Modern men have lost their ethics and morals based on the love of God and the fear of the devil, which induced men to be good and kind by holding out to them the promise of reward and the fear of torture. But they have not yet acquired the new ethics and new morals which are founded on the principles of the brotherhood of men and the community of interest in this inter-dependent world. As a result, civilized men live today in a vacuum, a transition period between the collapse of the old moral values and the establishment of new ones. Other things being equal, men's cruelties and ferocities will be likely to continue to grow until human beings acquire a new set of moral and ethical values, which cannot be done in a world of anarchy without an organized authority to decree rights and wrongs. Let us see then if civilized men, under the leadership of the Western nations, can create a new order in which they can survive without excelling others in war and barbarism.

Chapter IV

THE ANATOMY OF WAR AND PEACE

"Ah, peace, the blessed God's most beautiful, how long dost thou delay! I fear that old age will overwhelm me with burdens ere I see thee, graceful one, appearing with the beautiful dancing choruses and thy garlands in loving festal processions. Come to the city, August Queen, and drive from our dwellings the fearful tumult and strife which make merry with their sharpened steel."

Thus prayed Euripides of ancient Greece. But he died during the Peloponnesian War. Since then millions have offered similar prayers, only to perish in the arena of war. Should men always keep on dreaming for peace only to fall in the path of war?

As we have already examined, it was impossible for the savages to banish war. But it is not impossible for civilized men to swim literally in the river of peace and prosperity. Nevertheless, they have not yet found these on this side of the grave. One of the chief reasons for this appears to be the absence of a correct diagnosis of war. As disease cannot be cured without a correct diagnosis, so war cannot be eradicated without a correct understanding of its nature. Whether or not the white man can and will banish war and create peace will largely depend on his understanding of the nature of war and peace. So let us see if his understanding of the subject is sound.

Most savages believed that fighting was forced upon them by their quarrelsome gods, who demanded revenge on their enemies or flesh and blood for satisfying their hunger. Most wars, therefore, were waged in the name and for the sake of their gods. According to Robert H. Lowie, for example, of the seventy recorded battles among the Murngins of North Australia, sixty were fought for religious reasons and ten were over the kidnapping of women. Probably not all other tribes fought so much for their gods as the Murngins, but the important part which the spirits played in primitive warfare cannot be overexaggerated.

Many ancient peoples likewise believed that they were inspired by their gods to fight. For instance, the well-known Biblical story of the Tower of Babel is one evidence to show that men blamed their God for their own difficulties and troubles. The Greek legend definitely places the responsibility for starting the Trojan War on Zeus, who was believed to have started it for the purpose of solving the problem of over-population. As late as the fourteenth century, Legnano, a theologian, maintained that war was originated by God to chastise the devil. Even in our day, I think not a very small proportion of the world's population believes that wars have been brought about by God to punish the sinners. When you believe God is the creator of wars, there is very little that you can do about it except chanting and prayer, as many primitive savages have done.

Buddha, Lao-tse and a long list of religious mystics have blamed human nature, most specifically man's instincts, ambitions and desires for wealth, power and glory for all the evils of the world. Following this line of thought, many students of human relations have come to view man's drives for food, sex, honor, prestige, domination, adventure and the like as the chief causes of strife.

When you accept the theory that war springs from human nature, as many amateur students do, then one might as well give up all hope for peace and smile cynically when John Carter, who concluded in his *Man Is War* that the world will never escape the blight of war until man has ceased to be human, for man is war; he is war because he is born with instincts, impulses, desires and ambitions which cannot be eradicated so long as he remains human! Fortunately, however, few students of psychology today blame human nature for our failures.

Back in 1932 John M. Fletcher sent to some four hundred American psychologists this pertinent question: "Do you hold that there are present in human nature ineradicable instinctive factors that make war between nations inevitable?" Ninety-two per cent of the men answered "No" and only three per cent answered "Yes." Thus, practically all the psychologists seem to debunk the current idea that "man is born pugnacious; so long as children fight, peoples are bound to fight, and war is eternal."

Human nature is like water, which can be used in growing the meadows green, or in flooding a whole country district, causing untold damage in lives and property. As a matter of fact, all the sacred assets of any great civilization are the fruits of properly canalized expressions of man's instincts, emotions and desires, all the most horrible monstrocities in history are the works of the misguided and misdirected impulse of mischievous men.

It is true that man's apathy and indifference and his irredeemable selfishness are often blamed for the ills of the world. But neither of these seems incurable. Men have been taught to take precautionary measures against fire, flood, sickness and unemployment despite their apathy. They have been taught or forced to give countless billions of wealth and millions of lives in the name of national security, despite their selfishness.

Contrary to all popular notion, the reason why the world has no peace is not that men are selfish, but that they are not selfish enough—I mean in an enlightened way. Had the nations of the world been really selfish, they could have stopped Japanese aggression in Manchuria at the cost of a single battleship that went to the bottom of the ocean and could have saved in ten years, from 1931 to 1941, about $5,000,000,000,000 of the probable total cost of the last war. But they refused to do a thing to check the initial aggression and chose to fight a worldwide war, staking everything at their disposal. It is not their selfishness; no, it is their plain stupidity. If men were really selfish and did what was best for their self interest, they would have forgotten all their hatred and jealousy, their vain egotism and chauvinism, and would have formed a federation of all nations long ago. For by forming such a union, as did the thirteen American colonies, each and every one of the nations could have gained ten thousand times more than it would have sacrificed by joining such a union. Selfishness, therefore, is no insurmountable obstacle to universal peace.

As a corollary to the contention that human nature is the chief cause of war, some students of human affairs have maintained that what makes certain men, cultures and institutions more militant than others is food, climate, age and the like. For example, Colonel McHarrison, who was associated with the British Indian medical service, found that food is one of the chief factors which makes some peoples more belligerent than others. He came to this conclusion after making many interesting experiments with mice. He collected the food eaten by various British Indian tribes whose physical and mental make-ups were different from one another and fed mice on them. To his surprise, the mice showed in body and spirit the characteristics of the tribes whose food they ate. So interested was he by so absorbing an experiment as this that now he collected the food eaten by various nationals and made a similar experiment on the mice. Just as he expected, these mice showed in temperament and constitution the dominant characteristics of the race whose food they ate. For instance, those fed on the European diet grew big and fat and restless whereas those fed on Chinese diet grew small in size and gentle and passive in disposition.

Further proof that the difference in man's character and disposition may be due to diet has come from the fact that many Orientals who have been born and reared in the United States have lost their Asiatic characteristics and conform to those of the American people. Their limbs have grown tall and straight, their eyes deep and round and their nose bridges high and prominent when compared with those of their parents. They are likewise more energetic and restless than their Oriental brothers and sisters who were born and reared in the old country.

If food makes for war and peace, all you have to do is to

change the dietary habits of the people or just give them certain vitamin pills to make them either peaceful or warlike.

Ellsworth Huntington and his geographical school of political thought tell us that what makes men different and causes them to create different cultures is the influence of the climate. For example, both the Bahamans and the Canadians were originally loyal English with the same background, the same temperament, and the same disapproval of the cause of the American Revolution. But one moved to the tropical Bahamas and the other to temperate Canada. Within several centuries they have grown as different from one another as heaven is from earth. One is lazy, smug and passive and the other is energetic, progressive and vigorous.

Samuel Valkenburg maintains in *Elements of Political Geography* that age determines the temperament of the nations. In youth most nations want to be left alone; in adolescence, they grow cocky and rambunctious; in maturity they talk about law and order, security and protection.

It should be admitted that age, climate and food make some nations more energetic than others, but the mere abundance of energy, whether generated by age, climate or food, does not necessarily create war, for man's energy is neutral, like steam and electricity. How that vitality is spent makes for war or for peace. In the state of anarchy it is used for waging wars and therefore it creates warlike men, culture and institutions; but under the reign of law that energy is used for building peaceful men, culture and institutions. In the ultimate analysis, therefore, what makes men, culture and institutions peaceful or warlike is the state of order or chaos.

It has been stated often that the competition for life creates strife, and where competition is intense there is more war than in areas where it is less intense. But this contention seems to hold no water. In industrialized America the competition for life may be as severe as in Europe, but the forty-eight American states have not had as many wars as the European countries. It appears that it is not the absence or presence of competition but how that competition is carried out which makes for war or peace. Honest competition carried out according to the decent rules of fair play creates a progressive and yet peaceful society, whereas the competition which is practiced in a disorderly and predatory manner results in war and strife.

Some students believe that contact and isolation make for war or peace. But contact does not necessarily create war; it is the unruly and unregulated contact which creates conflict. Wholesome contact carried out through orderly channels, on the other hand, promotes peace and prosperity.

In this age of national states and complex industrial civilization, many Western students of history view war as a child of various conflicting forces such as nationalism, militarism, economic imperialism, and kindred factors. For instance, Herbert Hoover and Hugh Gibson list in *The Problem of Lasting Peace* seven dynamic forces which are believed to make for peace or war: ideologies, economic pressure, nationalism, militarism, imperialism, the complexes of fear, hate and revenge, and the will to peace.

Sidney B. Fay, learned professor of history at Harvard University, mentions in *The Origins of the World War* five underlying causes of the First World War: the system of secret alliances, militarism, nationalism, economic imperialism and false propaganda.

Devere Allen, editor of *World Over Press* and author of *The Fight for Peace*, believes the Second World War was brought about by nine human factors: Adolf Hitler, Neville Chamberlain, Joseph Stalin, Herbert Hoover's high tariff laws, President Roosevelt-Secretary Hull's failure to prevent the arming by the Axis, the selfishness of the American business interests who enabled the aggressors to prepare for war, the highhanded policy pursued by the Polish ruling class, French politics and the Versailles Treaty.

When you regard war as a product of these multiple causes such as nationalism, patriotism, sovereignty, imperialism, fascism, absolute states, empires, power politics and the like, you have to remove all these causes before you can expect to find peace. But the tragedy of it all is that none of these causes can be removed without destroying the ultimate source which breeds all these dangerous ideas and institutions.

So the modern compartmental method of studying the questions of war and peace so universally pursued by Western scholars becomes very much like the blind men examining an elephant. Instead of clarifying the true nature of war and peace in its proper perspectives, it has only complicated and confused the fundamental issues involved.

Fortunately, there have appeared in recent years a number of scholars who have recognized the utter futility of attacking the problem by this method. They have, therefore, tried to examine the subject as an indivisible whole and to reduce the confused mass of data into a simple understandable formula.

Mortimer J. Adler, of the University of Chicago, stated in *How to Think about War and Peace,* published in 1944, that international anarchy, namely, the absence of law in the realm of international affairs, is the sole cause of war.

Emery Reves maintained in *The Anatomy of Peace,* published in 1945, that the sovereignty of the nation-states is the only cause of war. It is needless to say that his contention is identical with that of Adler.

Although this approach to the problem of war and peace may seem a new one in our modern world, it is, in reality, a return to an old method followed by Confucius and Plato in ancient China and Greece. Confucius believed that the chaos of his day was due to the failure of the rulers to observe and uphold the laws of propriety. Plato appears to have thought that the absence of justice and law was the chief cause of strife among men. At any rate, this point of view holding anarchy, or lawlessness, or the absence of means of preserving justice as the ultimate cause of all wars appears to be fundamentally right and sound, when one examines how the struggle for survival in chaos has forced men to develop militant cultures and institutions which are regarded as the main causes of war.

As has already been pointed out, living in a world of anarchy, the savages were forced to develop for the sake of their survival all sorts of warlike ideas and institutions such as autocratic governments, belligerent gods and the militaristic sense of honor and glory. Similarly, civilized men, living in a state of international anarchy, were forced to develop all kinds of ideas and institutions, like militarism, imperialism, nationalism, patriotism and sovereignty, not materially different from those of the primitive peoples, for neither primitives nor modern man can survive in the state of anarchy without these ideas and institutions, however outmoded they may seem.

No people can survive in anarchy where there is no law and order. There can be no law and order without an organized authority like the state to enforce them. Nor can there be a state in this chaotic world without nationalism and patriotism because if its people, devoid of these ideas, refuse to fight against aggression, nothing else can preserve it. Nor can a state survive in anarchy without sovereignty, because without the exercise of absolute sovereignty, it cannot coerce its citizens or subjects to sacrifice their private interests for the safety of the state. Furthermore, in the world of chaos every state is sovereign; the only state which is not sovereign is that which is conquered or destroyed. Sovereignty in a state of anarchy, therefore, is the symbol of life and liberty and the inalienable right to survive. In other words, sovereignty is not the cause of lawlessness; it is the lawlessness which is the cause of sovereignty.

Nor can a people survive in a state of international anarchy without militarism and all that goes with it, such as war and the crude, barbarous sense of honor and glory, often sanctified by religious creeds. It is because in the state of anarchy, only the most powerful can survive, and whatever is indispensable for the survival of the group is honorable and glorious. Therefore, the institution of war, as stated by Heinrich von Treitschke, a forefather of Nazism, is sacred and is to be regarded as an ordinance of God.

Pride, power, the will to power, the will to overpower and the will to war, according to Friedrich Nietzsche, another forefather of Nazism, are the highest virtues of a superman, and the acts of conquest and domination and the ruthless elimination of other races are the most glorious achievements of a superior race. Thus we see our present-day Nazism is only a special brand of ideas produced by international anarchy.

Modern Japanese militarism and imperialism are likewise products of international anarchy. A century ago Japan was only a small isolationist country, wishing to mind her own business. But unfortunately, the veil of her isolation was lifted in a turbulent age of imperialism and war. It was the time when the imperialistic powers of Europe were conquering and occupying the poorly armed Asiatic states. Confronted with the danger of being conquered and dominated by the European Powers, the Japanese were obliged to build a powerful military empire. In other words, the modern Japanese empire, like all other empires in history, is only a bubble in the turbulent ocean of international chaos.

Unfortunately, however, most men have failed to see the woods for the trees. They have seen only the superficial causes of war such as militarism, nationalism and imperialism, without seeing the ultimate breeder of all these and other warlike ideas and institutions. As a result, they have erroneously, blamed their innocent cultures and institutions, their capitalists, their national states, their materialistic civilizations, their politicians and statesmen, their neighbors, their gods, even their own human nature for their troubles and wars. And at each generation they have found a scapegoat as a war criminal and have hanged and mutilated him, and then have gone to sleep thinking that peace will forever prevail. But anarchy has kept on breeding new war-makers without end. It is little wonder then that, despite men's relentless efforts to create peace, war has marched on century after century with only short truces.

As shall be shown presently in the following chapter, the failure of all the past peace efforts was chiefly due to a faulty diagnosis of war. Other things being equal, no peace plan which is not based on a correct diagnosis of war, and which does not strike directly at the heart of its ultimate cause, the state of international anarchy, can be expected to make a lasting peace among nations.

Chapter V

THE EARLY WESTERN CONTRIBUTION TO PEACE

1. Peace through Regulating War

The earliest attempt of men to save themselves from the horrors of war appears to be the regulation of war rather than the total banishment of it. We have already seen how the primitive peoples tried from time immemorial all sorts of devices regulating the conduct of war. Similarly, civilized men have worked out various rules and regulations to mitigate the horrors of warfare. The ancient Chinese, Indians and Greeks all developed an elaborate system of international law, not very different from modern international law. The Greeks, for instance, had customs and rules regulating the conduct of war, the functions of ambassadors, the formation of alliances, mediation, arbitration, neutrality, hostages, contraband, blockade, maritime law and scores of other subjects. The ancient peoples, unlike our sophisticated moderns, regarded those customs and rules as sacred and inviolable, and therefore, their attempt to control the horrors of warfare was more effective than today's.

Some ancient peoples likewise tried to lessen the cruelties of war by settling their disputes through a single combat. Instead of throwing into the arena all the able-bodied men, each party selected a single warrior and had him fight the battle for the people as a whole. As the decision of the single combat was regarded as an omen, the rival groups appear to have accepted it as final. The famous single combats between David and Goliath, Hector and Achilles, Aeneas and Turnus, and Horatii and Curiatii in Hebrew, Greek and Roman legend and history furnish some of the early examples of deciding the issues of national wars through chosen champions.

Herodotus relates an interesting attempt to solve national

issues through a group combat, instead of single combat, between the Argives and Lacedaemonians over a land dispute. The two opposing armies selected three hundred warriors each and these were left to fight among themselves. The rest of the army went back to their respective countries, so that no additional help could be given to the fighters. The selected men fought on until only three men were alive, two Argives and one Lacedaemonian. The two Argives believed that they had won the war, as only one of their enemy was alive, and went home for a rest. But the one Lacedaemonian remained on the battleground. When the two armies returned the following day to learn the outcome of the battle, both sides claimed victory. The Argives claimed victory on the ground that more of their men survived, whereas the Lacedaemonians claimed victory because their one surviving warrior remained on the ground, whereas the two surviving Argives fled from the scene. And so the two armies fought all over again, with heavy losses on both sides. Nevertheless, it was an interesting attempt, to say the least. Finally the Lacedaemonians won the battle, but their lone survivor from the first battle felt so ashamed to return home alone after losing his entire company that he committed suicide on the disputed ground over which the original battle began.

But the practice of settling national issues through a single combat was uncommon even in ancient times and became much less common as men grew more sophisticated, though it was not entirely abandoned until modern times. As late as the fifteenth century, Charles of Anjou and Pedro of Tarragona, who had been fighting about Sicily, agreed with the approval of the Pope to settle their dispute by a single combat. The Portuguese adventurers in the sixteenth century proposed to the Sultans of Batjan and Gilolo to settle their differences through a single personal combat. Single combats for the decision of individual disputes and for the vindication of personal honor have continued in Europe and America down to our own day.

Probably one of the most elaborate attempts to control war which has yet been made in history is that of the medevial church; and one of the means by which the early church sought to control war was by defining just and unjust wars and allowing the just wars while opposing the unjust ones. No sooner was this attempt made than came the controversy over what was and what was not a just war.

According to the early church fathers, St. Ambrose, St. Augustine and their followers, a war was a just one when it was waged by a proper authority for a just motive for a just cause. But what were the just causes of war? They were declared to be self-defense, the recovery of lost rights and the punishment of wrongs. But the average man was never sure whether he was fighting on the just or unjust side, as both belligerents were supported by equally able theologians. It was finally held, therefore, that if the soldier was not certain that his side was unjust he was regarded as fighting on the just side. As a result, all wars became just wars.

Thus what the early church accomplished in restricting wars was similar to that achieved by the signatories of the Pact of Paris, which was supposed to have outlawed all wars except those in self-defense. Since the conclusion of that pact, all wars have turned out to be wars of self-defense!

The medieval church, however, was much more successful in controlling wars through other means. It helped settle many disputes through arbitration and conciliation; it discouraged aggressive and unjust wars by upholding the laws of God and church; it limited the time and areas in which private wars could be waged by instituting the **Peace of God and the Truce of God**; it forbade the clergy and all the Holy Orders from bearing arms; it also forbade interest on loans made for economically unproductive purposes, such as fighting (see Peace through a Universal Religion).

Following the Renaissance, the Reformation, and the rise of modern states, the church lost its power and ceased to be a guardian of peace and justice. The whole of Christian Europe was thrown into an arena of unlimited and unrestricted warfare. The situation was so intolerable that some savants raised voices of protest against the cruelties of war and others proposed to control the horrors of warfare.

Hugo Grotius, commonly known as the father of international law, was one of the chief exponents, advocating the observance of certain laws of nations in the prosecution of hostilities. He believed that all controversies should be settled through conferences, or arbitration or by lot, but that if the rulers must wage wars, they should do so according to certain rules of warfare. In response to his plea, scores of jurists, scholars and statesmen echoed and re-echoed the voice of Grotius. Consequently, conferences were held, declarations were made, resolutions were adopted, conventions were ratified, all for the purpose of regulating wars. For instance, the agreements, conventions and declarations of Paris, London, Geneva and The Hague, all aimed at lessening the ferocities of inhumane warfare either by prohibiting the use of poison gas, dum-dum bullets and other dangerous weapons, or by providing for a fair and humane treatment of the wounded soldiers, the prisoners of war and the noncombatants. But for several reasons none of these measures has helped much the lessening of the horrors of warfare. First, war is the antithesis of all laws, human or divine, and cannot be controlled by rules and regulations. Second, because there has been no central authority to enforce the rules of warfare, all nations have broken their pledges under one excuse or another, whenever the breach of law has given them a promise of victory.

As the same situation will probably continue to prevail, other things being equal, all attempts to control the atomic bomb through rules and regulations will be as futile as trying to tie up the rainbow. Judging from the past experiences, there are only two ways to combat the menace of the bomb or other missiles. One is by creating an effective world authority to prevent international wars, so that there can be no occasion to use such bombs. The other is by inventing new weapons which will completely neutralize the effectiveness of the bomb, or which will be so destructive that the bomb will be as harmless as a firecracker in comparison.

At one time all Europe was terrified by the crossbow, but the discovery of firearms saved it from the horrors of that bow. At another time the civilized nations were as much terrified by the menace of poison gas as they are now by the atomic bomb. But they have abated that menace successfully, not by enforcing conventions outlawing the use of gas, as commonly understood, but by making it ineffective as an instrument of war. Willy Levy states in *Bombs and Bombing* that an ordinary bomb can cause seventy-five times more damage than a gas bomb of similar size known to the year of 1944. Therefore, should the scientists invent a new instrument of destruction many times more powerful than the atomic bomb, then we would not, at least, have to worry about the bomb as much as we do today.

2. Peace through Pacifism

The pacifists' attempt to build peace is worth considering because, despite their many shortcomings, they were the forerunners of our modern crusade against war.

There are various kinds of pacifists who are known under different names, like the Mennonites in the Low Countries, the Quakers in England, the Anabaptists, the Moravians, the non-resisters, the conscientious objectors, and Oxford Pledgers. In each of these brands of pacifists there are nearly as many different elements as there are among the Democrats and the Republicans. But they have one thing in common; all have sprung from the Christian religion and receive their inspiration from the teachings of Jesus.

There were, of course, pacifists even before the birth of Christ. For example, Buddha of India, who lived in the sixth century B.C. may be rightly regarded as one of the greatest of all pacifists. His command, "Thou shalt not kill," reached down to animals, whose souls were supposed to be as immortal as those of kings and princes, and were to migrate from persons to animals or vice versa, according to their merits, like human beings moving about from house to house, according to their fortunes.

At about the same time that Buddha was preaching in India, Lao-tse preached in China a kind of pacifism which is more akin to the ideas of the present-day non-resisters than that of most other thinkers. He was reported to have said, "The highest virtue resists nothing and water, which resists nothing, is always irresistible"; "The good I meet with goodness; the bad I also meet with goodness; the faithful I meet with faith, the faithless I also meet with faith"; "Heaven's way is to benefit, but not to injure"; "Good warriors are not warlike"; "A good man acts resolutely and then stops; he ventures not to take by force"; "Arms are unblest among tools and not the superior man's tools"; "Where armies are quartered, briars and thorns grow"; "Great wars unfailingly are followed by famines"; "Regulate things before disorder begins"; "Anyone who is anxious to lead the people should be behind them; anyone who wishes to arise above the people should stand beneath them." So far so good. But then he went on to say, "Don't keep treasure, don't boast, for they cause theft and provoke desire"; "The wise man who knew how to govern did not enlighten the people, for the sophisticated are difficult to govern." What a challenge to democracy!

Right or wrong, his teachings were obscured by the morass of superstition which grew around a religious faith known as Taoism. Furthermore, the realistic ideas of Confucius, who talked about preserving peace by upholding the laws of propriety and by recompensing evil with justice, pushed off the maxims of Lao-tse from the realm of practical politics.

Shortly after Lao-tse and Confucius, Moti, or Motse; came to ancient China with his immortal peace classic entitled *Universal Love*. Believing that "partiality" is the cause of all strife, he advocated the practice of universal love as a panacea of all conflicts. He said in substance: "If I love your family and your country as much as I do my own, why should I want to destroy your family and your country? If you love my family and my country as much as you do your own, why should you be wanting to destroy my family and conquer my country? If no one else wants to conquer and destroy the families and countries of others, why should there be conflict and strife in the world?"

Though an ardent lover of peace, he was not one of the so-called pacifists, because he advocated the wisdom of fighting defensive wars, as the failure to do so would encourage aggression. One might think that he took such a position because the adoption of his idea would aid his business, as he was a fortification builder by profession. But judging from his activities, he was not at all influenced in his thinking by worldly motives. For instance, once he walked ten days and nights to stop an impending attack on the state of Sung. He talked with the builder of the cloudladders with which the attack was to be made, and dissuaded him from undertaking such a move by pointing out the impregnable defense system of Sung. On the way back from his successful mission, he sought a shelter from a drenching rain while passing through the state of Sung, whose destruction he had just averted. He was not given a shelter, for no one knew that he was the saviour of that country. Was Moti displeased? No, he said he was happy that no one could recognize him, as he did not wish to be acclaimed as a hero. At least such was the record which he left behind.

A century or two after Buddha, Lao-tse and Confucius, Isaiah dreamed of a day when the nations should beat their swords into plowshares and their spears into pruninghooks. But his vision of universal peace, as pointed out by G. H. Gilbert, author of *The Bible and Universal Peace,* was a victor's peace, dictated by triumphant Jehovah to the vanquished world that would recognize him as their sole master and regard Israel as the center of God's universe. The men of Egypt and Ethiopia would come to pay their tribute to the chosen people of Yahweh; the kings and queens of other nations would bring their wealth as tribute to Yahweh's people and bow down to Israel with their faces to the ground, and would lick the dust of Israel's feet.

If the author of *The Bible and Universal Peace* is not mistaken, Isaiah was probably a pipe dreamer. Like an old man who had seen better days and who had very little to live for, Isaiah dreamed of a new world in which the chosen people of Yahweh would rise again to judge the wicked nations which had trampled down the proud and once powerful Israelites. Whatever the case, Isaiah planted a hope of a warless age which has never died from the hearts of men and women of the war-torn world.

When Alexander, the Greek warrior, swept into the Near East, Prophet Jaddua used the tactics of nonresistance and saved his people from being butchered. Let Alexander himself tell how that feat was accomplished. He said, "When I saw not a spear nor a sword, nor even an ax, I could not raise my hand against them. This is the only people that has met me peacefully instead of with arms. The more glory to their leader, Jaddua, who was brave enough and wise enough to do this."

Coming three centuries later, Jesus Christ gave his celebrated message of love, kindness, forbearance, humility and sacrifice. But fortunately or unfortunately, he left enough room in many of his isolated utterances for the rise of different interpretations by his followers. He said, in one place, for example, "Blessed be the peacemakers, for they shall be called the children of God," and in another place, he stated, "I come not to send peace, but a sword." He said on one occasion, "Put up thy sword in its sheath; for they who take the sword shall perish by the sword," and on another occasion, He declared, "He that hath no sword, let him sell his garment and buy one." To add more confusion, He did not make it clear just what He meant by these statements. Did He mean that His followers should or should not fight in self-defense, or in the defense of the meek and the helpless? Furthermore, what did He mean when He commanded His disciples to love their enemies and resist not that which is evil? Did He mean that a Christian man should love the devil and allow him to destroy the kingdom of God? There was no way of knowing just what position a Christian should take on this vital subject. As a result, the followers of Jesus have carried on a heated controversy on the position of their Master on the subject of war for two thousand years without a decisive victory on either side. Let us sample the nature of their arguments.

Tertullian, a Carthaginian writer in the second century, maintained that Jesus commanded his disciples not even to sue a wrongdoer in a law court. How could a Christian slay another man? He concluded that it would be better to be slain than to slay. Lactanius, a tutor in the household of Constantine, held as Leo Tolstoy and the modern non-resisters have done, that the shedding of human blood, whatever the excuse, was unlawful. George Fox, the leader of the English Quaker movement, contended that each man's life is guided by an "inner light" which transcended even the Bible; therefore, no one has the right to constrain anyone else. William Ladd, the first president of the American Peace Society, stated in 1838: "I do not believe that a Christian has the right to take life in self-defense. I ought not fight in defense of life, liberty or religion, much less for property; but to leave vengeance to God to whom it belongs."

On the other hand most Christians believe that to fight for justice against injustice, for the furtherance of the kingdom of God against the forces of evil, is not only a privilege but the sacred duty of all Christian men. Let Charles Kingsley, that famous English clergyman, give this side of the argument. Speaking in defense of the Crimean War, he declared:

> "For the Lord Jesus Christ is not only the Prince of Peace, He is the Prince of War, too. He is the Lord of Hosts, the God of Armies, and whoever fights in a just war against tyrants and oppressors is fighting on Christ's side, and Christ is fighting on his side. Christ is his captain and his leader, and he can be in no better service. Be sure of it, for the Bible tells you so."

Kingsley represents the majority of the Christian world and Ladd a small minority whose voice has scarcely risen above the noise of battle and the prayers for victory. But it is this small group of religious non-resisters who started to form the first peace society in the world. David Law Dodge, a Connecticut merchant living in New York, published in 1809 a pamphlet entitled *The Mediator's Kingdom Not of This World* and another entitled *War Inconsistent with the Religion of Jesus Christ*, published in 1812, in both of which he took the position of non-resister condemning all wars, defensive or offensive, as un-Christian and contrary to the Sermon on the Mount. He packed these pamphlets with the merchandise and sent them to his customers gratis. Finally on August 14, 1815, he formed with a few of his friends the world's first peace society. About the same time, similar societies were founded in New England, Ohio, and also some in England. All the peace societies in America came together in 1828 and formed the American Peace Society with William Ladd as their first president.

Before banishing wars, these men of peace started a new war of their own on the eternal controversy of whether or not a Christian man should fight in self-defense. During this controversy, a certain Mr. Lovejoy, in Illinois, was killed in 1837 while repelling a burglar. The uncompromising non-resisters considered it God's penalty for violating the teachings of Jesus as revealed in the Sermon on the Mount. Henry C. Wright, William Lloyd Garrison and his followers withdrew from the American Peace Society and formed the New England Non-Resistance Society the year after the Lovejoy incident. This group unequivocally opposed participation in military service for whatever purpose and the use of force in defense of property, life, liberty or religion.

But the most colorful and spectacular non-resistant group was the League of Universal Brotherhood which conducted in 1846-1855 a series of stirring anti-war campaigns in America and Europe. Its founder was Elihu Burritt, a cobbler by profession, dubbed by the *London Times* "The Yankee Cobbler." His study of the anatomy of the earth revealed to him the unity of the world and his study of the Bible and the roots of language taught him the unity of all mankind. Under his energetic leadership, the League had over 50,000 men and women, most of whom were working men, sign the pledge "never to enlist or enter into any army or navy, or to yield any voluntary support or sanction to the preparation for or prosecution of any war, by whomsover, or for whatsoever proposed, declared, or waged." The idea was essentially the same as the Oxford pledge adopted by the Student's Union of Oxford University which was popular on the eve of the Second World War; it read, "This House will in no circumstances fight for king or country."

In his peace crusade, Burritt circulated monthly a million copies of *Olive Leaves,* a fortnightly publication printed in several European languages. On one of his pamphlets entitled *The World's Working Men's Strike Against War,* published in 1855, he even advocated an "organized strike of the working men of Christendom against war" as the only alternative to the creation of a congress of nations leading to disarmament. He likewise promoted a series of universal peace congresses held in Brussels, Paris, London and Frankfort in different years. Some of these meetings were attended by an audience of 8,000, a remarkable feat of demonstration. In due time, even some kings and princes and such personages as Victor Hugo and Thomas Carlyle came to give their support to the movement.

Although the early peacemakers spent most of their energy on painting the ugly un-Christian character of war, they likewise introduced some constructive measures, which they thought might work even without physical sanctions. For instance, Noah Worcester, founder of the Massachusetts Peace Society in 1815, advocated the creation of a Court of Equity and Confederacy of Nations in his *A Solemn Review of the Causes of War,* published as early as 1814. William Ladd campaigned for the establishment of a Congress of Ambassadors for the preparation of a code of international law and a Court of Nations for the arbitration of disputes according to the law. Burritt's peace crusaders likewise favored a congress of nations, arbitration, disarmament, international communication, postal reforms, the revision of weights, measures, coinage and education and practically all the programs which have been adopted subsequently by various peace organizations, numbering some 425 by the end of the century.

The hopes and dreams of the peace crusaders of that time were beautifully set forth in a masterly address delivered by Victor Hugo, president of the universal peace congress held at Paris in 1849 before 840 delegates from various countries. He declared:

"A day will come when you, France—you, Russia—you, Italy—you, England—you, Germany—all of you, nations of the continent, will, without losing your distinctive qualities and your glorious individuality, be blended into a superior unity, and constitute a European fraternity, just as Normandy, Brittany, Burgundy, Lorraine have been blended into France. A day will come when the only battlefield will be the market opened to commerce, and the mind opening to new ideas. A day will come when bullets and bombshells will be replaced by votes, by the universal suffrage of nations, by the venerable arbitration of a great sovereign Senate, which will be to Europe what the Parliament is to Engalnd, what the Diet is to Germany, what the Legislative Assembly is to France."

The dreams of these dreamers were shattered by the outbreak of the Crimean War in Europe and the Civil War in the United States. After the storm, new men and new organizations emerged to carry on the pacifists' fight for peace, but more wars have marched on. It may be largely due to the fault of the sick old world; but it may likewise be due to the faulty principles and methods used by the peace crusaders.

The chief weakness of the Pacifists lies in their conviction that wars can be prevented by peaceful means only without physical sanctions against the wrongdoer and that they can preserve peace through the principles of nonresistance and nonparticipation in the armed forces because "if you fight for peace, you get war, not peace, and if you fight against war, you get war, not peace."

It is granted that if all peoples and nations in the world adopt the same brand of pacifism, and settle their disputes through peaceful means only and refuse to take up arms under whatever circumstances, the world will of course enjoy a perfect peace. But if it is adopted only by certain groups, as has always been, and as will always be, there is nothing more dangerous than pacifism, not only for the peace of the world, but for the very survival of the peaceful nations. Just consider what a dangerous situation the whole world faced when the democracies pursued pacifism while the totalitarians prepared for war. Consider more specifically into what a perilous danger Great Britain was thrown when Hitler unleashed his fury against her. And why was she so pitifully helpless against Hitler's barbarism?

It may be unfair to blame the pacifists for everything, but it is a fact that there were some twelve million English pacifists who did the best they could, as all the pacifists in other countries did, to prevent their own government from building a bigger army, navy and air force, to propagate the doctrine of non-resistance and nonparticipation in the armed forces, and to persuade their fellow-countrymen not to fight under any circumstances for king or country. But what have they accomplished? They only encouraged military aggression in Europe, Africa and Asia by giving the Germans, Italians and Japanese the assurance that the British would fight for no one, not even for their king and country. Furthermore, they helped slaughter millions of peace-loving peoples, at home and abroad, by making them helpless against the barbarism of Hitler, Mussolini and Hirohito.

The pacifists, of course, can laugh at all those who take up arms because they know that he who rises by the sword perishes by the sword. They can smile cynically at all the armed hordes marching by in pride because they know that they can outlive those who take the sword. They know that the militant Assyrians vanished in 150 years but the peaceful Sumerians lasted 4,000 years. They know that the Chinese, the Jews and the Indians, all of whom have renounced their warriors and have followed philosophers and prophets, have outlived scores of their conquerors. They know, too, that all the pacific civilizations have survived much longer than the militant ones which have wasted their energy on conquest and have met with premature deaths.

But do they know that longevity is not the only virtue worth living for? Do they know that Jesus Christ lived on earth only about thirty-three years and yet gave more than anyone who slumbered over a hundred years? Do they know that there is more value, more joy and life in one year of freedom than there is in a century of slavery? Do they know that all the terror, misery, torture and massacre which countless millions of unarmed and helpless Chinese, Indians, Jews and numberless other peoples suffered at the murderous hands of their savage oppressors have failed to achieve peace on earth? Do they know that peace can never be established by refusing to defend our rights against armed criminals and by preferring to be enslaved and tortured by them forever?

It has been said often that fire is not quenched by fire, nor is a war stopped by war. But one of the most effective ways of putting out a big forest fire is by starting a counter fire, and the most effective way to control the tide of barbarism is to meet it with the combined moral and physical forces of the entire civilized world. Maybe Emery Reves was right when he stated in *A Democratic Manifesto* that if the nations of the world care about peace so much as to fight for its preservation, then the world will find it.

The refusal to participate in war on the ground that there is neither a good war nor a bad peace is likewise sheer nonsense. The world has had as many good wars as it has had years of bad peace. Consider the peace of 1931, which was purchased at the cost of sacrificing all the sacred principles of international decency and fair play in the face of Japanese aggression. That peace was bad because it was purchased at the cost of the Second World War, many times more destructive than the one which might have resulted from an attempt to restrain the lone aggressor, Japan.

The contention that moral sanctions are enough to constrain an aggressor has also proved fallacious. Neither Japan, nor Italy, nor Germany bowed to the public opinion or moral sanctions of the civilized world. You cannot prevent wars through moral sanctions alone any more than you can prevent crime through public opinion alone.

The argument in favor of nonresistance rather than active

resistance has likewise proved ineffective. It is true that in some cases nonresistance and non-co-operation have been effective, as proved by Jaddua against Alexander, the Hungarians against Austrian oppression, the Indians in Natal against the South African government, and the Finnish in their refusal to submit to conscription. But these are only exceptions rather than the rule. The French Indo-China non-co-operation movement collapsed when the French shot down the demonstrators by the thousands. The Korean nonviolence movement failed when the Japanese mowed down the Koreans like rats. The nonresistance movement of Mohandas Gandhi collapsed when the British Lion roared and scratched and killed thousands of his followers. And after all Pascal may have been right when he said, "Justice without power is meaningless."

The belief that the good Lord takes care of the wrongdoers is a useless mysticism. If the burglars and baby kidnappers cannot prosper in our society, that is only because we have organized a society in which they cannot prosper. No one should expect that the Lord will organize the world and deliver up peace on a silver platter to us when we have failed to do our part.

There have been thousands of communities which have enjoyed peace and prosperity through the establishment of an authority with the power of sanctions to enforce the rules of fair play. But there has never been a single community organized exclusively on a pacifist model without law backed by sanctions that has enjoyed peace and prosperity. Bronson Alcott and his idealists once planted a colony, Brook Farm, in New England. They planted some fruits and vegetables for food, as they would not eat the flesh of animals. The worms soon began to feast on the fruits and vegetables. But since they were true pacifists, they could not kill the worms. As a result, the colony, faced with famine, dissolved itself. That is a fair indication of what might happen to any society of exclusive nonresisters.

William Penn, though a Quaker himself, did not completely repudiate the idea of employing coercion. He made a treaty with the Indians and settled disputes through an arbitral tribunal composed of six Indians and six whites. He enforced not only the treaties and arbitral awards, but the regulations of the commonwealth with the minimum employment of coercion. Benefiting from this "holy experiment" in America, he advocated in his peace plan for Europe the settlement of disputes through a diet or parliament with sanctions to enforce its decisions. Should any sovereignties "refuse to submit their claim or pretensions to them or to abide and perform the judgment thereof, and seek their remedy by arms, delay their compliance beyond the time prefixed in their resolutions, all other sovereignties, united as one strength, shall compel the submission and performance of the sentence, with damages to the suffering party, and charges to the sovereignties that obliged their submission."

What a pity that the pacifists have not followed experienced men like William Penn, instead of following inexperienced religious mystics like William Ladd and Elihu Burritt, who believed erroneously that the ruthless and cruel aggressor nations could be persuaded by the power of ballyhoo and hot air without the backing of physical sanctions to observe the principles of honor, justice and peace.

It seems to me that we must do all in our power to influence men to be good, law-abiding citizens, but we still have to have police and the ugly jail because there are usually one or two men out of a hundred who cannot be made good or harmless without the power to restrain, and the failure to restrain one person makes it impossible for the rest of the hundred to enjoy law and order. Similarly, we must do all we can for the promotion of friendship and understanding among the nations and for the peaceful settlement of international disputes, but we must still have an effective central organization empowered with sanctions to uphold the principles of fair play against a few ruthless aggressor states, or else all the civilized nations cannot enjoy peace and security in the world any more than an individual person can in a community without an established authority.

3. Peace through Disarmament

As battles are fought with instruments of war, how can men fight without weapons of destruction? And so it appears on the surface that the simplest way to peace is through the road to disarmament. There is a more important reason why many men think disarmament is one way out of war; it is their belief that wars are created largely by the business interests, chiefly arms-makers, for the purpose of making the almighty dollar. Many seekers after peace, therefore, have struggled to banish wars by controlling the merchants of death or by reducing national armaments.

As early as 546 B.C. the fourteen warring states in ancient China held a disarmament conference under the leadership of Hsiang Hsu, a minister of the state of Sung. It brought to an end a seventy-two year old war between two rival states and gave a brief breathing spell to the war-torn states. But the attempt to preserve a lasting peace through disarmament was no more successful in ancient China than in the modern world.

Twenty-five centuries after Hsiang Hsu, Czar Nicholas II of Russia called a world-wide peace conference for the primary purpose of reducing the armaments of various countries. Ninety-six delegates representing twenty-six states assembled at The Hague, and after wasting more than two months, May 18-July 29, 1899, all they could accomplish for the cause of disarmament was the adoption of a pious resolution that the reduction of military budget is "extremely desirable" for the welfare of mankind. All were willing to disarm, if the other party did too, but there was no other party willing to disarm. The Kaiser of Germany was frank enough to say that he could trust no one but God and his sharp sword. The second Hague Peace Conference, which was held in 1907, when the representatives of forty-four states of the world talked themselves almost to death for four long months, accomplished not even as much as the first conference.

The Washington Disarmament Conference of 1921 called

by President Warren G. Harding at the instigation of the British, who were very hard pressed from the First World War, fared slightly better than the previous conferences. The leading naval powers of that time agreed to scrap—and they actually did scrap—some battleships, though most of them were obsolete ones bound for junk yards. They also agreed not to build capital ships over ten thousand tons except according to the fixed ratio which was 5-5-3-1.75-1.75 for American, England, Japan, France, and Italy respectively. This arrangement gave Great Britain and the United States a short respite from the building of capital ships. But it by no means stopped the naval race; actually it created a new naval race for the building of ships below ten thousand tons, with Japan taking the lead. Had the conference not been called, the situation could not have been worse. The late Will Rogers explained the situation well when he remarked that if another disarmament conference was called there could not be found enough ocean to float all the battleships. The naval conferences which were subsequently held in Geneva and London were no more fruitful than the old Hague conferences.

The attempt to achieve peace through disarmament has been singularly ineffective because the whole movement was based on the false assumption that armament is the cause of war, instead of war being the cause of armament. This assumption is false because it is very much like regarding the umbrella as the cause of rain, instead of considering rain as the cause of the umbrella. The attempt to banish war by the reduction of armament, therefore, is like trying to control the rain by the abandonment of the umbrella.

It is admitted that the arms-makers have much more to do with wars than umbrella-makers have with rain. No rain has yet been made by umbrella-makers, whereas numerous wars have been promoted by arms interests for the purpose of swelling their dividends. Besides, the production of umbrellas has had little effect on the downpour of rain, whereas the race for armament has often precipitated conflicts. But the fundamental point to be remembered is that almost all wars are created, not by arms interests, but by the necessity to survive in the state of anarchy without an organized authority to preserve justice. So long as there is such a necessity, the mere reduction of armament, or the abandonment of it, will no more banish war than the abandonment of umbrellas will stop rain. In order to be convinced of the soundness of this assertion, just look at the animals and savages.

The animals do not have Krupps, Vickers or du Ponts among them, but they fight with tooth and claw. The savages had no armament to speak of until the coming of the white man, but they were engaged in endless wars. Other things being equal, therefore, mere reduction of arms will make war less destructive and more frequent, but will not banish it.

Furthermore, until the world is organized into a single unit for the enjoyment of peace and justice, nothing can prevent the various nations from arming themselves. It is because in the state of chaos, the possession of superior arms has been the only means of defense against aggression.

We have seen the tragedy of China's unarmed millions slaughtered like rats by the Japanese and other armed barbarians who had preceded the Japanese. We have reviewed the tragedy of the wandering Jews who have been kicked and whipped, downtrodden and maltreated, robbed and murdered century after century. We have wept over the suffering and sacrifice of the peaceful Danes and Norwegians, groaning under the tyranny of the Nazi terrorism. We have shed glassy tears of sympathy and regrets for hundreds of other peaceful, unarmed peoples who have suffered a similar fate. After all this, how can any nation afford to abandon or reduce its arms?

In any community where there is no law and order it has been impossible to prevent the people from carrying arms because there is the necessity to protect themselves and their interests by the force of arms. But in any society where the reign of law and justice prevails, the people voluntarily have discarded their weapons of destruction because there is no necessity to resort to arms for the defense of their rights. The only way to bring about disarmament, therefore, is through the construction of a new civilization in which the vindication of honor, justice and right by armed forces will be no longer necessary.

4. Peace through Gentlemen's Agreements

All attempts at preserving peace through the conclusion of treaties and conventions, whether the subject of the agreement is the humane conduct of war, the reduction of armaments, the pacific settlement of international disputes and what not, are characterized as the methods of making peace through gentlemen's agreements, because all of them are based on the assumption that the contracting parties will observe their commitments voluntarily even though there is no way to enforce them.

As early as 1280 B.C. the kings of the Hittites and of Egypt made one of these gentlemen's agreements renouncing war as an instrument of their policy: "There shall be no hostilities between them forever. The great chief of the Hittites shall not pass over into the land of Egypt, forever, to take anything therefrom; Rameses, the great chief of Egypt, shall not pass over into the land of the Hittites to take anything therefrom, forever."

Thirty-three centuries later some of our modern idealists made a similar attempt to preserve peace through the conclusion of a gentlemen's agreement in which all the signatories voluntarily renounced war as an instrument of national policy and their disputes were to be settled through peaceful means. Thus came about the so-called "Pact of Paris," commonly known as the "Kellogg Anti-War Pact." In his message to Congress in 1928, Calvin Coolidge declared that, "The observation of this covenant, so simple, so straightforward, promises more for peace of the world than any other agreement ever negotiated among the nations." With similar optimism, the pact was hailed and adhered to by practically every country under the sun.

Between the conclusion of the Hittite-Egyptian treaty and the Pact of Paris, literally thousands of treaties and conversations of peace were concluded. Some provided for the maintenance of peace and friendship and others for nonaggression, mutual aid, arbitration, conciliation, and judicial settlement. In spite of all these, wars have relentlessly marched on, century after century. There must be something inherently wrong in the attempt to create peace through this kind of method.

One defect seems to be that treaties between states, unlike private contracts between individuals, cannot be enforced because in the realm of international affairs, unlike in an organized community, there is no organized authority to enforce the treaties. Therefore, agreements among the sovereign states, whether they are called treaties or conventions of alliances, arbitration, or nonaggression, are mere gentlemen's agreements, which can be kept or broken at the pleasure of the contracting parties. This explains, then, why thousands of these treaties, most of which were meant to remain in force forever, survived on the average not more than two years.

One of the reasons why the Articles of Confederation failed to preserve peace among the thirteen American states was that the government set up under that covenant could only legislate laws without the power to enforce them. Similarly, the main reason why countless peace treaties have failed to preserve peace on earth appears to be the absence of the means of enforcing them.

Of course, it would be wonderful if all the nations acted like gentlemen and voluntarily observed the rules of decency and respected the rights of others. Then we could have peace on earth and good will toward men without a union, council or league, whatever it may be called. Some civilized nations, in fact, have abided by these rules of fair play whether there were police or not, as the majority of good people do. But there have always been, and there will always be, some nations which would not do so voluntarily. The world, therefore, should be organized to handle just such cases. Until then, millions of peace treaties and conventions providing for thousands of different peaceful means of solving disputes will not save the world from perpetual anarchy. All the talk of making treaties and alliances without organizing the world for their enforcement, therefore, would amount to nothing more than a kind of WPA to provide jobs for the unemployed diplomats and paper and ink manufacturers.

What the world needs is faith and confidence among the nations. There can be no faith and confidence when the contracting parties can break their covenants with impunity and without corresponding penalty. But the powers of the world will continue to do as they please, regardless of what treaties they make, so long as the world is not so organized to enforce treaties as private contracts are enforced. So long as the nations act according to their momentary whims, nothing will create a feeling of security, and therefore nothing will prevent the race for armament, alliances and counter-alliances, leading to perpetual war. And so we should not place false hopes in peace treaties and conventions for arbitration, nonaggression, mutual assistance and the like until after we have organized the world for their enforcement.

5. Peace through Universal Religion

Many honest, sincere and well-meaning men of God have been saying often that there will never be peace on earth until all men accept one and the same God as father of all mankind, and learn to love one another like brothers as Jesus Christ taught us. But a more careful review of history casts some doubts on the validity of these apparently sound statements.

It is a fact that some savages who believed in the same spirits lived together peacefully like brothers, but some other primitives worshipping the same deity waged eternal wars against one another. Believe it or not, it has been the same with the ancient and the modern peoples.

The ancient Hebrews lived together like brothers with Jehovah as their sovereign, but this strong religious tie could not prevent them from waging centuries of fratricidal warfare.

The ancient Greeks formed the celebrated Amphictyonic League, which meant a union of the people who dwell around a temple. They worshipped the same god and lived together like friends and allies, waging wars in common against the trespassers on the temple, or on any member of the league. But this wholesome unifying influence of religion failed to preserve peace in the Hellenic world.

Of all religions, Buddhism is most noted for its pacifism. For Buddha's command, "Thou shalt not kill," applied to animals as well as to human beings. In the reign of Asoka, the famous Buddhist emperor of India in the third century B.C., some of the pacifistic doctrines of Buddhism were actually put into practice. He renounced war as an instrument of his policy, when his armies were winning victories everywhere. He propagated the teachings of his master by peaceful means only. He likewise abolished or restricted the killing of animals. He abandoned royal hunting expeditions and prohibited the capture or sale of fish on fifty-six days a year. The castration of bulls, he-goats, rams, and boars was restricted to certain days. The daily slaughter of animals for making royal curries was reduced from hundreds of animals to two peacocks and one antelope. He ordered the planting of trees and medical centers for the animals as well as for men.

Asoka ruled forty years. His dynasty lasted 137 years, ninety years of which were glorious. Buddhism itself flourished in India for more than a thousand years and then was absorbed by Hinduism which conquered it by adopting its best elements. There are today only twelve million Buddhists in India, as compared with some 250,000,000 Hindus.

Buddhism was not confined to India. It spread far and wide throughout Asia, leaving similar pacific influences everywhere, except Japan where it failed to make pacifists out of the Japanese. The pacifying influence of Buddhism, however, has not succeeded in banishing warfare to any appreciable degree, primarily because of its lack of social engineering, which is indispensable for the building of lasting peace: Buddhism spent most of its effort in teaching men how to attain the peace of mind and the harmony of the soul by sacrificing their worldly ambitions and desires, instead of teaching them how to build a better and finer world of peace and harmony by skillfully directing the dynamic human and social forces.

Undoubtedly, the most outstanding religious attempt to create international peace is that of the medieval Catholic Church when, following the collapse of the secular political authority, it emerged as a sovereign power in both spiritual and temporal matters.

R. F. Wright maintains in *Medieval Internationalism* that there was a striking similarity between the medieval church and the League of Nations in the field of international relations. The League was a permanent organization with its headquarters at Geneva; the church was, and still is, a permanent organization with its headquarters at Rome. The League had a council and an assembly; the church had the college of cardinals corresponding to the council, and the Oecumencial Council corresponding to the assembly. The papacy likewise served as an international tribunal, comparable to the Permanent Court of International Justice and carried out an extensive program of humanitarian work as the League tried to do. Like the secretariat of the League, the papal chancellary served as a depository of documents where the international treaties were registered. Above all, the papal church was endowed with powerful sanctions to enforce its orders against kings or princes. The use of excommunication and interdict, for instance, was far more effective in those days than the economic sanctions provided in the covenant of the League.

A modern internationalist cannot help feeling a sense of shame and humiliation when he compares the papal sanction against Emperor Henry IV with the League's sanction against Mussolini of Italy. Following Pope Gregory's excommunication of Henry IV, the emperor stood in penitence for three days, barefooted in the snow outside the castle at Canossa, praying for Gregory to remove the excommunication. On the other hand, when the League enforced economic sanctions against Italy, Mussolini growled and defied and threatened, whereupon the League's representative stood in penitence outside Il Duce's office in Rome, begging and praying for forgiveness!

Equipped with almost a perfect organization, backed by powerful sanctions, religious, political and economic, as the church owned and controlled one-third of all lands in Christian Europe, and supported by millions of faithful subjects who were presided over by resident bishops in various localities, the Catholic Church actually banished many wars on various occasions. For instance, the Pope induced Richard of England to make truce with Philip Augustus of France and settled the dispute between Spain and Portugal by dividing the world between them.

The church likewise forbade the clergy and all the Holy Orders from bearing arms; it converted all the churches into sanctuaries where the peace of God was preserved; it instituted the Truce of God, which prohibited private wars at first only on Sundays but later from Wednesday evening till Monday morning, leaving only three days a week for private warfare. Even these three days a week were ruled out during Lent, Advent, the great feasts of Our Lady, and the feasts of the Apostle and other saints. The Truce of God remained effective for about two centuries, from the eleventh to the end of the twelfth century, and its effectiveness waned in the thirteenth century, owing to the needs of the popes themselves to forget the Truce of God in their struggle against the House of Hohenstaufen. The church likewise forbade interest on loans made for economically unproductive purposes, such as fighting. "If the church had maintained the authority which it had in the twelfth century," states R. F. Wright, "it is possible that it would gradually have extended the Truce of God and the Peace of God until there was a complete outlawry of war."

Although the church controlled or banished many wars, both public and private, it did not succeed in beating many swords into ploughshares. One reason for it was that the servants of the church, like all those of secular institutions, succumbed to the temptation of power; they grew abusive, mundane, corrupt and tyrannical. As a result, they failed to gain the confidence and trust of their people: and peace and security do not flourish in a land where there is no faith and trust in men. Another main reason was that several of the ambitious and worldly-minded popes created a series of armed contests with the secular princes for power and supremacy. Still another main reason was that the church promoted the famous, or infamous, crusade against the infidels which lasted over several centuries, costing untold lives and treasure, and sponsored most cruel and barbarous wars against the so-called heretics in the name, and for the sake, of the ever-kind and merciful God. Thus, the medieval church, like most of the national states of our times, prevented many petty wars only to create bigger and better ones.

Even if it is assumed that the ancient and the medieval religious institutions were very successful in restraining wars, as they undoubtedly were in many instances, it cannot be expected that they can serve as an effective instrument of restraining warfare today, when the promise of heaven and the fear of hell can no longer prevent the people from resorting to violence.

Besides, as we have already seen, the worship of the same god does not necessarily mean peace. On the contrary, the people who worship one god have had more religious wars than those who believe in different gods. It sounds strange, but it is rather logical. When you recognize only one god, the god whom you conceive of as a true god, you cannot respect other gods or tolerate different interpretation of the same deity. You must therefore conquer the other gods or annihilate the so-called heretics whose interpretation of the same deity does not agree with yours. It is natural then that most religious wars have been waged by the monotheists, either against each other or against alien faiths.

It is unthinkable that any intelligent people could have kept killing each other off by the thousands over such trifling arguments as whether God's name was Allah, or Jehovah, Johnny or Billy; whether his nose was an inch longer or shorter; whether the color of his eyes was blue or brown; whether he wore a hat or a turban, a gown or a suit; whether he created the universe 6,000 years ago or 5,999 years; or whether he made the earth round or flat. But that is precisely what the monotheists have done for centuries and all for the glory of God, who is a merciful Father of all.

On the other hand, when you believe in many gods, or in the

right of others to interpret the same deity differently, according to their own taste, there is little room for religious intolerance and bigotry. This explains why most of the polytheists have lived together harmoniously with the followers of different faiths. Even among the people who recognize the existence of many gods, religious conflict has not been entirely absent because the followers of one faith, at times, have tried to place their deity over and above those of other beliefs. For instance, the famous Tang Emperor Wu Tsung, who was a Taoist, was reported to have destroyed 4,600 temples of Buddhist, Christian and Zoroastrian faiths and secularized 260,00 priests and nuns. His persecution of other religious followers, however, constitutes an unusual exception in the land which has been so long noted for its religious tolerance.

What has created religious peace is not the acceptance of one faith, but the recognition of a complete religious freedom and tolerance. The Near East, for instance, was bathed in blood when the Mohammedans sought to propagate their faith with the sword as taught in the Koran, which reads, "When ye encounter the unbelievers, strike off their heads, until ye have made a great slaughter among them." But peace and harmony returned when the followers of Allah abandoned their hideous practice of butchering men to save their souls. Christian Europe likewise was torn by religious war for centuries when the Catholic Church insisted upon the acceptance of its own interpretation of God, but religious strife ceased with the recognition of the right of the Protestant countries to interpret God to suit their consciences. Few lovers of peace, therefore, should press for the repetition of the bloody drama of religious crusades in the name of universal peace or for the sake of saving a few stray souls from hell-fire.

Furthermore, so long as the present state of international anarchy continues to exist, it will be impossible for men to accept one and the same god. This is because man can see god only so far as his mind fashioned by the environment allows him to see. Fashioned by the primitive environment in the primitive stage of development, he learned to conceive of god as the god of tribes. In the national stage of development, he learned to think of him as the god of a state. To most men today God is just that and no more, else why should they pray to him for their national victory against other states?

Moreover, until all mankind is organized under a single authority to preserve justice, it will be impossible for men to live according to the precepts of love, charity and justice. For how can they learn to love one another like brothers when they are constantly forced to hate, despise, rob and murder their fellowmen in the name of national honor and self-preservation? Twenty centuries of preaching have failed to prevent the so-called Christian nations from slaughtering one another like beasts of prey. The fault does not lie in religion; it lies in international anarchy. So long as the present system of world anarchy exists, a million years of preaching will not teach men to live as Jesus taught us to live.

What all sincere men of God should do, therefore, is not merely to shout that there will be no peace on earth until all men accept the same God, and love one another like brothers, but it is to combine all their spiritual and physical forces and drive forward toward the establishment of a new world authority in which men can live in peace and justice as Jesus taught them and the nations can prosper without wasting their energy and resources for mutual slaughter.

6. Peace through Universal Education

From Confucius and Plato down to John Dewey and Robert Hutchins, many educators have regarded ignorance and misunderstanding as the roots of most troubles. They have, therefore, endeavored to create peace and harmony on earth through the promotion of education and understanding. Their educational crusade has made a great stride with the assent of democracy which recognized all human beings as equals and with the introduction of modern science which has made it possible for everyone to get an education.

They introduced a system of universal education in every

civilized country in the world. They lured or forced every boy or girl, even the deaf and the dumb, into the schools and taught them world geography, world history, and world economic problems, in the hope that they would grow bigger and better morally and intellectually. They also introduced a means of exchanging students and faculty members with other countries, and of holding peace conferences under various auspices. As a result, any fool in the modern world has come to possess more knowledge, though not wisdom, than any philosopher in the ancient or medieval world. But this amazing advancement of education, unprecedented in all history, has failed to preserve peace among the nations. On the contrary, it has helped men wage the most cruel and destructive wars in all ages. One cannot help wondering if the fault lies with the educators, or the militant and materialistic system of education, or the general world conditions which shape the educational policies of all nations.

It is a fact that many educators have too often forced their poor students to learn their hair-splitting details of all sorts of dead, putrid and unimportant things in the world without helping them to acquire and cultivate the vision and wisdom to understand the fundamental principles of life in our ever-changing world.

It is also a fact that Western education has been too materialistic and too pragmatic to teach man the great moral, intellectual and spiritual values of life. It has taught man how to make money and how to make all kinds of inconceivable things except himself. So he has developed science and inventions, but not his mind and soul. He has built great machines, factories and fortifications, but he has not improved much of his morals and manners, and his mental and spiritual outlook on life. He has multiplied a thousandfold his scientific powers to create or destroy, but he has not widened to the same extent his compassion, kindness, sympathy and willingness to serve his fellow-men. In other words, modern education has taught man the science of war, not the arts of peace. As a result, he is but a savage armed with modern science. It is natural then that man uses his science and inventions for building battleships and bombing planes instead of for developing a peaceful culture and civilization, for waging wars of conquest and expansion instead of for preserving peace and justice, for mutual slaughter and destruction instead of for mutual aid and co-operation.

The chief responsibility for the failure of education to inculcate in men the great moral and spiritual values of life, or to teach them the arts of peace instead of the science of war, does not lie in the laps of the poor, innocent educators as much as it does in the state of international anarchy in which all nations are constantly pressed by the necessity of mobilizing all their moral, material, educational and religious forces for the purpose of waging wars in defense of their honor, justice and right.

Education is only an agency of teaching and learning. It can teach man to be good and kind or cruel and barbarous. It can teach men to build and help as well as to destroy and kill. In the state of international anarchy, all it can do is to teach men to love and respect only those settled in the same watertight compartment but to hate and despise all those who live under a different flag. It can teach the principle of the brotherhood of man and the fatherhood of God, but such a faith should not interfere with the belief in pseudo patriotism, jingoistic nationalism and self-centered egotistic chauvinism. It can discourage men from committing little crimes, such as stealing chickens or toys, or murdering one or two persons belonging to the same nationals, but it must still teach them to commit big crimes like stealing big states or massacring thousands of their fellowmen in the name of patriotism and national honor.

We have heard often that this double standard morality, rather the lack of international ethics and morals, is the main cause of all troubles in the world. But morality is a product of organized communal living. There can be no ethics and morals in the state of international anarchy where there is no authority which can decree what is good and what is bad. Where there are no universal ethics and morals, no education can cultivate international morals broad enough to apply to all peoples. In other words, education in the present state of anarchy is incapable of teaching the principles of universal peace and cooperation.

Perhaps Herbert Spencer was right when he stated that unless men have a better social system than the present one, it will be impossible for them to attain a higher degree of moral and intellectual development. For you cannot grow a big man with broad international love and friendship within four walls, any more than you can grow a whale in a puddle.

Intelligent though they were, the ancient Greeks, locked up behind their impenetrable city walls, could learn to think and live only as citizens of a certain city, Athens or Sparta, not as proud citizens of all the Hellenic world. The Romans, on the other hand, were not nearly as intelligent as the Greeks, but they learned to think and live as citizens of the Mediterranean world because their mental and spiritual development was not hampered by the prejudices of the city states as was the Greeks'.

It is not only men who accommodate themselves to shifting environments. The gods do also. Jehovah was little more than a tribal god within the framework of Israel, but he was transformed into a God of all Christendom when he was introduced into the Roman World State.

One hundred and fifty years ago there was little difference between the mental and spiritual outlook of the American and the European peoples. But today the Americans can think and live in terms of a world state, the United States of America, not in terms of Virginia, Texas, Wisconsin; therefore, they have enjoyed a state of comparative peace, whereas the Europeans still think and live in terms of France, Germany and Poland, not in terms of the United States of Europe, and therefore they have suffered a state of perpetual war.

Any student of human relations can readily see what has brought about this amazing mental and spiritual revolution of the American people within a century and a half. It is, of course, the formation of a more perfect union, possessing a preponderance of power, which banished anarchy among the several states. Had the fathers of the American Union waited until their constituents learned to be broad enough to welcome a more perfect union, it is very doubtful if the conditions in America would be any different from those in Europe today. But thanks to their wisdom, they did not wait. They just went ahead with the formation of a more perfect union and banished international anarchy, and then their educators taught and their people learned to fit into the larger framework.

In view of the foregoing facts, we can see the absurdity of the contention that there will be no world peace until men learn to love and respect all human beings as brothers. The truth is that men will never learn to live with other peoples as they do with their own nationals until the whole world is organized into a single unit. It is because in the present state of international anarchy, educators must teach and the peoples must learn how to kill and destroy, instead of learning how to love and respect each other. So long as the present state of chaos continues to exist, then, a million years of schooling will not beat many swords into ploughshares.

7. Peace through Economic Reforms and Communism

Many students of human relations, especially since Karl Marx, have believed that the economic factor is the most fundamental cause of war. They have maintained that all wars fought in the name of gods, morals and ethics, states and empires, have been motivated by economic interests and have been waged on account of the almighty dollar. With this kind of assumption, they have struggled for centuries to build peace and prosperity through economic reforms.

They have tackled the question by attacking the unsound taxing system, the unfair profit system, the ruthless competitive system, and the merciless exploitation of the workers. They have tackled it by introducing measures of relief for the poor, by developinig scientific farming and manufacturing and by facilitating free trade between the nations. In spite of all these, poverty and war have plagued mankind at an ever-accellerating rate.

Those who have been disillusioned by the failure to save mankind from poverty and war through these reform measures have abandoned all hope for a better world under the capitalistic system, and cry aloud for communism and socialism. But one wonders if the road to peace and prosperity through communism or socialism will not lead them to the same disappointment.

Long before Karl Marx and even Plato, the ants and bees introduced a sort of state socialism, and yet they still wage atrocious wars, comparable to those fought by our capitalistic states. Most of the primitive peoples likewise practiced various forms of communism, but they enjoyed neither peace nor prosperity. So other things being equal, it may be only an illusion to believe, as Harold Laski and his associates do, that Socialism or Communism will insure peace and prosperity.

There are several reasons why these economic measures have uniformly failed to create peace and prosperity. First, the ultimate cause of war is not economic, but international anarchy and therefore peace cannot be created by economic means without banishing the state of anarchy. Second, the chief cause of poverty in our times is not the lack of wealth, but the misuse of it and therefore the problem of poverty cannot be solved without preventing the misuse of wealth for mutual destruction.

There was a time when men's search for food, shelter and clothing constituted a major cause of strife. For instance, where there were no scientific means of production and no equitable methods of exchange, the warring for loot and plunder was one of the few available means of gaining economic objectives. Hence many wars were waged for economic reasons. But in this age of science the motive for economic gains is not and cannot be regarded as a necessary cause of war, because with the aid of science and invention there is no nation under the sun which cannot make both ends meet. Besides, the nature of warfare has undergone such a change that no nation can attain its economic objectives through conquest. Finally, the interests of the world are so interwoven that no nation can enrich itself by looting or destroying other countries. Let me amplify these points briefly.

The Anheuser-Busch Company, St. Louis, Missouri, has worked out a method of making synthetic beefsteaks, which if perfected, will make cows and pigs museum pieces. The new food is produced by mixing molasses, ammonia, water, air and yeast. By this process a ton of synthetic meat can be produced every twelve hours in a vat one thousand cubic feet in size. At this rate of production a factory covering the area of a large aircraft corporation in the United States can produce enough food to feed the whole country.

Dr. W. F. Gericke, associate plant physiologist of the University of California, has succeeded in growing tomato plants as high as orange trees and tobacco plants as large as oak trees! He produced at the rate of 217 tons of tomatoes per acre and 2,465 bushels of potatoes against the present United States average of 116 bushels. He did this by the following methods: he filled the shallow tanks with a liquid composed of chemicals. Over the tanks he spread wire screens covered with straw, excelsior or moss, in which the seeds are planted. The roots of the plants thrust down into the water, not into the ground, to draw nourishment. If food is grown at this rate, the peoples of the world will need no farms at all; all they will need is a small victory garden, the size of lawns in the metropolitan residential districts.

Some scientists go so far as to maintain that with the aid of science, and as long as there is air, water, and sunlight, men can swim in plenty. Dr. G. F. Nicolai, for example, maintains in *The Biology of War* that if man could utilize all the energy liberated from the sun, then instead of eleven human beings, twenty millions can make a living out of each square kilometer. He elaborates on his assertion by giving the approximate number of population which can be supported by the earth in each of the four periods as follows:

Barbaric period	100,000,000
The present agrarian period	1,500,000,000
Maximum agrarian period	20,000,000,000
Period of full utilization	3,000,000,000,000

THE EARLY WESTERN CONTRIBUTION TO PEACE

Besides, the nature of war has so changed that it has become impossible to attain economic objectives through war. When men fought with bows and arrows they could stage profitable raiding parties with little or no capital. Even in modern times the imperialistic nations occasionally seized valuable territories with little difficulty because they were very poorly defended. But even these territories which were seized at no cost have not proved economically profitable to most controlling countries. It is not difficult to understand why political and territorial expansion did not add much to national welfare and prosperity.

Let us suppose the city of Chicago conquers and annexes the city of St. Louis. In order to conquer St. Louis, Chicago must invest billions of dollars for the preparation of the war, and St. Louis will have done the same to ward off attacks. In the ensuing struggle much wealth will have been destroyed and many people will have lost their lives. Finally, when the victor takes over the city of the vanquished, he is obliged to take not only the wealth of the captured city, but the people who own the wealth, and the responsibility to preserve peace and order, and the obligation to defend it against attacks from other aggressors. Consequently, the victor spends not only all he gets out of the conquered city, but much more from his own pocket. Hence the theory that empires founded on conquest are essential for national welfare is a "great illusion." Such is the substance of the message which Norman Angell gives in *The Great Illusion* and Grover Clark gives in *The Balance Sheets of Imperialism*.

Furthermore, science has made the world literally one small community. The Atlantic and the Pacific, which were once unfathomable, are now only small ponds, and America, Asia and Europe are so close to each other that they can talk across the ponds as easily as one can talk across the table. Their economic life is so integrated that no nation can enrich itself by robbing and destroying others.

The ancient Romans were very jealous of the prosperity of Carthage, especially so since the Carthaginians joked about the Roman senators being so poor that they had to borrow silverware from their neighbors when entertaining guests. So they conquered Carthage, massacred its inhabitants and ploughed over the ruined city and scattered salt over it. But they could not capture the prosperity of Carthage, which died with the destruction of its people. If the Romans could not swim in plenty through plunder in the ancient world, how could anyone, except morons and lunatics, hope to promote the welfare of their countries today by robbing and conquering other peoples? So all the talk that wars are waged for economic necessity is a fraud and an inexcusable lie.

It should be admitted, however, that many imperialistic wars have been promoted by selfish business interests, such as arms makers and allied industries, in their relentless search for profits. They have promoted such wars in the name of national honor and national interests, and at the cost of millions of lives and billions of dollars of their fellow countrymen, they have made millions for themselves. But the main reason for them to make profits by such antisocial methods is the favorable condition of waging such predatory wars created by the absence of a world organization to safeguard the legitimate interests of various nations. Had there been a capable central authority to protect the common interest of all mankind, the war for economic gains among the nations, whether waged by Germany on England and Russia, or Japan on China and the United States, would be no more conceivable than similar wars being waged by New York against New Jersey or Illinois against Indiana. But there has been no such world organization to safeguard the common interests of all nations. Naturally, many unscrupulous business interests have sought to make fortunes by promoting such predatory wars, as many adventurous men try to solve their economic problems by robbery or banditry whenever there is an even chance to do so.

Several years ago there was widespread bank robbery throughout the United States, the richest and most prosperous country in the world, where few men could not solve their economic problems by honest means even in the depression. Robbery swept the country like a plague, and there was hardly a decent bank in the land which was not visited by these daring bandits. Almost any superficial student of social science would say that the cause of the robbery was economic, but the real cause was the failure of the authorities to protect public interest. I know that was the cause of it, because no sooner had the law stepped in with an effective force than bank robbery ceased. Robbery ceased not so much because of the improved economic situation, as because the chances for a successful holdup had grown so slim that few daring men tried to make a fortune by holding up the banks.

This case alone seems to show that in any community however prosperous, where the central political authority is absent, or inefficient, or corrupt, the harmful enterprises like burglary, robbery, theft or war can be profitable at least for a few successful hoodlums, and therefore they can and will flourish. But when the community is firmly established for the enjoyment of peace and justice by the majority of the people, none of these destructive elements detrimental to the welfare of the community can prosper. In other words, all the so-called economic wars, like all other wars between states, are born of international anarchy. Without banishing the state of anarchy, therefore, even if the whole world were made as rich and prosperous as the United States, it would not help materially to banish strife among the nations. On the contrary, it would only enable the war lords of the world to wage bigger and more destructive wars, as the increased production and freer exchange of goods did to Germany and Japan.

Furthermore, as modern wars consume or destroy in a few hours what has taken centuries to save and build, it would be impossible to lift up humanity from poverty and starvation without preventing the civilized nations from wasting most of their resources for war. Nor is it possible to prevent the people from sacrificing their wealth for war without organizing the world for peace and security. For how can anyone convince the people of the wisdom of using their resources for bread and butter when they cannot enjoy their bread and butter without powerful bullets and tanks? How can you persuade them to beat their swords into ploughshares when they know that without the sword, they cannot keep what their ploughshares will bring?

So long as the fear of aggression hangs overhead like the sword of Damocles, all the peoples, however peaceful, will keep on spending most of their energy and resources for wars and for preparation of more wars. So long as the nations keep on working and producing for destruction, even if they work day and night, weekdays and Sundays, 365 days a year without vacation, and always working overtime, no nation will enjoy a lasting prosperity, for the harder they work for destruction, the poorer the world will grow. Other things being equal, therefore, none of the attempts to solve the economic and social problems, like the Russian Five-Year Plan, Beveridge's Social Security Plan and Wallace's Sixty Million Job Plan, will save the world from poverty and bankruptcy. All one has to do to convince oneself of the soundness of this conclusion is to review the present situation in Europe and the world at large.

But when the question of security against aggression is solved all other apparently indissoluble problems, including the economic one, can be solved automatically. It is because when the fear of aggression is removed, all science and inventions, all energy and resources, all manpower and wealth of the world can be released from the field of destruction and impoverishment into that of reconstruction and rehabilitation. When all science and resources are employed for the welfare of the peoples, instead of mutual destruction, there is no man or country which cannot literally swim in plenty. No man or woman or child, either with or without position, will have to suffer from want of anything. No man will have to worry about jobs, nor will he have to work more than a few days a week or a few weeks a year, unless he chooses voluntarily to work more. But he will enjoy luxury and comfort unheard of except among the kings and queens, millionaires and labor union leaders of our times because when he produces for living instead of killing, he will actually enrich the world, even if he works only a few hours a week, whereas when he works for destruction, even if he works his head off, he and the rest of the workers will grow poorer and poorer.

When the question is examined from this angle, one can readily see the absurdity of the statement which we hear daily that no world peace can be founded without reorganizing the economic system of the world to provide every man with a good job which will lift him up from misery and poverty. The truth is that until the world is organized for peace and all the powers of production are converted into peaceful purposes, untold millions of human beings, no matter how desperately they struggle, will always rot and decay in the seas of misery and poverty. It is likewise absurd to maintain that, without solving the economic problems of the world, it will be impossible for the nations to organize the world for peace. The truth is that, without organizing the world for peace under a centralized authority to preserve justice among the nations, it will be impossible for men to solve any of the major economic problems of the world.

To put it bluntly, it is sheer nonsense to talk about peace and prosperity through the overthrow of capitalism or through the introduction of Communism or Socialism. If the world is organized to prevent the misuse of energy and resources for war purposes, even capitalism will give us prosperity and peace. But in the continued state of anarchy, even Communism and Socialism and all other isms will not give peace and prosperity. Unfortunately, however, many men believe that socialism and communism will give what capitalism has failed to give because they do not understand that the reason why capitalism has not given us prosperity is not so much due to its own fault as to the state of anarchy in which it is forced to yield its fruits of labor for destruction rather than for consumption.

Other things being equal, there is even less chance to enjoy peace and prosperity in a communistic society than under a capitalistic system. There are several reasons for making such an assumption. In the first place, the capitalistic system as an agent of production has found no equal to it. I think even the Russian Communists admit this, or else they would not have introduced into their country some of the features of the capitalistic system, for example, the present wage-scale used in Russia. It is clear that the failure of capitalism to give mankind prosperity is not due to its inefficiency as to the state of international anarchy in which capitalism is forced to yield its fruits of labor for destruction rather than construction.

Secondly, even if it is assumed that communism is equal, or superior, to capitalism in the field of production and distribution, there is no assurance that men will enjoy a greater degree of peace and prosperity in a communistic world. As communists believe in overthrowing established governments by bullets rather than ballots, there will be more wars in communistic society than in a capitalistic world where people believe in orderly processes of government. Since war is the greatest single cause of poverty and misery, there could be no more prosperity in a communistic world than in a capitalistic society.

Karl Marx maintained that in the socialist millennium the government itself will wither away. When there is no government, how can anyone wage a revolutionary war against a government which does not exist? But the time will never come when men can live without a government. Even among the angels there must be a government to restrain the bad angels for the benefit of the good ones. The promise of a socialist millennium without a government is only a fraud designed to sanctify the dictatorship of the few for the ruthless oppression and exploitation of the common men; it is far more fraudulent than the primitive concept of heaven and hell which was used as a means of exploiting millions of wretched men in the Dark Ages. Unless the whole world is organized under one authority for common security, the search for peace and prosperity through Karl Marx and his communism is doomed to eternal failure.

8. Peace through Democracy

Those who believe that wars are created by the totalitarian powers naturally expect that peace will reign when dictators are gone. But I wonder if universal peace will automatically prevail even when all states have been transformed into democracies.

The animals, states Allee, have both democracy and dictatorship. The ants and bees, for instance, have a sort of democracy, with each member assigned to certain functions without recourse to war. But hens and some fish practice dictatorship, establishing their pecking order through physical combat. The democratic animals, however, have not banished warfare altogether, although they have fought less than those practicing dictatorship.

Among human beings, whether democracies have been more peaceful or more warlike is a difficult question to answer. It is a fact that some primitive peoples, living in a democracy, were more peaceful than those under a dictatorship. But some others, like the Iroquois, were very warlike although they practiced democracy. In general, one could say that democratic primitives were somewhat more peaceful than the other savages. But was their peacefulness due to democracy, or their democracy due to their peacefulness? I am more inclined to think that their democracy was due to their peacefulness than the other way around. For democracy cannot flourish in the atmosphere of war, as war means regimentation and regimentation means dictatorship, not democracy. As democracy can thrive best on peaceful soil and at peaceful times, it flourished with some primitives when they enjoyed peace through isolation or some other fortunate circumstances, but faded and withered away, even though temporarily, when war came like frost. So the relative peacefulness of a few primitive democracies fails to prove much of anything, except the contention that democracy is a product of peace rather than peace being the product of democracy.

Quincy Wright gives in his *A Study of War* the number of major wars which the leading states fought between 1480 and 1941:

| Great Britain | 78 | Savoy (Italy) | 25 |
| France | 71 | Netherlands | 23 |

Spain	64	Prussia (Germany)	23
Russia	61	Denmark	20
Empire (Austria)	52	United States	13
Turkey	43	China	11
Poland	30	Japan	9
Sweden	26		

If the foregoing figures represent the relative warlikeness of the states, Germany, Italy and Japan do not seem as warlike as most people of our times believe. Nor do the so-called democracies seem to have been half as peaceful as some people claim them to be. But fortunately, the numbers do not appear to represent the nations' comparative peacefulness for several reasons. First, the figures do not state whether a certain war has been fought in self-defense or for an outright aggression. As even peaceful states often fight in self-defense, the mere number of wars does not explain the degree of warlikeness of the states. Furthermore, as Wright states, the numbers do not include all the numerous minor wars. For instance, the United States is listed as having fought only thirteen wars, but she has been engaged in over 170 distinct military campaigns. As the same may be true of some other countries, a complete list of all revolutions, insurrections, interventions, punitive expeditions, pacifications and explorations involving the use of armed force would make many times this number for some countries, without much affecting the figures for some other states. Pending the appearance of complete data for all countries, any talk on the relative warlikeness of democracies and totalitarian powers will have to remain largely guess work.

Nevertheless, it appears to be the general conclusion of most discriminating students of history that the so-called peace-loving democracies have been nearly as warlike as the totalitarian powers. Democratic Athens was as warlike as oligarchic Sparta, except some thirty years under Pericles when Athens was beautified. Democratic France and England have been as militant as totalitarian Germany and Russia down the pages of history. What of the United States of America, the torchbearer of peace and justice? Wright states cautiously that the United States has "perhaps somewhat unjustifiably" prided itself on its peacefulness, as it "has had only twenty-years during its entire history when its army or navy has not been in active military operations during some days, somewhere."

If democracies are as warlike as the totalitarian powers, what prospects are there for winning the peace through democracy? Probably not much, but we must know the reason why the democracies have been as warlike as the dictatorships. It is due to the fact that both systems existed in the same state of international anarchy in which both were equally pressed by the same necessity to defend their rights and to insure their survival by armed forces. So long as this state of international anarchy continues to exist, the mere overthrow of the totalitarian powers by the so-called democracies will give us no more peace than the overthrow of the absolute kings has.

In the days of absolute kings and tyrants, who carried out an eternal struggle for dynastic ambitions, many philosophers like Locke, Rousseau, Kant and a whole chain of them regarded the institution of absolute kings, namely, of dictatorship, as the chief cause of war. They, therefore, tried hard to restrain the power of the kings and tyrants by advancing the democratic principles of government—the government of the people, by the people, for the people. Subsequently, many of the kings were either hanged by the mobs or were drowned or swept away by the tide of democracy. Hardly a king or queen who was important enough to be assassinated was left free to wage wars for dynastic motives. But new dictatorships arose from the ashes of the old ones and have continued to wage wars without end.

It is obvious why such a tragic situation has developed time and again from the days of Alexander down to today. It is all due to international chaos in which war is a normal occurrence. Where war is normal, dictatorships flourish and democracies either die out or imitate the totalitarian ways and grow belligerent. As the same situation will continue so long as the old state of international anarchy remains intact, the only hope for the triumph of lasting peace and democracy seems to lie in the banishment of international anarchy through the creation of an organized world authority.

Assuming the soundness of the foregoing conclusions, it is not right to maintain that democracy must be spread throughout the world before we can have peace. The correct view is that in order to enjoy freedom and democracy we must organize the world for peace through the co-operation of all forces, democratic or totalitarian, as we did in defeating the Axis in the war. Because democracy can prevail best in peace and dictatorship in war, given a century of uninterrupted peace, all forms of dictatorship, be it German, Japanese or Russian, might be as dead as dodo bones.

It should be admitted that peace does not necessarily create democracy, nor does war necessarily result in dictatorship. The Americans and the British have preserved democracy despite the numerous wars they have fought. The Japanese, the Siamese and many other Asiatics failed to develop it although they enjoyed a comparative state of tranquillity until recent years. Nevertheless, peace is more favorable for the development of democracy because in the absence of war, or threats of wars, most people would naturally prefer democracy as it is a superior way of life. When faced with the threats of war, even the free peoples are obliged to sacrifice their democratic way of life. The greater the danger, the more democratic freedom they are obliged to yield. In the state of constant war, therefore, the enjoyment of democracy is very difficult, if not impossible.

9. Peace through Conquest and Domination

All the lessons from history show that there are only two effective ways of creating order out of chaos. One is through voluntary co-operation whereby several independent political units federate themselves under a supreme organization created by mutual agreement. The other is through armed domination by which the conqueror imposes the rule of law upon the vanquished.

In not a few cases in history both savages and civilized men have succeeded in banishing anarchy by federating several tribes or states in the face of an overwhelming danger. The Greek unity in the face of the Persian invasion, the Swiss federation amidst the warring states of Europe, and the American federation of the thirteen states against European domination are some of the glowing examples of this. But the number of such voluntary federations is very small. In about ninety-nine cases out of a hundred, intertribal and international anarchy has been cured only through brutal conquest. It may be due to the tragic fact that human beings in general have been too stupid, too short-sighted and too much obsessed with fear, hatred and jealousy to achieve a union through voluntary co-operation and, therefore, only the cold, merciless force of iron and steel could bring them under the authority of law for the enjoyment of peace and security.

The ancient Chinese, for instance, suffered a long period of anarchy between 722 and 221 B.C. The period of unrest began with the growing impotency and corruption of the celebrated Chou Dynasty which began its reign in 1100 B.C. With the collapse of the central authority some 150 feudal states started their struggle for power. But in due time, most of the smaller states were either conquered or absorbed by the powerful ones. By the time of Confucius there were only some fourteen states against about twenty-seven states in Europe on the eve of the Second World War. These warring states in ancient China duplicated the history of modern Europe in almost every detail. They played power politics and gambled with the balance of power system; they produced great thinkers and philosophers like Lao-tse, Motze, and Confucius; they held peace conferences similar to The Hague conferences and developed a system of international law. In short, they tried to rescue themselves from anarchy and chaos by the same methods tried by the modern nations. But wars marched on.

At last there arose Chin Shih Huang Ti, the ruler of a semi-barbarous state. He was a counterpart of modern Hitler—cold, calculating, murderous and efficient, hardly a person but an instrument of inscrutable destiny. Employing precisely the same methods which Hitler used, he conquered all the warring states. The secret weapon which enabled him to carry out his blitz was the cavalry, which was superior to the clumsy chariots of his enemies.

Following his successful conquest, he abolished feudalism and moved all the surviving noble families to Shensi, where their movements could be watched and controlled. He unified the whole country under one centralized authority and divided the new empire into thirty-six provinces controlled through governors appointed by him.

When the Confucian scholars criticized his cruel and inhumane methods and opposed his drastic reform measures, he burned the Confucian classics and executed some 460 scholars. The burning of the classics and the execution of the scholars were probably more offensive to the Chinese than most of the crimes committed by Hitler's gang are to modern men. He earned so much ill-will and hatred of the Chinese people that his dynasty lasted only from 221 to 206 B.C. But in that short period, he destroyed all things with such thoroughness and efficiency that old China could never again arise on its feudal foundations. Ever since, China has had many days and nights of unity and dissension, but she always recovered her unity in the end.

Were it not for Chin Shih Huang Ti, the man who has been hated and condemned for twenty-two centuries, I wonder if China could ever have been united. For in any country in any age, when the people are so incurably obsessed with centuries of accumulated hatred and jealousy as ancient China was, nothing but cold, cruel force could have created order out of chaos.

Similar stories could be multiplied by the hundreds from the pages of other nations' history books. The anarchy of the Hellenic world was cured, not by the wisdom of Plato and

Aristotle, but by the military might of King Philip of Macedon, who was comparable to Chin Shih Huang Ti of China. It was the unsurpassed military prowess of the Romans rather than the philosophy of Seneca or of Marcus Aurelius which preserved peace and order in the Mediterranean rimlands for several centuries. It was not so much the wisdom and intelligence of Europe as the overwhelming military forces of the several princes which crushed some two thousand warring sovereignties in sixteenth century Europe and molded them into several national states, which preserved peace within their respective dominions. With one or two exceptions, there is hardly a nation in the modern world which has not been rescued from interminable civil wars by heroes armed with swords. Modern France was formed out of eighty separate warring states through the effective use of force; modern Germany was created out of some nine hundred warring territories by the same means; modern Japan was created out of some three hundred feudal states by similar methods.

The story of how the Tokugawa Shogunate preserved peace in feudal Japan for nearly two and a half centuries is unique, to say the least, not only because the Japanese are a belligerent people but because feudalism has often been synonymous with strife. Following the unification of the country by Iyeyasu's military exploits, the 262 daimyos, or feudal chiefs, were obliged to move their families to Yedo, modern Tokyo, the seat of the Shogun government. The chiefs themselves were required to live in the capital for at least half of the time lest they plot revolts from their fiefs. Ordinarily the diamyos were to pay no contributions to the Shogun government, but in time of crisis, they were to supply military forces at their own expense. When some diamyos grew wealthy and powerful, the central government bestowed on them such honors as controlling the rivers and building castles for the purpose of preventing the powerful feudal lords from conspiring and rebelling. The building of the famous castle of Nagoya drained the treasuries of twenty diamyos. The lord of Satsuma was ordered to repair the levees of the Kiso River, 750 miles from his fief. His samurais went so far as to borrow money from Osaka bankers to complete the work, lest their lord receive the punishment from the Shogun. Undoubtedly, many of the Shogun's repressive measures were harsh and unjust. But it is questionable if any method less drastic could have preserved peace among the belligerent islanders so long as it did.

There are, however, a few fundamental weaknesses in the method of banishing anarchy through militarism, imperialism and domination. The first is that the peace under a dictatorship, whether Roman or Japanese, has been the peace of the grave without freedom, without progress, without all the blessings of life, without which peace is not worth preserving. The second is that the cost of war has been too great to bear. The third is that the peace obtained through armed domination has always been short-lived and has been followed by more disastrous conflicts on an ever-increasing scale.

When Athens and Sparta took turns in seeking domination of their smaller neighbors, there was no peace in ancient Greece. Pax Romana, based on the principle of armed domination, gave more wars than peace except for about two centuries between 27 B.C. and A.D. 180.

Unlike the Romans, the old Chinese did not go strongly for conquest and domination. On the whole, they sought to build a superior civilization at home instead of empires abroad. As a result East Asia has been more peaceful than Europe. But even then, occasionally when ambitious rulers of China sought to dominate the smaller kingdoms, war and strife resulted.

There was no peace between England and her colonists when the mother country sought to dominate them. Only when the British substituted after the independence of the United States co-operation on an equal footing for armed domination by the mother country did the Anglo-Saxon world come to enjoy an enviable degree of co-operation.

Peace in the new world, even after the formation of a union by the United States, was not much more enviable than that of Europe. There were wars and rumors of wars in both Americas until the United States renounced the old ideas of conquest and domination and adopted the policy of the good neighbor, an old Chinese policy dressed up in American style. And, if the United States as a leading power adopts the same policy which Germany and Japan adopted, namely, refuse to respect the rights of the smaller nations and seek conquest and domination, the New World will probably be no more peaceful than Europe, regardless of how many Pan-American Unions work, how many treaties are made and how many peace conferences are held.

Anyone who still has some doubt about the futility of attempting to create peace through this old method should just consider for a moment what Hitler, Mussolini and Hirohito have done to the world with their attempt to create peace of their own choosing through the principle of conquest and domination. Thousands of years of struggle by other warriors to create eternal peace and security through the same principles have only made mankind progressively more belligerent and destructive. Any attempt to establish peace by this age-old method by the Big Three or Big Five, jointly or separately, is bound to produce the same result: more catastrophic wars.

It should be pointed out, however, that the desire for conquest and domination springs largely from the fear of insecurity. The greater the fear of insecurity, the greater the desire for domination, because in domination there is a sense of security, even though only temporarily.

W. E. Caldwell, author of *Hellenic Conceptions of Peace*, believes that Athenian imperialism was born of the fear of insecurity, as the Athenians were dependent on imported grain for food. According to Virgil, the early Romans preferred the ploughshares to the sword, but they were obliged to take up the latter because of the hostile savage tribes who had menaced their safety. Similarly, modern British imperialism was born of the same parentage, the fear of insecurity in the struggle for survival against hostile Spain and other continental empires. Modern Japanese imperialism is likewise a product of the fear of insecurity created by Czarist Russia and the European powers. The present Russian drive for domination in Asia and Europe is largely born of the fear of attack by the capitalistic nations.

The comparative absence of the desire for conquest and domination in the old Chinese and the modern Americans may have been due to the position of security which few other nations enjoyed. For even these peoples have been obliged to resort to policies of domination whenever their security has been threatened by enemies. When menaced by the northern barbarians, the Chinese conquered them and annexed their territories until China came to cover most of Eastern Asia. Confronted by the "Western Barbarians" in the nineteenth century, they sought to tighten their hold on Indo-China and Korea, over which countries China had seldom exercised any authority.

The present-day Americans sent their troops all over the world in the face of the totalitarian threat to American security, and conquered the Axis Powers and controlled their countries for no other purpose than insuring American security.

Were it not for the fear of insecurity, the Athenians probably would not have sought for the domination of the Hellenic world; the Romans probably would not have obliterated Carthage; Hitler and Tojo probably would not have cared to risk all they had for world domination. Similarly, were it not for the threats to their security, the Americans would not want to play any part in the European and Asiatic affairs; the British would not be reluctant in relaxing their control over their colonial possessions; nor would the Russians be so vigorous in pushing for their domination of Europe and Asia. But because of the fear of Russian aggression both Britain and America have found it necessary to keep their troops in all parts of the earth. Because of the fear of attack by the capitalistic states, Russia insists on controlling, by hook and crook, all lands and seas from which an attack might be launched.

In the absence of means to guard the nations against the fear of attack, nothing will prevent them from struggling for domination. The best way, therefore, to prevent Russia and other nations from pursuing the old policies of conquest and domination in Asia and Europe is through the development of a world security organization which will remove the fear of insecurity from the hearts of all nations, large or small.

10. Peace through the Balance of Power

The balance of power is a system of power politics which was born of anarchy, is nourished by anarchy and is maintained for the perpetuation of anarchy.

In any region where there was an organized authority in place of anarchy, there was no system of balance of power politics. Neither in the Mediterranean region under the Roman domination nor in the Far Eastern area under the Chinese hegemony was there a balance of power politics. In the first place there was no need for it and in the second place it was impossible to maintain a balance of power in a world of preponderance of power. But in the state of anarchy, without an organized authority possessing a preponderance of power, there was for the first time a place and the necessity for introducing such a system. It was because in the absence of a preponderant authority to preserve justice, all the various groups were forced to form alliances and counter-alliances for protection against other groups, or for the domination of other groups, which means the same thing in a world of chaos.

So the balance of power system, like nationalism and patriotism, was born of anarchy, and its object has been self-preservation against hostile groups. Its method of accomplishing this objective has been by preventing the rise of any power or combination of powers which might become powerful enough to dominate other groups. But since no one group has felt safe in an ever-shifting balance of power system, all nations have struggled for a superior balance of power either through superior arms, resources or alliances. The balance of power in its ultimate analysis, therefore, has become synonymous with the struggle for mutual domination; and the struggle for mutual domination has perpetuated a state of international anarchy. Thus, the system of balance of power was born of international anarchy and has been nourished and preserved by perpetuating anarchy.

These are the reasons why wherever and whenever the system of balance of power has prevailed, the battlefields have never been dried of the blood of the victors and the vanquished. Such was the case in ancient China and ancient Greece, and the same has been true of modern Europe and the modern world at large.

Some students of power politics maintain that the system of balance of power under the leadership of England has given Europe the best two hundred years of peace since the Roman Empire. If Europe had respite from incessant wars, it must have been despite the balance of power, not because of it. For a state of comparative peace existed in Europe because of the fact that since the age of discovery, the white men have carried out their eternal wars not so much in Europe as outside of it. Taking the world as a whole, there probably has never been an age which has suffered more or bigger and better wars than the past two hundred years. Most of these wars fought over the four corners of the earth have been brought about by the rivalry among the European nations, including England, France, Germany and Russia in their struggle for a superior balance of power.

What has created peace anywhere and in any age has been, not the balance of power, but the preponderance of power unaccompanied by abuses. The existence of an overwhelming power ever ready to uphold the principles of justice and right has always created faith and confidence in men, and where there have been faith and trust, peace and security have invariably prevailed. It is because confidence is the mother of peace and faith is the father of security.

The peoples of Eastern Asia enjoyed a state of comparative peace for centuries not through the balance of power but through the preponderance of it. Old China, somewhat peaceful and refined, held the position of a superior power for thousands of years, and no other power, save that of a few northern barbarians, challenged her superior position. As a superior state,

China did not go strongly for conquest and domination, as Rome did. She restrained her designs on her smaller neighbors and sought to guide them through the use of cultural influence without political and military domination. As a result, there was faith and confidence among the Asiatic states, and peace and tranquillity prevailed longer than in almost any other region in the civilized world.

Peace and harmony have so far prevailed among the twenty-one republics in the Americas even though for a short period of time not because of the existence of balance of power, but because of the absence of it. Had there been some balance of power among the republics, particularly between the United States and Argentina, the new world would have been torn by strife. But fortunately, there is no such balance, and the state which holds the preponderance of power, namely, the United States of America, has tried to live according to the principles of law and order. As a result, faith and confidence have developed among the republics and peace and harmony have prevailed.

In view of the foregoing, the only way to create peace among the nations is by creating an overwhelming authority to banish chaos, and the best and surest way to perpetuate international wars is through the preservation of the balance of power. If the post-war statesmen adopt the first course, the world might be blessed with peace, but if they adopt the second, nothing will give us international peace and justice.

Let us suppose that the old system of balance of power were adopted, as advocated by the late Nicholas John Spykman, chief of the Institute of International Studies of Yale University in *America's Strategy in World Politics,* and by many other amateur students and statesmen of Europe and America. Under this old system, Germany will be encouraged to rearm, as she was after the last World War, and Japan also will be invited to rearm, as she was encouraged to arm before, so that the defeated states can help to balance the power against Russia, or China, or any nation which might emerge on the horizon with a potential power to disturb the ever-changing balance of power. And the last war, like all other wars, will have been fought in vain; we will have defeated the Axis only to help them rise again tomorrow; we will have disarmed them and dismembered them only to help them rearm and reconstruct for their domination of tomorrow's world.

However unsound and dangerous, the nations will not abandon this cursed policy of power politics so long as international anarchy continues to exist. It is due to the fact that this system of power politics affords at least one means of defense in the state of anarchy. The only way to end this system, therefore, is by organizing the world for peace and justice under an effective authority, so that there will be no room, nor necessity, to resort to such a policy for survival. In other words, it is erroneous to maintain that world peace can never be created until the nations abandon their power politics. The truth is that no nation will abandon it until the world is organized for peace and security.

11. Peace through the Spheres of Influence

The ancient Hebrews tried to preserve peace by dividing their land into two spheres, Judah and Israel. The result was ceaseless internecine warfare. The ancient Greeks made an attempt to preserve harmony by dividing the Hellenic world into two rival spheres, dictatorship and democracy. The result was as disastrous as the Hebrew experiment. The Roman Republic when divided into three spheres of Antony, Lepidus and Octavius created the same war of rivalry and domination. When Old China was cut in twos or threes, the empire seldom enjoyed the kind of tranquillity which it enjoyed under a unified control. The modern European nations made an attempt to preserve peace in Africa by dividing that continent into various spheres of influence. The result was rivalry and conflict. They made the same attempt in America and Asia, but the results were the same.

The chief reason why the policy of the sphere of influence has failed to preserve harmony is that its practice precludes the establishment of an over-all central authority to co-operate for the preservation of peace. Where there is no such co-operative agency embracing all spheres, rivalry and conflict between several groups are inevitable. The policy of the sphere of influence in its final analysis, therefore, is one of conflict and rivalry, not of peace and harmony.

Other things being equal, the pursuance of the same policy will not give any more benefits in the future than it has in the past, whether the world is divided into four spheres as Walter Lippmann suggests in *U.S. WAR AIMS,* or into five "power aggregates" as William B. Ziff advocates in *The Gentlemen Talk of Peace,* or into eleven regional federations, as Ely Culbertson proposes in his *World Federation Plan,* or into two spheres, democratic and totalitarian, as Henry Wallace suggests, unless such divisions are no more than administrative divisions under an over-all central authority.

Let us suppose that the earth is divided into four main zones or spheres as envisaged by Walter Lippmann in his *U. S. War Aims.* There will be an Atlantic sphere, a Russian sphere, a Chinese sphere and a Middle Eastern sphere. The Atlantic sphere, or "Atlantic Community," will include, according to Lippmann, Australia in the west and Greece in the east and all the lands and waters between the two points. It will cover more than two-thirds of the earth's surface and will become the most powerful sphere in the whole world. It can lead, direct, or even dominate the other spheres, if it chooses to do so.

Whether there is, or is not, any such danger of domination by this community, all the other spheres would feel uneasy because the fear of the Anglo-Saxon domination will never be absent from the minds of the leaders of those spheres. There are, therefore, only several things for them to do. They would either try to combine the three spheres into one, or they would try to break up the Atlantic Community, or both. They would spread false rumors, if nothing else, to play up the United States against Great Britain, France against Italy, and so on. The Atlantic Community in turn would try to prevent the three spheres from combining their strength by playing them up against each other. Therefore, the world divided by Lippmann's system can no more enjoy peace than could ancient Greece and ancient Israel, divided into two hostile spheres.

Whichever way the earth is divided, the interested powers will not be satisfied with less than what was asked for by a modest old farmer who said, "All I want is the land adjoining my farm." All which the British Empire, the United States, Soviet Union, China, France and others will want within their spheres may not be more than the land adjoining their territories from which a hostile power can launch an attack on them. But in the future, in fact even today, an attack can be launched against any nation from any spot on the earth. And so none of these powers would feel secure unless they bring the whole world within their own sphere of influence.

Strange as it may seem, Japan, like other empires, started her career of conquest precisely in this manner. When she was a small island state, she claimed her life line lay in Korea, for that peninsula constituted a dagger pointed into the heart of Japan. Having brought Korea under her sphere, she then claimed Manchuria was her first line of defense. Having brought Manchuria within her sphere, she then claimed the whole of China and everything east of the Suez to be within her "East Asia-Co-Prosperity Sphere." No one can deceive oneself into believing the course of other nations will be any different from that of Japan when they pursue the same policy.

12. Peace through Isolation, Neutrality and Preparedness

Isolation, neutrality and preparedness, which I call the unholy trinity, usually work together as the three legs of a stool. To remain isolated from the troublesome world, you must adopt measures of neutrality, as did the United States of America in 1935-37 under the spell of the isolationists. When you remain isolated and neutral, you will have no friends to count on in time of trouble, and you must prepare to stand alone against the whole world, if necessary.

There was a time when the states could adopt some of these

measures with good results. But in this day and age, when the whole world is integrated into a small village, it has become difficult for the states to enjoy peace and security by adopting these measures. Isolation has become physically impossible. Neutrality, if successfully adopted, would make the neutral countries safe from the embroilment in unwanted conflicts. But few nations in our age of universal wars can remain neutral because the beligerents will not let them. Preparedness likewise no longer gives the same comfort for peace and security which it gave before the days of the robot bombs and the atomic bomb.

Formerly the superiority in army, navy and air forces gave a margin of security because if you had more of these than the enemy, you could defeat him in the field of combat and leave the home front secure. But today the scientists are doubtful if the superiority in the atomic bombs will give the same margin of security because, even if you had 10,000 bombs and the enemy only 1,000, he can destroy you in a few minutes, provided he strikes you first. So both the big and the small, the prepared and the unprepared, can no longer feel secure by the possession of more weapons of destruction.

In the continued state of chaos, the policies of isolation, neutrality and preparedness, futile as they are, will still be pursued by the nations because they give at least the illusion of protection. These obsolete measures, therefore, cannot be discredited by merely attacking the isolationists like Gerald Nye, Gerald Smith and a whole chain of blind mice, or the militarists and imperialists who cry for bigger armies, navies and air forces. The only way to combat the evils of this unholy trinity is through organizing the world for peace and justice so that there is no need for isolation, neutrality or preparedness.

13. Peace through the Oriental way

Following each catastrophic war, not a few white men are so disappointed and disillusioned in their own civilization that they cast their longing eyes beyond the blue seas to look for guidance and inspiration. They feel that their materialistic civilization, built on the basis of iron and steel, commerce and trade, has failed to solve the complicated problems of our modern world; therefore, they must import some foreign ideas, the spiritual values of Eastern civilization which give them the flavor of Oriental mysticism.

At the same time, many Orientals, who have witnessed time and again the insane carnage of suicidal warfare among the so-called Christian nations, have come to the conclusion that the white men with their materialistic concept of life, with their militant cultures and institutions, are incapable of creating peace among themselves, let alone among other peoples. For instance, Lin Yutang, author of many delightful books on Eastern culture, states in *Between Tears and Laughter* that the materialists of the Occidental world, with their mechanical way of thinking and with their "swine-and-slop" economic plans, cannot end wars or devise a peace. He concludes, therefore, that there is "more hope in a heather rose than in all the tons of Teutonic philosophy."

After giving a brilliant expose of the shortcomings of the Western system and the failures of the Occidental statesmanship, Lin reintroduces in a delightful manner Confucius, Lao-tse, Mencius and their followers. But when one examines the teachings of these great philosophers one finds very little political and social philosophy in them which cannot be found in the wisdom of Plato, Aristotle and a galaxy of other Western philosophers. For instance, the Confucian principles of government based upon justice and law administered or exemplified by the superior men or philosopher kings is not substantially different from the political principles of Plato and Aristotle. Lao-tse's idea of nonresistance and of recompensing evil with kindness, or Moti's principle of universal love, or Buddha's kindness and pity for all creatures, either men or animals, all can find a counterpart in the teachings of Jesus and his followers. The democratic ideals of the ancient Chinese, their respect for intangible values such as philosophy and literature, their love for peace, purity and tranquillity—all these are not absent from the fabulous wealth of the materialistic culture and civilization of the West. In fact, Hu Shih, one of the most profound scholars of modern China, contends that there is more spirituality in Western material civilization than there is in the so-called spiritual civilization of the East. So those who are looking for some Oriental magic which will cure all the age-old evils of human society with the wave of the wand are bound to be disappointed at the end of their painful search for such a panacea.

Even if it is admitted that the East is more richly endowed with wisdom and philosophy than the materialistic West, it has contributed little more to the cause of good government than the West. The chief reason for this is that the Orientals, unlike the Occidentals, have formed the habit of putting their faith in men, not in organizations based upon law. As a result, they have failed to cultivate their ability to develop organizations and to devise ways and means of translating sound philosophy into mass action.

For instance, theoretically, the emperor of China ruled with the mandate from heaven. That sounds very much like the divine right of kings in the West. But according to Chinese democratic philosophy, heaven sees as the people see and heaven hears as the people hear, a concept not foreign to the Western maxim that the voice of the people is the voice of God. But how could they tell what the wishes of the people were? They had no Gallup Poll, no secret ballots. The only practical way to ascertain whether the emperor had the mandate to rule or not was through a forcible revolution. If the revolution was successful, it was held that the emperor lost the mandate to rule. If the revolution failed, it was contended that the emperor still held the mandate, and, therefore, he was entitled to rule.

Some twenty-five major dynastic changes were made in the past 3000 years. Practically all of them were brought about by violent revolutions. It is needless to say that this kind of practice was tantamount to sanctifying the doctrine that might makes right.

It is a fact that the Asiatics in general have been more peaceful and have developed more peaceful and passive cultures and institutions than the Europeans who have been more warlike and have developed more militant cultures and institutions than any other race in the world. For those who might question the soundness of this statement, I quote from *A Study of War* by Quincy Wright who grades the degree of warlikeness from the highest to the lowest as follows: The White Race, Negroids, Hamitoids, Brown Race, Yellow Race, Red Race Australoids, and the Pigmies. But what has made the white man more belligerent than other races and has caused him to develop more militant cultures and institutions than others?

As has already been pointed out, what has made the white man more belligerent is not because he was born that way, or because he is by nature more warlike than others, but because he has suffered the state of international chaos longer than other races. To reinforce this contention, I compare the history of China with that of Europe.

The Chinese were fortunate enough to have a ferocious and yet clever and powerful ruler, Chin Shih Huang Ti, who obliterated the feudal foundations of old China and unified the whole empire under a central authority twenty-two centuries ago. Since then they have passed through many periods of dissension, but they have always succeeded in recovering their unity under one authority which banished internecine warfare. As a result, they have been able to devote most of their energy to developing a peaceful civilization to such a stage that they could worship the scholars and degrade the soldiers.

To some extent, the same is true of India. Since the third century B.C., when Asoka unified a large part of India, to the fall of the Mongul Empire to the British, India witnessed many conquering races and also suffered numerous periods of internal disorder. But as pointed out by Jawaharlal Nehru, the country as a whole enjoyed a far more peaceful existence for a longer period of time than Europe has had. This explains why the Indians, like the Chinese, were able to produce a civilization which scorned soldiery and elevated the prophets.

Europe, on the other hand, lost her unity after the collapse of the Roman Empire and has never been able to recover it. Several times it was almost unified under a central authority, once by the medieval Catholic Church, once by Napoleon and another time by Hitler. But none was so powerful as to whip divided and hostile Europe into a firm, unshakable empire or union. As a result, the white men have suffered international chaos longer than the Chinese have, and have been forced to use most of their energy and resources in developing militant ideas and institutions, militant art and literature, militant political and religious institutions for the sake of survival.

One should not entertain the deluded notion that other races would not have grown warlike under the same international atmosphere which has prevailed in Europe for centuries. As a matter of fact, even the Asiatics, including the Chinese and the Indians, have already grown considerably more belligerent since they were thrown into the whirlpool of modern international chaos. To wit, the cherished idea of nonviolence is losing its hold among the Indians, and the contempt for soldiery has received a jolt in the land of scholar-worshippers. Lin Yutang himself has demonstrated this tendency when he declared that China must learn how to give a black eye before she can hope to gain the respect of other nations.

In other words, it will do no good to shout against the warlike men, cultures and institutions, be they British, French, German, Japanese or Russian. The world must be organized under an all-embracing authority to banish international anarchy, so that it will be unnecessary for the nations and the races to build militant cultures and institutions for the sake of survival. Assuming the soundness of this approach to the problems of world peace, there is a more practical guide for the building of international order in the short history of the United States than there is in tons of Oriental philosophy and literature.

Chapter VI

THE FIRST STEP TOWARD WORLD PEACE

The examination of all the foregoing highways to peace leads to the conclusion that none of these measures will give us the blessed peace which we dream of until the whole world is sufficiently organized under a central authority to banish the state of international anarchy. The one vital question before us then is how to create such a world authority in this age of nationalism and sovereign states.

As has been pointed out before, there are only two direct and effective ways of creating such an authority. One is through outright conquest and the other is through voluntary co-operation of the separate groups. If the first course to unity is preferred, all that is necessary is to just let the present international situation take its natural course. Then the world might be united under one supreme power after one or two more world wars. But if the second course is desired, the best approach to the problem appears to be this: accept the thesis that all breeders of war spring from the one ultimate cause—international anarchy—and concentrate our attack on that ultimate source of all conflicts, instead of worrying about scores of contributary factors such as militarism, nationalism, imperialism and other militant ideas and cultures, all of which are the children of the same parentage, international anarchy. In other words, it would seem wiser to approach the subject of peace as did old Confucius and Plato who focused their attention on the principles and methods of maintaining justice and law, instead of worrying about countless products of injustice and lawlessness, as do the modern students of international relations.

But how can a world authority be created to uphold the principles of justice and law without removing the various forces which prevent the establishment of such an authority? So we try to destroy militarism, nationalism, patriotism, sovereignty, power politics, economic barriers and what not through treaty making, education and religion. At the end of a long, long tortuous journey, we finally arrive at the same conclusion—that none of these forces can be removed without banishing international anarchy by creating an organized world authority. Then how and where should we start toward the making of international order?

The best way, in fact the only way, to tackle the problem of world peace is through the old and tried way by which every city, state and country in the world have found peace and security, even though only locally.

The American pioneers who blazed their trails into the western frontiers used this method of creating order out of chaos: When the lawlessness in their unorganized frontier hamlet became unbearable, a group of thoughtful men created a semblance of authority by forming a small vigilance committee. This committee, with the blessings of most good people, temporarily exercised the power of an organized authority. They ordered the lawless men to cease their acts of violence. When such orders were ignored, they punished or shot down the offenders. When the demonstration of authority on the side of law was strong enough, violence subsided. The committee then was replaced later by a staff of officers chosen by the people, who moved about with their activities in an atmosphere of peace and tranquillity.

The men of the community were not a fraction different from what they had been before. They were still guided by their same drives for food, sex, glory and honor; they were still selfish, vain and egotistic, with all their original mental and physical characteristics; they were not an inch nearer to God morally and spiritually, not a bit higher mentally and intellectually. The town itself was not any different from before, as all the same disruptive forces, economic, cultural, political and religious, still operated. But after the creation of an authority to preserve justice the people behaved like decent human beings although they had failed to do so before.

The honorable fathers of the American Republic did not

start the formation of their union through the elimination of the so-called causes of war, such as cultural, economic, political, psychological, moral and religious, or nationalism, patriotism, sovereignty and power politics, or men's struggle for power, profits or honor. They just went ahead with the formation of their union and set up an over-all central organ to maintain the principles of justice and fair play; then most of the apparently incurable causes of friction dissolved like a bubble.

The narrow provincialism and sectionalism of the people which appeared to be insurmountable obstacles to unity gradually melted within the larger framework of the union. The insatiable love for freedom and the cherished ideals of sovereignty were no longer incompatible with the idea of national union because the people learned in no time that at the sacrifice of a small amount of local freedom, they could enjoy a greater freedom and democracy which was inconceivable before. The commercial rivalry and economic competition which had divided the colonies into thirteen hostile camps no longer impeded the development of the union, because the business interests also learned that their particular interests could be best promoted through the union. So the union of the thirteen colonies, which seemed to Josiah Tucker "the idlest and most visionary notion that ever was conceived even by writers of romance," became an accomplished fact.

There are several important reasons why this kind of approach to the problem of peace is the best and the only sound one. In the first place, it is due to the fact that what really makes order or disorder in any society is not the absence or presence of man's instincts, ambitions or desires for food, sex, glory and honor, or of such conflicting economic, cultural, political and religious forces, or of the integrated system of basic values and the harmonious patterns of conduct, or of contact and isolation, homogeneity and hetrogeneity, as has been held by almost all the learned authorities of social sciences; but it is the absence or presence of an organized authority capable of upholding the principles of justice and fair play.

Where there is such an authority, myriads of forces, economic, cultural, psychological, national or racial, can exist peacefully side by side, but where the central authority is absent, or too weak and corrupt to preserve the principles of justice, not only these powerful social forces, but almost any little incident or accident can cause endless strife. It is because the march of social forces is like the movement of vehicles. Where there are traffic rules all vehicles can move on with little friction, but where no such rules are observed, few vehicles, however good, can move through the streets without a collision.

Similarly, where there is an authority to safeguard the traffic regulations of life, all man's desires and ambitions, his drives for food, sex, honor and justice can be expressed through orderly processes without bloodshed, but where no such authority exists, none of these can be satisfied without violence; in one case all economic, cultural, political and religious forces, however diverse, can be directed to function smoothly with little friction, but in the other, none of these forces can exist side by side without creating collision. Therefore, wherever and whenever there has existed such an organized authority, peace and order have prevailed, but in its absence, war and strife have never ceased to curse mankind.

In their long years of history, the Chinese have enjoyed peace at times but have suffered bloodshed at other times. The main difference between the peace years and the war years has been the presence and absence of a just and efficient central government, not so much the difference in their ethics and morals or their economic, cultural and religious matters. When the dynastic government, presided over by men with high character and integrity, governed wisely and justly, the people enjoyed peace and security at home even in lean years with a surplus population. But when the central authority fell into the hands of corrupt politicians and wicked eunuchs, they waged and suffered civil wars even in times of plenty with rich harvest. So Plato was right after all when he said that chaos appears in the souls of men where there is no just rule in the commonwealth.

China is no exception in this case, as most other peoples have had similar experiences. For instance, the ancient Romans and their allies enjoyed peace and order when the rulers of Rome governed their state honestly and justly, but they suffered civil wars at home and the invasion of the barbarians from the outside when their authority grew corrupt and impotent and failed to preserve justice among the Romans or their allies. Contrary to all popular opinion on the subject, the empire appears to have collapsed primarily because its organized authority failed to function, not so much because its economic system had collapsed, or because the Romans as a whole had degenerated morally and ethically, or because the Roman mothers could not compete with those of the barbarians in their output of baby crops, or because the Romans failed to guard themselves against the fifth column activities of the barbarians. The belief that the breakdown of the organized authority appears to be the chief cause of Rome's downfall is greatly strengthened by the fact that many Romans and their allies deserted Rome and joined the Huns for the purpose of obtaining justice and legal protection which they could not find in Rome.

One can maintain that the Roman authority grew corrupt because the Romans as a whole were corrupt. But even the most honest and the least corrupt peoples have had corrupt governments locally or nationally, although the greater proportion of their peoples have not degenerated morally and spiritually.

There are as many corrupt and selfish people in the United States as in Europe; there are as many conflicting religious, cultural, and racial groups in the United States as in Europe; there are as many economic, political, cultural and religious activities in the United States as in Europe; there is as much mixing and rubbing of various men, ideas and institutions in America as in Europe. But peace has prevailed among the forty-eight American states, whereas war has continued to rage among the European states. The main reason for this is the presence and absence of an all-embracing central government to preserve the traffic rules for social forces.

Similarly, the main reason why there is no peace in the world is that the world is not like the United States, with a central authority to preserve justice among the constituent states, but it is like Europe, without an organized agency to safeguard the rules of fair play among the various national and racial groups. In the absence of such an authority it is natural that all the conflicting social, national and racial forces of the world move about aimlessly in all directions, causing countless clashes in the march of history. So Emery Reves is right in maintaining in *The Anatomy of Peace* that law is the only remedy for our troubles.

Assuming the soundness of such a contention, the way to world peace is not through the attack on various human, social and cultural forces, but through a direct attack on the state of anarchy where no men, or culture and institutions can exist without clashing against one another.

The second reason why the direct attack on anarchy through the creation of authority is the only sound way to lasting peace is that war and peace do not depend on the character of men, culture and institutions as much as the character of men, culture and institutions depend on the state of war or peace. It is because in a state of anarchy where there is no organized authority to preserve justice among the nations, all men must of necessity learn to use their energy and power, all their moral, material, economic and religious forces for the purpose of waging wars for the sake of survival. But in any region where anarchy has been banished by an established authority which upholds the principles of law and order, it is neither possible nor necessary for the people to use their energy and power, their spiritual and physical forces for mutual slaughter.

The ancient Egyptians were peaceful and developed a peaceful culture and civilization when they were ruled by an organized government, however crude, and when their lands, guarded by the deserts and seas, were free from invasion, namely, from the necessity to be warlike. But following the Hyksos' invasion, they grew more warlike and developed a more militant culture and institution than before.

Even the belligerent Athenians remained comparatively peaceful and developed in thirty-odd years under Pericles a most glorious civilization, so famous through legend and history, when they were given a blessed state of peace preserved by the power of their empire, and were not threatened by external invasion or internal strife.

The Chinese grew peaceful and developed a peaceful civilization when their country enjoyed peace and security under a unified authority which banished anarchy, but grew militant and developed militant ideas and institutions whenever they were thrown into a state of chaos. The Japanese were very belligerent and developed a belligerent culture when the country was torn by strife, but grew more peaceful and produced a more peaceful culture, when they were freed from internal anarchy and external invasion. The excessive warlikeness of the present-day Japanese and their cultures and institutions appear to be largely the result of the prevailing state of international anarchy in which few nations can survive without cultivating warlike ideas and institutions.

The American people could not live together any more peacefully than their European brethren when they struggled for life and security in the state of international anarchy, but following their unification under a central authority, they used their energy and power in the peaceful pursuits of life and almost succeeded in making the whole continent a blessed isle of peace. Even such a people has never failed to be warlike and to develop a militant spirit and militant organizations whenever their security has been threatened by the evil forces of anarchy.

So even if it is assumed that no lasting peace can be brought about without changing the sensate men, culture and institutions of our times, as does Pitirim A. Sorokin, of Harvard, it is clear that no such changes can be brought about without changing the chaotic world situation which has produced these sensate men, cultures and institutions. It is a dangerous fallacy, therefore, to maintain that the world cannot be organized for peace under a central authority without changing the warlike men, cultures and institutions, or without curbing or destroying militarism, nationalism, imperialism, absolute states, empires, or men's desires for conquest and domination. The truth is that none of these can be modified or destroyed without banishing the state of anarchy through the creation of an organized agency. If world peace were to wait until men, cultures and institutions change, it will always remain only a dream.

It would be very difficult, of course, to create a world organization through voluntary co-operation in this age of nationalism and sovereign states. As a matter of fact, many students of world affairs hold the view that it would be impossible for the sovereign nations, with different standards of values and different patterns of civilization, to form an effective world organization in our times. So they would leave the task to the distant future when men will have reached a higher moral and intellectual development, without realizing that men will not rise much higher under the present environment.

But it seems to me that the creation of a workable world authority in our times should not be impossible for several reasons. In the first place, the world is so small and the means of communication and transportation are so good that the representatives of various political and racial groups can get together as easily as the leaders in a primitive village could. Secondly, although there is no universal language to serve as a medium of exchanging ideas, this constitutes no insurmountable obstacle because there are enough linguists in the world who can translate any language spoken by man. Thirdly, ideological and cultural differences and the economic, educational, religious and racial antipathies present no unbreakable barriers to world unity. In almost any city or state on earth there is as much difference in such matters as there is in the world, but it has not prevented the workings of the local and national governments.

Contrary to all popular views on this subject, what is most indispensable for unity and co-operation, local, national or racial, is not the cultural or ideological similarities, as commonly understood, but it is the willingness of the people to co-operate with other groups; and their willingness to co-operate for common destiny springs, not so much from the community of ideas and institutions, as from the conviction that mutual co-operation is indispensable for security and survival. For example, the thirteen American states started co-operating despite their mutual antipathies, clashing interests and their difference in governments and habitudes because they had the conviction that they could not survive in the chaotic world without pooling their power and resources. Their conviction that they could survive as a free people only through unity was explained most clearly and vividly in Benjamin Franklin's cartoon of a snake cut in thirteen pieces with the caption that they must hang together, or they would have to hang separately.

England and Japan were allied against their common enemy, Czarist Russia, despite their cultural and racial differences. The United States and China co-operated against Japan; America and Russia fought together against Hitler's Germany and Tojo's Japan, not because of their community of ideas and cultures, but because of their conviction that none of them could live in peace and security without crushing the Axis Powers.

There have been many peoples who would rather perish than live together with those whom they hate and despise. But such peoples have been limited in all ages and in all countries. When faced with certain annihilation most human beings have preferred to co-operate actively or passively even with their inveterate enemies. When their will to co-operate was strong enough to result in action, they have overcome their hatred and prejudices and have created an instrument of co-operation through which they could work together. When they have worked together under the same co-operative agency for a sufficient time, they have often developed a common language and common ideas and institutions, all of which have helped preserve peace among the co-operating groups.

However, where the people are too stupid to understand the value of mutual co-operation or too obsessed with hatred and jealousy to work together for their common destiny, force has been the only means of bringing them together. Following the subjugation of the weak by the powerful, the victors have imposed upon the vanquished their own language, ideas, cultures and institutions. After the lapse of time, both the victor and the vanquished have frequently merged into a single cultural and institutional unit, with a common language and a community of ideas and interests.

The common bonds of ideas and cultures have helped preserve the unity of the people, but even such ties have failed to prevent civil wars. So it appears that the similarity in ideas and cultures is largely the result of a prolonged communal life, instead of being the necessary condition of co-operation.

If the best way to world peace is to take the bull by the horns and start organizing a world authority instead of worrying about myriads of other factors, then the creation of the League of Nations was probably the right approach to the establishment of international peace. But the League failed. Why did it fail? Did it fail because its principles were unsound, or because its organization was imperfect, or because the leadership of the Western powers was poor, or because the participating nations had not yet acquired the conviction that no nation, however powerful, could enjoy peace and prosperity without such a world authority? If we knew correctly why the League failed, we might be able to foretell whether the United Nations Organization will succeed or fail, because it is based upon the same principles of the League. So let us examine carefully the peace which failed between the two World Wars. I think the re-examination of this question is necessary because it has been one of the most misunderstood and misinterpreted subjects among the Western students of international relations.

Chapter VII

THE GREAT EXPERIMENT

1. Prelude to the Great Experiment

The movement to preserve peace among the nations through an organized world authority has largely been the attempt of the Western world. I do not mean to give the impression that there was no peace movement among other races, as there were many such experiments among the ancient Chinese, Indians, Muslims, American Indians and even among the African savages. But what I maintain is that this modern movement toward universal peace through an organized authority has been largely Western in its origin and development.

The incipient peace movement which laid the foundation for the present world-wide drive against war was started by the Christian pacifists of America and Europe. The crusades for the adoption of arbitration, international law, international courts of justice, the League of Nations, and the Dumbarton Oaks and the San Francisco security conferences were all engineered largely by the American and European statesmen.

One reason for this, I think, is that the white men have waged more wars in the past three or four hundred years than all the rest of the races have fought in the same period. It is natural that they should have started such a peace movement because the desire for peace is more intense in the midst of war, as the desire for wealth is greater in the midst of poverty. Another reason seems to be that the white men, especially the Anglo-Saxons, trust no one, neither their God nor their kings and princes. Whatever they undertake to achieve, therefore, they always form an organization for that purpose. It is very natural then that the white man should have started the movement to banish war through an organized authority, instead of talking vaguely about establishing peace through the cultivation of wisdom and virtue, through the suppression of selfish desires and ambitions, as most Oriental philosophers have. Another reason is that from the dawn of the modern period the Western nations, equipped with superior methods of destruction and production, explored and conquered most of the world and became masters of the globe. The problem of preserving peace and order throughout the world, therefore, became their immediate national problem.

Whatever the case, there have certainly been more thinkers in Western history of the past three or four hundred years who have thought of more peace plans than in the history of any other part of the world. Beginning with Pierre Du Bois of the fourteenth century, scores of peace plans have been proposed in almost every generation. Erasmus, Henry IV and the Duke of Sully, Hugo Grotius, Emeric Cruce, William Penn, St. Pierre, Rousseau and Kant are only a few of the outstanding men to make plans for perpetual peace. But none of these peace plans has been tried for the preservation of peace in Europe, and the ceaseless warfare continued to exact a heavy toll of lives and treasure.

At the close of the Napoleonic War, Czar Alexander I of Russia made a proposal for a "Holy Alliance" among the Christian sovereigns of Europe to abide by the precepts of Jesus and to live in peace like brethren with God as their sovereign. His proposal became a mockery of the crafty old European statesmen and the Czar himself died a martyr as Woodrow Wilson did a century later. But another Czar, Nicholas II of Russia, called the Hague Peace Conference of 1899, the first universal peace conference in which the representatives of not only Europe and America, but also of Asia, took part in the deliberations for the eradication of war. Of the twenty-six participating nations, five were Asiatic states: China, Japan, Persia, Siam and Turkey.

The world's first public universal peace conference failed to accomplish what it was called upon to accomplish. How could it? All the delegates and their governments were so ignorant, stupid, self-centered and egotistic that they simply could not even grasp the nature of the great task before them. All they thought, wished and did was to advance the vanity and pride and the honor and glory of their own kings and princes or states. All it achieved on the subject of relieving the world of the unbearable cost of armament was the adoption of a meaningless resolution to the effect that it is "extremely desirable" to reduce the armament budget of the participating states. On the subject of warfare, it adopted several conventions and resolutions providing for the prohibition of certain projectiles and the humane conduct of warfare, but nothing was done to create an agency to preserve justice and to prevent endless wars except the establishment of the so-called Permanent Court of Arbitration, which was neither permanent nor a court. It was a mere international bureau of communication and a depository of the names of jurists, designated by the several states separately, not including more than four jurists from any one country. From that list of jurists, arbiters were to be selected, if and when the parties to dispute submitted their differences for arbitration. And this was the product of more than two months' labor of ninety-six delegates from twenty-six so-called civilized countries. Certainly no one expects to find a less fruitful labor than this even in a WPA project!

The second Hague Conference held in 1907 accomplished little more, although nearly twice as many states participated and consumed twice as long a time as the first conference. The most important proposal, in fact the only proposal worth considering, was that of creating a real court of arbitration suggested by the American delegation. It failed to materialize, due to the difficulties of electing judges. Nevertheless they adopted fourteen measures, conventions or rules of intercourse, twelve of which dealt with the conduct of war and only two of which had a remote bearing on the subject of preserving peace. Thus, as John Dewey remarked, the delegates of the "civilized" nations, who were assembled to devise ways and means of preserving peace, wasted all their time in talking about how humanely they should kill each other in the next war.

The tragic failure of the Hague Peace Conferences inspired

Edward Everett Hale to write the following verse, which is called *I am the Hague Tribunal, I have come to say good-by*:

Pray, Soldier, drop a tear for me, and bless me ere I go;
I tried to take your job away, but you'll forgive, I know.
Men petted me and cherished me, and cried me for a boon,
But now I see that I was born a century too soon.
We part and may not see again; I bid you my farewell,
And when again you see the Powers, soldier, you may tell—
Tell them—his voice was broken and he smothered a great sob—
Just tell them when you saw me, I was looking for a job.

The failure of the first and the second world peace conferences to work out some system to preserve justice among the states left unchecked the continued race for armament, the endless gambling with power politics, the shuffling and reshuffling, forming and reforming, of alliances and counter-alliances, all of which were inevitable in the state of international anarchy without an organized authority to preserve justice. Step by step, the sick old world moved closer and closer to the catastrophic of 1914. Nothing retarded or deterred the fatal march into the war. All the combined voices of millions of men and women, representing more than 425 peace organizations, had no more influence in stopping the war than the singing of a mosquito could have in preventing the eruption of a volcano. And so four years of unprecedented orgy of blood and carnage followed.

2. The Great Experiment

The war that cost untold billions in lives and treasure seems to have done at least one good thing—that is to force the people to think more about the ways of eradicating the age-old evils of mutual slaughter. More men and women did more serious thinking on the subject of future peace than ever before. The men on the front, the woman behind the lines, the statesmen, scholars, and almost every Tom, Dick and Harry scratched their heads and tried to figure out how future conflicts could be postponed or prevented. They all hoped, wished and said, "It must not happen again."

One of the most significant peace movements during the conflict, which had a considerable influence on the formation of the League of Nations, was that of the League to Enforce Peace, sponsored by such prominent Americans as William Howard Taft, Theodore Roosevelt, Andrew Carnegie and A. Lawrence Lowell. The League was formed on June 17, 1915, at Independence Hall, Philadelphia, where the immortal fathers of the American Republic formed a more perfect union to enjoy life, liberty and the pursuit of happiness. With Taft as its president, the League advocated the use of economic and military powers to restrain an aggressor waging a war against another before submitting the dispute to arbitration, conciliation, or judicial tribunal. The members believed that civilization was still too crude to outlaw wars altogether and tried to restrain it in several stages, as England did with private war. It may be recalled that at first the Crown sought only to prevent men from avenging their wrongs before going to court, but when the hands of the Crown grew stronger and the concept of man's honor and justice more refined, all private wars were banished. Adopting the same method, the League advocated the use of force only against those who would go to war before going to court, leaving them free to fight out their issues after exhausting pacific means of settling disputes. It is interesting to note that this idea was adopted by the framers of the League of Nations.

I do not mean to state, however, that the League to Enforce Peace was the only peace movement which had any effect on the formation of the League. There were literally hundreds of peace organizations throughout the world, all of which probably had some effect on the drafting of the covenant in one way or another. Nor do I contend that the League was the product of any particular country or statesman. It was a product of accumulated knowledge and the experiences of all mankind from ancient to modern times. But the chief credit for the formation of the first universal League of Nations must go to the United States of America and her President Woodrow Wilson, who someday will be looked upon by all mankind as the Father of All Nations, as George Washington is looked upon as the Father of the United States of America.

Some students of the League maintain that Jan Christiaan Smuts should be honored as the real father of the League and Woodrow Wilson only as a stepfather, for they contend that Wilson saw Smuts' pamphlet on the League and borrowed his plan "lock, stock and barrel." There is no denying that the principles and the structures of the League of Nations closely resemble those outlined in Smuts' pamphlet entitled *The League of Nations* published on December 16, 1918. But to state that Wilson borrowed everything from Smuts betrays the complete ignorance of Wilson's political philosophy which he formed long before the publication of Smuts' pamphlet.

Ray Stannard Baker states in *Woodrow Wilson: Life and Letters* that Wilson had the idea of a League of Nations as early as 1887 when he was an associate professor at Bryn Mawr at the age of thirty-one. In an article published in the *Political Science Quarterly,* June 1887, he stated that modern political tendency was towards the American type—"of governments joined with governments for the pursuit of common purposes, in honorary equality and honorable subordination." Baker reports a conversation of Wilson with Dr. Axson, his brother-in-law, in which he translated his old idea of a league into a more definite form. In that conversation held shortly after the outbreak of the First World War, Wilson declared that one of the essentials to preserve future peace was the creation of "an association of nations, all bound together for protection of the integrity of each, so that any one nation breaking from this bond will bring upon herself war, that is to say, punishment, automatically."

Besides, on January 4, 1915, Wilson wrote to Heath Dabney, his college friend, that he was very much interested in creating a "world federation" but he did not think it an opportune moment for him to propose such a federation. These then contradict most of the loose talk that Wilson is only a stepfather of the League.

Contrary to all the unfair and unjust criticisms raised by the die-hard Republican opponents of his day and many popular writers of our times, Wilson's understanding of peace and his method to preserve it were absolutely sound and beyond reproach. Unlike the loose thinkers and superficial demagogues, who usually capture the eyes and ears of the indiscriminating mass with false promises, Wilson did not pin all his hope on the vague, idealistic and humanitarian sentiment of the peoples, or on the constantly changing alliances and counteralliances, or on the ever-shifting balance of power, so dear to many politicians and statesmen. He rightly placed all his hope for world peace in the creation of an organized authority, which he characterized as a "Community of Power" in contrast to the balance of power. He declared, "Mere agreements may not make peace secure. It will be absolutely necessary that a force be created as a guarantor of a permanency of the settlement so much greater than the force of any nation now engaged or any alliance hitherto formed or projected that no nation, no probable combination of nations, could face or withstand it. If the peace presently to be made is to endure, it must be a peace made secure by the organized major force of mankind."

He likewise foresaw what was to come from the failure of the League: "I can predict with absolute certainty that within another generation there will be another world war, if the nations of the world do not concert the method by which to prevent it." He further warned that the First World War, with all its terror and destruction, would be nothing compared with the Second World War, because "What the Germans used were toys as compared with what would be used in the next war." With such a clear understanding and definite conviction, he mustered all his power and energy for the successful creation of the League of Nations.

Perhaps he was too poor a politician and the world was too blind with prejudice and stupidity for him to put across his ideas in their entirety. But considering the circumstances, he did fairly well in selling his ideas and methods of preserving peace. He succeeded in persuading the representatives of the twenty-one nations then assembled at Versailles to set up the first universal peace organization, a thing which had been talked about and dreamed of by philosophers for centuries. The machinery known as the League of Nations was not much different from the World Security Organization drafted at Dumbarton Oaks and revised at the San Francisco Conference. It was composed of an assembly, a sort of parliament representing all the member states, a council, a kind of executive body in which the big powers played a dominant role, not without the co-operation of the smaller states; a permanent secretarist serving as an administrative body of the League; numerous social, economic and intellectual bureaus and departments to carry out the League's social and humanitarian activities; and a judicial organ known as "Permanent Court of International Justice," working independently of, but in conjunction with, the League.

The members of the League pledged themselves to "undertake to respect and preserve as against external aggression the territorial integrity and existing political independence of all members of the League." They agreed to submit their disputes to arbitration or judicial settlement or to inquiry by the council, or to the report by the assembly and in no case to resort to war until three months after the award. They further agreed not to resort to war against a member of the League which submits disputes to arbitration or judicial settlement and complies with the award or decisions. But they reserved the right "to take such action as they shall consider necessary for the maintenance of right and justice," if the council fails to reach a report for the settlement of a dispute by a unanimous vote, excepting the parties to the dispute, or if the assembly fails to make a report by a majority vote concurred in by all the states represented in the council, exclusive of the parties to the dispute.

Should any state resort to war in disregard of the covenant, they agreed to "undertake immediately to subject it to the severance of all trade or financial relations, the prohibition of all intercourse between their nationals and the nationals of the covenant-breaking state, and the prevention of all financial, commercial or personal intercourse between the nationals of the covenant-breaking state and the nationals of any other state, whether a member of the League or not." In the event that such political and economic measures should fail to produce the desired effect,, "it shall be the duty of the council to recommend to the several governments what effective military, naval or air force the members shall contribute to the armed forces to be used to protect the Covenant of the League."

The covenant was not an ideal document. Nor was the League created in accordance with this covenant a perfect organization. But it was about the best one could hope to find in a world of bigotry, hatred and stupidity.

The loss of its parent, the United States, made the League an orphan at the very start of its life. But had its stepparents taken good care of it, the League might yet have proved a success as many orphans do. And the possibility that its adopted parents might make the orphan a success was not altogether absent, for there were both federalists and antifederalists in the League's adopted household, as there were in the early days of the United States of America. The federalists wanted to make the League a strong and powerful machine with muscles and teeth, whereas the antifederalists wanted to make it a harmless talking shop. The high-water mark of the federalists was the celebrated Geneva Protocol of 1924, which would have had the effect of making the League the most powerful instrument of peace known in history. But the whole attempt collapsed tragically when Stanley Baldwin, Austen Chamberlain and his Conservatives replaced Ramsay MacDonald and his laborite government, which promoted the move. The federalists made several more attempts, but never had a better break, always fighting the losing battles.

Unfortunately for all mankind, the antifederalists gained the upper hand from the very start and were most cruel and unkind to the poor little orphan. They scorned him, beat him and tried to knock out all his teeth even before they were cut, so that he could not eat a few morsels of their precious bread or bite anyone that might prove detrimental to the peace of the world; they did all this without the slightest forethought that some day his strong arms would protect them against a wholesale massacre, had he been brought up properly.

One of the moves to knock all the teeth out of the League was the attempt to strike out Article 10 of the covenant, providing for the preservation of territorial integrity and political independence of the member states against external aggression. The proposal was made by the Canadian representatives at the League for the ostensible purpose of freeing her from the obligation to send her boys overseas to fight in defense of foreign countries. After four years of fight, Canada gained the support of only three states—Austria, Bulgaria and Hungary. After losing the fight, the Canadian representatives forced the assembly to adopt a resolution which asked the council to consider the geographic situation of each state in recommending the application of military sanctions. The solution lacked the required unanimity. Twenty-nine states voted in favor of it; thirteen abstained from voting, and one state, Persia, voted against it. So that was the end of this fight.

But another move to knock all the teeth out of the League met with a considerable degree of success. The representatives of Denmark, Sweden, Norway and the Netherlands proposed to make the automatic and obligatory application of economic sanctions provided in Article 16 into optional and discretionary. After a long and sustained debate, they succeeded in causing the assembly to adopt an interpretive resolution modifying the article in the following manner: when the council would inform the member states that a certain member had violated the covenant, each state was free to judge whether the council's decision was right or wrong. If it disagreed with the decisions of the council, the member was to be free from the obligation of applying economic sanctions, regardless of what others did. But if it accepted the council's judgment as correct, then the member states must fulfil the duty as a member of the League. In other words, any state could refuse to join in the application of economic sanctions by merely disagreeing with the judgment of the council.

In spite of all these and other blows, the League refused to die. It weathered badly the stormy seas of political controversy created by the Polish seizure of Lithuania, the Italian occupation of Corfu and scores of other disturbing incidents. But it still survived, enjoying at least the blessings and sympathy of the world, if not health, power and glory. Then came the Manchurian Crisis, the major test case which was to decide, once and for all, the fate of this unfortunate orphan.

The Manchurian Crisis was created by the Japanese Army which opened an attack on Manchuria on September 18, 1931, and subsequently seized a territory larger than Germany and France combined. The Japanese committed this act of aggression in the name of self-defense by charging the Chinese with aggression: they alleged that the Chinese had caused an explosion on the evening of the eighteenth and blown up thirty-one inches of the Japanese railway tracks in Manchuria. The seizure of such a large territory in self-defense for the destruction of thirty-one inches of railway tracks would be going a little too far in any language, even if it were admitted that the Chinese had actually done so. But all evidences pointed to the conclusion that the whole incident, if there was one, was cooked up by the Japanese Army to justify its attack on China. It is interesting to note that, at the International War Crimes Tribunal held at Tokyo in the summer of 1946, the Japanese Army officers admitted that they had started the Manchurian incident.

There was a definite and indisputable case of flagrant aggression committed by a militaristic power against a friendly neighbor, violating all the principles laid down in the covenant of the League, in the Washington treaties and in the Pact of Paris. The peace of the entire world and the fate of all mankind were dependent on the outcome of the Manchurian settlement. Naturally, the whole world looked upon the handling of this test case with keenest interest. Both the peace-loving peoples and the reactionary militarists, the pacifists and internationalists in America and England as well as the Nazis and

Facists in Germany, Italy and Japan were all equally interested in the case, because if it was handled successfully it would have enhanced the power of the peace machinery so much as to leave no room for the triumph of Hitler, Mussolini or Hirohito.

What the members of the League should have done was to discharge their duties as imposed upon them by the covenant of the League, namely, place Japan under political, economic and financial embargo as provided in Article XVI, which was still in force with a slight modification in the method of application. In the event that such measures failed to produce the desired result, they should have moved for the employment of military and naval powers.

Japan then was the lone aggressor, not so powerful as she was ten years later. She was poor economically and financially and could not have waged a long war without the accumulated vital materials. Then, too, the forces of liberalism in Japan could have been counted on for co-operation against the encroachment of militarism. So had the members of the League moved in the direction mapped out in the covenant, the Japanese military clique could have been crushed, the rise of similar forces in Germany and elsewhere could have been frustrated, the peace of our generation and many generations to come might have been saved at the cost of a single battleship sunk in the Pacific and certainly at a small fraction of the cost of the Second World War. But the civilized nations of the world completely failed to act in the interest of peace in that most vital test case, the greatest in all history. Their failure to act in this case was a great catastrophe to all mankind, for it encouraged the rise of similar evil forces of aggression in Germany, Italy and elsewhere to pursue the same course which the Japanese had paved for them to follow.

Many volumes have already been written on the question of why the great experiment failed. But few have understood the real cause of its collapse. It does not seem possible that the nations of the world will do any better in preserving peace than before, unless they know correctly why that great experiment failed. I shall, therefore, attempt to give the true reason, in fact, the only one, for the failure of the last peace.

3. The Collapse of the Experiment

A. The Alleged Cause of Its Collapse

Most students of world affairs blame the failure of the League on its faulty principles. They contend that the system of confederation has never worked anywhere it has been tried. It failed in the early days of America, Canada, Australia, and South Africa. It was bound to fail, and it failed. Such, for instance, was the explanation given by Clarence K. Streit in *Union Now*. It may be noted here that the same kind of argument has been used against the United Nations Organization by various so-called federalists.

It is needless to say that this kind of contention does not agree with historical facts. The Boeotian League of ancient Greece, with Thebes as its capital, survived more or less for six centuries. The Peloponnesian League, the Aetolian League and the Achaean League all continued to function from one to two centuries. The Hanseatic League, organized largely for economic collaboration, carried out its activities for three centuries. The confederation of the Swiss cantons survived the stormy political climate of Europe for five hundred years before it was converted into a closer federation in 1848. The Iroquois League of five Indian nations, though an association of sovereign nations with the retention of veto by all the chiefs of the participating nations, worked nearly three centuries despite all the political crises which battered upon it. The British Commonwealth of Nations, though more loosely organized than even a confederation, has survived many unprecedented crises in history, including the two world wars.

It is true that many confederations did not work. Nor did many other forms of government. Many confederations died a premature death. So did countless other forms of political units. The members of a confederation often quarrelled with each other. So did the people living in empires and unions.

For instance, the United States of America, with a union government, had one of the worst civil wars known in history. It is, therefore, an inexcusable distortion of historical facts to contend that all leagues of sovereign states are foredoomed to failure whereas a union of peoples is preordained to success. It is most unfortunate that many honest but sadly misinformed people have jumped to such an erroneous conclusion and have sabotaged both the League of Nations and the United Nations Organization in a more shameful way than even the Hearst Press and the Midwest isolationists would have dared to do.

One cannot deny that union or federation has certain advantages over confederation or association of sovereign states. For instance, the union government does not have to depend on the support of the several states for the execution of its orders, as it can operate independently of the constituent states. Had there been a world union instead of the League of Nations, the situation might have been better. But to expect that, because of this constitutional difference, a union would have succeeded where the League failed, under the kind of political atmosphere which prevailed between the two wars, betrays the complete ignorance of the real cause of the League's collapse.

Following Streit's line of thought, Emery Reves contends in *The Anatomy of Peace* that the League failed because it was based on the fallacy of the sovereignty of nations and the self-determination of races, both of which are regarded as anachronism in our age of interdependency. He says that the Second World War came about "not because Wilson's doctrines were not carried out, but because they were!"

While agreeing with Reves that unbridled sovereignty and the over-exaggerated claims to self-determination have created many evil consequences, I cannot accept the view that the Second World War came because Wilson's ideas of self-determination of races were carried out, or because the political independence of nations was preserved. Did the war come because the civilized world preserved Chinese sovereignty when Japan invaded Manchuria? Did the war come because the civilized nations upheld the independence of Ethiopia when

Italy attacked that country? Did the war come because the powers preserved the independence of Czechoslovakia and Austria against Hitler? Did the civilized nations fail to check the aggressor nations because they had recognized the sovereign right of the totalitarian powers to do what they willed, including the right to conquer their neighbors?

Some students of international relations blame the collapse of the League on its imperfect organization. One of the major faults of the organization was declared to be the unanimity rule. But I do not think it was the main obstacle against taking action in the Manchurian crisis. The unanimity rule, for instance, did not prevent the members of the League from applying economic sanctions against Italy during the Ethiopian War in 1935-36, when their action was backed by powerful members like Great Britain and France. Fifty out of fifty-four member states agreed with the council's finding that Italy violated the covenant, and applied economic sanctions against the lawbreaker. Three states, including Albania, Austria and Hungary, all of which later suffered the fate of Ethiopia, refused to join in the sanctions by holding that Italy had done no wrong. The fourth state, Switzerland, while admitting the guilt of Italy, refused to apply sanctions on the ground that it would expose her neutrality to "real danger." The United States did no more than place an arms embargo on both Ethiopia and Italy, and warn American tourists to travel on Italian ships at their own risk. Besides, the participating members did not apply sanctions to oil, the most critical war material needed by Italy, largely due to the opposition of the French who wished to retain Mussolini's friendship against the German threat. In spite of all these, the economic sanctions imposed upon Italy by fifty member states produced a telling effect. Within six months Italy lost half of her gold reserve and half of her total imports and exports. Had the sanctions been continued, the aggressor could have been crushed in due time. But the British and French, now faced with the menace of German power, reversed their stand and sabotaged the sanctions to retain Italy's good will. Thus, the two leading members hanged the League's executioners and helped the criminal recover to enjoy what he had robbed his murdered victim of. In the face of such a record, who can maintain that the civilized nations could not take action against Japan in Manchuria because of the imperfect organization of the League?

Consider also the tragedy of Pearl Harbor. According to experts, Pearl Harbor was one of the best naval bases, equipped with about the best means of defense known to science. In spite of all this, the Japanese could destroy in a little over one hour the major portion of America's Pacific Fleet, built at the cost of billions of dollars! Who can maintain that the failure at Pearl Harbor was due to a defect of the mechanism of defense?

I admit that even the best surgeon cannot perform a delicate operation with a pickaxe. But even the best surgical instruments cannot save the life of anyone, if the user is incompetent or unwilling to employ the instruments to the best of his ability.

Walter Lippmann maintains in *U. S. Foreign Policy* that the main cause of the collapse of the League was the absence of a nuclear alliance among America, Britain and France to underwrite the maintenance of the collective system of security. Such an alliance undoubtedly would have helped preserve peace. But then even similar alliances based on similar principles, like the Locarno Pacts, for example, failed to function because the contracting parties were unwilling to assume the risks involved in executing the agreements. It is doubtful, therefore, if the mere absence of a triple alliance was the main cause of the collapse of the League. Had the members of the League been willing to live up to their pledged words in the covenant, no such alliances would have been necessary for the triumph of peace. But without such willingness and determination, not even scores of alliances could have produced results.

Many Europeans and not a few charitable Americans blame the United States and Woodrow Wilson for the collapse of the League. They contend that the failure of the United States to join the League sealed the fate of the organization at the very start, and for America's failure to join the League, some blame

Wilson, some criticize Lodge and others assail the American people as a whole. For example, Thomas A. Bailey, author of *Woodrow Wilson and the Great Betrayal,* places the responsibility for the failure of the United States to join the League almost entirely on Wilson's uncompromising attitude "to get it all, or nothing." Undoubtedly, Wilson's uncompromising disposition in the matter was one of the causes of the League's defeat in the American Senate. But to hold that Wilson alone was responsible for the defeat is very much like maintaining that the Roosevelt administration alone was responsible for the Japanese attack on Pearl Harbor. If the Roosevelt administration alone were responsible for the Pearl Harbor tragedy, the Japanese are completely innocent. Similarly, if Bailey were right, Senator Lodge was not at all responsible for the League's defeat, and, therefore, the Senator was wrong in claiming the credit for defeating it.

Walter Lippmann likewise attacks Wilson without mercy in his *U. S. Foreign Policy* and *U. S. War Aims.* He says that Wilson failed to win the American people for the cause of the League because his arguments in favor of the League were "moralistic, legalistic and idealistic, not substantial or vital to American security." Such charges as these are very amusing when one reviews Wilson's appeals to his people with the solemn warning that without an organized authority such as the League, the world would suffer in a generation another war which would be so terrible that what the Germans used in the first war would be only toys!

Carl L. Becker—author of *How New Will the Better World Be?*—blames the American people for the failure of the United States to join the League. He maintains that the people were tired of war and troubles abroad and wanted to forget all of them and return to normalcy, in other words, isolation.

But Ruth Cranston, who made a painstaking study of Wilson's fight for the League, debunks all this popular myth that the American people "turned the League of Nations down cold" because they wanted to return to normalcy or because Wilson failed to win the American people for the cause of the

League. She points out in *The Story of Woodrow Wilson* that eighty per cent of the people wanted the League as a safeguard against future wars. In other words, Wilson, who, according to Lippmann failed to persuade his people that the League was vital to American security, succeeded in persuading eighty per cent of his people that the League was indispensable for the preservation of peace and democracy throughout the world. Why then did the United States fail to join the League?

Senator Henry Cabot Lodge, chairman of the Senate Foreign Relations Committee, told in *The Senate and the League of Nations* how he sabotaged the League and prevented the United States from joining the other nations in a concerted drive against international anarchy. Lodge frankly admitted that he would have been defeated and the League would have gone through the Senate had he allowed a direct vote to be taken on the subject. He therefore decided to kill it piecemeal through a slow, lingering death by the use of indirect political means. He packed the Committee on Foreign Relations by appointing four new anti-League senators to fill vacant seats. By doing so, he even violated the sacred seniority rule by rejecting Frank Kellogg, a pro-League Senator who was the first to be on the committee. With support of this packed committee he introduced numerous reservations which would have nullified all the principles of the League and staged a two-months' long debate, jabbing, slashing and tearing the League to a mere skeleton. He also carried the fight into the whole country with the support of the Hearst papers and the Midwest isolationists and the financial support of Andrew Mellon and Henry Frick. In spite of all this maneuvering, the League failed to go through the Senate by the lack of only seven votes for the required two-thirds.

But no fair-minded student of world affairs should single out the American politicians for the blame. The stubborn fight for the spoils of war, the consistent refusal to abandon power politics and join in an honest-to-goodness co-operation for international justice by the other allied and associated powers gave the American politicians an excuse to fight against their participation in the League, which they deemed an instrument of domination and exploitation, designed to use American lives and property for their own selfish ends.

With America in the organization, the League might have had a better chance of success, but even without her, the League members could have made a success of it, as shown in the abortive economic sanctions imposed on Italy during the Ethiopian War. The American absence, therefore, appears to be only a convenient excuse for, not the real cause of, the failure of the civilized nations to concert their action against aggression.

Some students of world affairs blame the harsh treatment of Germany for the collapse of the last peace. But the peace of Versailles was many times more liberal than that of Brest-Litovsk which Germany imposed upon vanquished Czarist Russia. The amount of indemnity which Germany was to pay the Allies was considered high. But Hitler's Germany, which was too poor to pay her indemnity, was able to squander many times that amount for her rearmament. Judging from what liberal treatment of Nazi Germany did, had the victorious powers been more lenient than they were, Germany could have started her war of revenge much sooner than she did.

Many students of economics blame the great depression and the failure to solve the urgent economic problems for the collapse of the peace machinery. But the fallacy of such a contention is self-evident when one understands that the main reason for failing to solve the economic problems was the inability of the civilized world to solve the problem of peace and security.

Furthermore, what should be remembered is that when a man or a nation is faced with a dire economic necessity, he or it would make an attempt to meet it either through thrift and industry, or through a direct attack on the bank or the rich people, provided that there is a chance for a successful loot without facing the consequences. Had the power of the world organization been upheld during the Manchurian crisis, it is very doubtful if Germany would have had the temerity to attempt to solve her economic ills through international banditry. But when the civilized world condoned Japanese aggression and let Japan get away with her fabulous loot, that, of course, gave the Germans a temptation to emulate Japan. The result was the rise of Hitler to power. It is significant to remember the dates: Manchurian crisis began in the fall of 1931, Hitler arose to power in 1933, and Mussolini opened his attack on Ethiopia in 1935.

And so, all these and hundreds of other alleged causes, including bad weather, amount to little more than manufactured alibis to cover up the sins of the civilized nations for their pitiful failure to act in defense of peace and justice in that historic case, the Manchurian crisis. What are then the chief causes of the failure of the League? Who is responsible for the ultimate collapse of the peace machinery? As their failure to preserve the principles of collective security during the Manchurian crisis brought about the last war, the trial of war criminals should begin with the saboteurs of peace, if there are any.

B. The Retrial of the Alleged Saboteurs of Peace

The first person who should be called on the witness stand is Henry L. Stimson, then Secretary of State of the United States of America. His country was not a member of the League, but she had much to do with the success or failure of peace. Because she was the most influential nation in that period, the peace of the world and the fate of all mankind largely depended on her attitudes and policies. What her statesmen did or did not do, therefore, was of vital importance to the whole world. Now let us see what Stimson did or tried to do in that significant test case.

On September 23, five days after the outbreak of the Manchurian crisis, the council of the League took up the question of dispatching a neutral commission to Manchuria to supervise the withdrawal of Japanese troops. Stimson objected to the sending of such a commission for fear that such hasty action might arouse the whole Japanese Nation. He wanted the League to go slowly and cautiously so as not to jeopardize the fate of the liberal government of Japan. However good his intention was, the adoption of the moderate course which the council subsequently took did not help the situation. It only emboldened the military clique to pursue their policies of conquest with great vigor and determination. Many European observers maintain, therefore, that Stimson spoiled it at the very beginning of the case.

When the Japanese Army carried out a major war of aggression, both the United States and the League members changed their tune. The American Government sent at the invitation of the League's council its representative, Prentiss B. Gilbert, to sit in at the council deliberations against the objections of the Japanese Government. Fortified by the American support, the council adopted a strong resolution on October 23, boldly requesting the withdrawal of the Japanese troops from Manchuria. The resolution, however, had no restraining influence on the Japanese military action, which by that time became a full scale war.

The council met again in the middle of November to discuss ways and means of coping with the grave situation in the Far East. At this time the American Government drew back a step. It refused to have its representative, then Charles G. Dawes, to sit in at the council meetings; it merely asked Dawes to be present in Paris, where the council met, to be available for consultation if necessary.

By that time it was clear to everyone that empty words and futile gestures would have little effect against the determined Japanese. The question of economic sanctions, therefore, was aired, not seriously but casually. All the encouragement Dawes could give the League was his assurance that if the League members imposed economic sanctions against Japan, the United States would not discourage them or "put any obstacles or dangers in their path." This was another way of saying that the United States, which had as much trade with Japan as the rest of the world did, was not prepared to go so far as to join them in an outright economic boycott against Japan. William Star Myers states in *The Foreign Policies of Herbert Hoover* that President Hoover made it clear to Secretary Stimson that his administration should not be committed to more than moral suasion to deter Japan. It is little wonder that Dawes could not give the League more encouragement.

It is questionable if economic sanctions could have been considered seriously by the members of the League even if the United States were actually prepared to join them. But as she was not, the others were greatly relieved, for they could say, and actually did so, that economic sanctions without the co-operation of the United States would be a futile attempt foredoomed to failure. Thus, Hoover, Stimson, Dawes and the United States as a whole were blamed for the failure of the peace efforts.

With the question of economic sanctions thrown out of consideration, the Japanese felt free to go ahead with their program of conquest without any serious threat of penalty. The council, however, adopted on December 10, a resolution creating the so-called Lytton Commission to inquire into the sources of the Sino-Japanese conflict.

As expected, the situation in the Orient grew from bad to worse. So on January 7, 1932, Stimson sent to the signatories of the Nine Power Treaty his famous but ineffective note, enunciating the so-called Doctrine of Non-Recognition. In it he declared that his country would not recognize the fruits of the Japanese military conquest. The enunciation of this policy was a substitute of economic sanctions, the least which any civilized country with honor and decency could have done. Rightly or wrongly, Stimson believed at that time that moral sanctions, if adopted in the form of non-recognition by the entire world, could have halted Japan, or any other aggressor. Had other signatories followed suit, it might have produced some effect, but no other state did. The British Government, on whose co-operation Stimson relied heavily, replied politely that, as a member of the League, Great Britain could not send such a note to Japan alone. Whatever action she took must be taken with other members of the League. In this, the British Government must have been right. But the Japanese Government, for reasons which should have been clear to it, interpreted this British reply as a rebuff to Stimson and believed that it could, as far as Great Britain was concerned, do virtually as it pleased in Manchuria.

The British refusal to go along with the United States in this move created much stir in America, as well as in England. Public agitation against the government in Great Britain grew to an embarrassing proportion. The British Foreign Office, therefore, tried to remedy its blunder as well as it could. Sir John Simon, the British Foreign Minister, supported Stimson's Doctrine of Non-Recognition in the League's council meetings held on January 29 and February 16, and caused the adoption of the principle by all members of the League on March 11, 1932.

In the meantime, the undeclared war in Manchuria spread to Shanghai, the citadel of Western interests. The Japanese attack on Shanghai created a stir throughout the world. Stimson grew impatient and worried. He thought something more than his Doctrine of Non-Recognition was needed. Acting at the suggestion of President Hoover, Stimson telephoned from Washington on February 11, to Sir John, who was then attending the League's council meeting at Geneva. He made a momentous proposal for a joint Anglo-American demarche under the Nine Power Treaty. Contrary to popular understanding, it was not a proposal for an outright application of joint sanctions against Japan. But it appears that it was much more than a proposal for an invocation of the Nine Power Treaty in mere words, for Stimson explained to Sir John "fully and at length" that the main purpose in making such a joint demarche was to "make clear our faith in and intention to live up to the covenants of the Nine Power Treaty respecting the future sovereignty and integrity of China."

It appears that Stimson suggested the taking of such a joint Anglo-American demarche because the League had failed to handle the case in the interest of peace and justice, and there was little hope that the League could do better. Nor was there any chance for joint action against Japan by all the signatories of the Nine Power Treaty, for France was openly in sympathy with Japan and against the invocation of the treaty. What Stimson proposed to Sir John amounted to saying that "even if the League should fail and even if all the signers of the Nine Power Treaty refused to act, we, the two greatest democratic nations, the United States and Great Britain, must make a joint demarche under the Nine Power Treaty and see what could be done to check the Japanese aggression, without jeopardizing the prestige of the League in some way satisfactory to all." Now let us see what response Sir John gave.

One can easily imagine what a warm reception Stimson's proposal could have had if one were familiar with the sad fact that at the very time when Stimson made such a proposal, Sir John, the man who was charged with the most important task in world history, the task of safeguarding the peace of the world against international banditry, was making an eloquent plea in defense of Japanese aggression!

Sir John was courteous but cool in his proposal. So Stimson telephoned to him again the next day, February 12, and cabled him a tentative draft for a joint demarche in the hope that he would discuss the matter with the prime minister and the whole cabinet on February 13, when Sir John was to return to London for a cabinet meeting. Stimson telephoned him again on the thirteenth at London and once more on the fifteenth, and then set down the receiver in the belief that he had failed to secure British co-operation. Did the British Government actually turn down the American proposal? Or did Stimson voluntarily withdraw his proposal?

All that Stimson said in his book, *The Far Eastern Crisis*, published in 1936, was this: "While no explicit refusal to my suggestion was ever made, I finally became convinced that for reasons satisfactory to it, and which I certainly had no desire to inquire into or criticize, the British Government felt reluctant to join in such a demarche. I, therefore, pressed it no further." But the British spokesmen, official or unofficial, maintain that the British Government was "most anxious to co-operate with America," but Mr. Stimson himself abandoned his proposal for a joint Anglo-American demarche under the Nine Power Treaty.

If the British contention is correct, the United States, not Great Britain, must assume the responsibility for the ultimate collapse of the collective system of security. Let us then examine briefly the British side of the story of the peace move that failed.

The best defense of the British Government is to be found in the works of Sir John Pratt, formerly consul general in China and later adviser on Far Eastern Affairs in the British Foreign Office for thirteen years, including the time of the Manchurian crisis. His letters published in the *London Times* on the position of the British Government have been widely read in Europe and America and his book *War and Politics in China,* published in 1943, has had several printings and enjoyed a popularity which Stimson's *The Far Eastern Crisis* has yet to attain.

Pratt maintains that both Sir John Simon and the British Foreign Office, instead of cold-shouldering, welcomed Stimson's offer for a joint demarche. He supports his statement with an undeniable document: a written statement of the Foreign Office for transmission to Stimson, which was delivered to Ray Atherton, American Charge at London, on February 16, the day after Stimson held his last telephone conversation with Sir John Simon. In that statement they assured him that they were "most anxious to co-operate with America" in the matter.

It is a fact that such a note was actually delivered to Atherton. But rightly or wrongly, the note was interpreted in Washington as meaning that Great Britain would only follow the American lead if the United States invoked the Nine Power Treaty, but that the British Government would not make a joint demarche which is tantamount to the rejection of the American proposal in a polite language.

Pratt then goes on to maintain that there is no proof to support the contention that Sir John cold-shouldered Stimson's offer for a joint demarche because there is no record of the telephone conversation, and there is no way of telling just what Stimson said and how Sir John replied. Besides, Sir John's speech in defense of Japanese aggression, delivered at the Anglo-American Press Association luncheon at Geneva, was confidential and no record exists to hold against the British Foreign Secretary.

It is true that Sir John spoke at a private luncheon without the right of quotation; in other words, his remarks were off the record and highly confidential. But his speech was so startling and reckless that few of those present could forget it. And some went so far as to let the world know what Sir John said.

Raymond Gram Swing gives in *Ken* magazine, November 17, 1938, the substance of the British Foreign Secretary's speech delivered at the Press Association on February 12, on the day when Stimson made his second trans-Atlantic telephone call to him. Here it is in substance: "Sir John did not think that anyone, Britain in particular, should find fault with what Japan was doing because that is the way the British built their empire. The only difference he could see was that Japan was doing it when the rest of us have stopped doing it. He made a particularly strong case for Japan's need for expansion on the continent of Asia."

Swing adds that everyone who heard that speech on that day "could write with confidence that so long as Sir John Simon remained at the foreign office, Great Britain would never raise a finger to restrain the Japanese aggression."

Even if no one had "spilled the beans," Pratt's position is still untenable because the record of Sir John's activities in Geneva is well known to everyone. He made such a great defense of Japan at the League of Nations as to receive the public thanks and praise of the Japanese representatives for having spoken more effectively for Japan than the Japanese representatives themselves. He blocked all the attempts to take strong action against Japan so openly throughout the Manchurian crisis that even the newspapers of that period are filled with the dilatory tactics which Sir John employed.

There probably is some justification for the contention that Sir John was not enthusiastic to Stimson's overture because nothing short of economic or military sanctions could have halted Japan, that the United States was not prepared to go so far. It may be true that the United States was not willing to go so far at that moment, but in the event that the proposed joint demarche should have failed to produce the desired results, no one could tell how far this country would have gone. The entire American Navy was concentrated in the Pacific, and a joint naval demonstration could not be ruled out entirely. Bills were introduced into Congress empowering the government to impose economic sanctions against the aggressor. No one but God could guess how far the American Government and people would have gone.

It has been maintained that the resort to economic sanctions or naval demonstration would have led the two countries into a war in which Japan could have easily defeated both America and England, because the Washington treaties made Japan a master of Asia, rendering England and America helpless. But this was another alibi. If the United States and Great Britain could defeat Japan after exhausting so much power and energy on Hitler, certainly they could have crushed the Japanese easily enough at that time with the co-operation of the entire world.

Perhaps the strongest defense of the British Government as a whole is the disclosure of the inquiry, showing that the British Cabinet was not informed of the true nature of Stimson's offer. According to this inquiry made by a former member of the British Cabinet, whose name has been withheld for the time being, Sir John Simon, for the reasons not hard to guess, did not tell the Cabinet the whole story, although he did so to a few colleagues. All that he told the Cabinet was that the United States wanted to invoke the Nine Power Treaty, but did not stress the offer of an Anglo-American demarche, "with all it implied." The Cabinet members, therefore, made a historic decision blindfolded. If one accepts this finding, it is Sir John alone, not the British Government as a whole, who should be held responsible for the failure to make a joint demarche.

But I do not think it fair to put all the blame on poor Sir John, who did the best he knew how. What the foreign minister said and did was not entirely different from the general tempo of British politics. The influential *London Times* editorialized against its country's participation with America in invoking the Nine Power Treaty by reminding the British Foreign Office that it was not their business "to defend the administrative integrity of China until that integrity is something more than an ideal," in other words, worth preserving. The powerful business interests in England, as well as in other countries, believed that Japanese conquest and exploitation of Manchuria would be beneficial to their business. The Federation of British Industries actually sent a trade mission to Manchukuo in 1934, begging for the crumbs of trade which the Japanese war lords might throw to them like bones to dogs. I think Colonel Leopold S. Amery, Secretary of State of India, expressed the prevailing sentiment of many British politicians of that time when he declared:

"I confess that I see no reason whatever why, either in act, or in word, or in sympathy, we should go individually, or internationally, against Japan in this matter.... Who is there among us to cast the first stone and say that Japan ought not have acted with the object of creating peace and order in Manchuria and defending herself against the continual aggression of vigorous Chinese nationalism? Our whole policy in India, our whole policy in Egypt, stand condemned if we condemn Japan."

Jan Christiaan Smuts, who has been honored as one of the most enlightened statesmen in the British Commonwealth of Nations, predicted that the Far Eastern political cloud, though not greater than a man's hand then, would "come to overshadow the whole international sky in time." But he was opposed to the taking of any measure which might antagonize Japan. He would only appeal "most earnestly and in the friendliest spirit to Japan to pause before she destroys the concert in the Pacific." After seeing what Smuts advocated, how much more could one expect from Sir John Simon!

Whether it was due to Sir John's excessive sympathy for Japan, or to the coolness of the British public to Chinese nationalism, or to the impatience of Stimson, or the indecision and vacillation of the democratic governments, or the general apathy and indifference of the nations of the world at large, the United States and Great Britain failed to make a joint demarche against the lone aggressor, Japan. When the two greatest democracies, guardians of peace and justice in that period, failed to assume a vigorous leadership in a world crusade against aggression, there was little hope for the preservation of peace and justice against the relentless onslaught of war and barbarism.

C. The Final Verdict on the Collapse of the League

Having reviewed the performances of the actors of the peace drama now we can say definitely what caused, or did not cause, the collapse of the League. It is clear that the defect of the peace organization was not the chief cause of its failure, for under the kind of leadership and in the kind of atmosphere throughout the world, even a more perfect union government would have collapsed. And if a butcher fails to operate on a patient successfully, or if a murderer fails to save the life of his victim, one should not blame the innocent instruments. Nor were the hundreds of other reasons given for the failure of the collective system more than manufactured alibis.

There was only one big reason why the League collapsed; that was the absence of the will to act in common security. Rappard was right when he concluded in *The Quest of Peace* that "what was lacking for the preservation of peace was not the instruments but the universal will to use them."

Lord Robert Cecil, who knew probably more about the inside workings of the League than any other living person, believes that the League was sabotaged by those who had control of it. In his autobiography entitled *A Great Experiment*, Lord Robert tells that no British Prime Minister who had held office between the years 1920 and 1939 really believed in the League. They regarded it, he said, "as a kind of excrescence which must be carefully prevented from having too much influence on our foreign policy." Although he was too much of a gentleman to blame other nations, he did say that that summed up the official view of the League "in almost all countries."

The League which Lord Robert knew resembled a perfectly good automobile in a convenient garage. There was nothing wrong with it except that it could not be driven without a chauffeur at the wheel, without gasoline, oil, water and tires, or the passengers who were willing to step inside the car for a trial run. Lord Robert concludes, therefore, that the League did not succeed because the forces and the men in command of the organization "never really wanted it to succeed."

Had there been a strong, determined will to act together in common defense, there was no defect in the covenant, or outside it, which could not have been overcome. But there was no desire or determination to act together in common defense because the civilized nations of the world believed that, regardless of what happened to others, they could still enjoy peace and prosperity, protected by their armies, navies, air forces, geographical position, power politics, neutrality, or just good luck.

The British had great faith in their mighty empire, in their matchless navy and their skillful balance of power system, all of which appeared sufficient for their enjoyment of peace and prosperity, regardless of what happened to the League. The Americans believed that their geographical position, protected by two unfathomable oceans, could continue to give them peace and security, and the success or failure of the League was none of their business. The French had an undying faith in their unconquerable army and their indestructible Maginot Line. Even the smaller nations of the world, which had no navies or armies to protect their interests, believed that they could again enjoy peace and tranquillity by remaining neutral in the event of another war. So both the big powers and the little ones failed to do their part for the preservation of the League. The big powers, however, should assume a greater share of responsibility for the collapse of peace, because with their vigorous leadership there was nothing that could not have been accomplished, whereas without it, nothing was capable of accomplishment.

The failure of the collective action in that test case reminds me of a well-known Manchurian bandit story. At a primitive corner of undeveloped Manchuria there was a small village where five families were huddled together in five adjoining houses. Cut off from the rest of the world, there was no shadow of law, no means of protection. One dark, stormy night the bandits invaded this little village. They first attacked the house at the farthest end. They crept over the walls, broke through the windows; they split the heads of the occupants with axes and mutilated their bodies with butcher knives. The screams and cries for help aroused the whole village but the timid village folk did not come to help their neighbors; they held their breath and shivered in fear and trepidation; they only hoped that the bandits would go away after looting the first house, leaving the rest of them unmolested, as they had done nothing against the bandits. In the meantime, the robbers wiped out the entire family, gathered up all their valuables and were ready to depart. But they did not leave. Flushed with victory in their first attack, they flung into action against the next house and repeated their ignoble deeds, and then the next, and again the next until all the villagers were exterminated. They then retired at leisure to the green forest to enjoy the fruits of their atrocious crime.

There is a striking similarity between what happened in that little Manchurian village and in the world community. The Japanese attack on China was comparable to the attack of the outlaws on the first house. Mussolini's invasion of Ethiopia was similar to the assault on the second house. Hitler's encroachment on Austria, Czechoslovakia and Poland was comparable to the attacks on the third, fourth and fifth houses in the row. In all these cases, the so-called civilized nations did precisely what the inhabitants of that primitive village did: they heard the cries of the victims but failed to mobilize their forces for the rescue of their neighbors. Worse still, the so-called civilized nations not only failed to help their neighbors, but they aided the aggressor nations by supplying them with arms, money and vital war materials, in the vain hope that the international highwaymen would leave them alone to enjoy peace and prosperity!

In both cases peace and order could have been preserved, had the inhabitants of the respective communities, the Manchurian village and the world community, joined their forces for their common defense. But they failed to, and so invited calamities upon themselves and their fellowmen. So why blame the League of Nations? Why blame the business interests or the poor politicians? Why blame Henry L. Stimson or Sir John Simon? Why blame Hitler, Mussolini and Hirohito? The inhabitants of that primitive village were as much responsible as the outlaws for the tragic fate fallen upon them, and the so-called civilized nations of the world were as much responsible as Hitler, Mussolini and Hirohito for the deadly bombs rained over London, Paris, Moscow, Chunking and Tokyo, and for the baptism of blood and the carnage of destruction which cursed mankind through the length and the breadth of the entire world.

In both the Manchurian village and the world community, the failure to take concerted action for the preservation of peace and justice was the same—the lack of will to act in common security; and the lack of will to take concerted action was born of a mistaken belief that, regardless of what happened to others, they could still live in peace and prosperity. Had they known that, without a common defense against the criminal elements, all of them would have eventually fallen victims of the murderous gangsters, they certainly would have had the unconquerable will to act together; had they had that will to act, nothing, not even the League of Nations, could have prevented their taking joint action at the first sign of disturbance. Therefore, the most dangerous saboteur of peace was the seemingly harmless, superstitious belief that civilized nations could enjoy peace and prosperity protected by their military, naval and aerial forces, or by power politics and good fortune without concerted action for the preservation of peace and justice throughout the world.

Misguided and misled by this dangerous, unseen saboteur of peace, the civilized nations remained smug and indifferent while the world was being set on fire. As a result they suffered the

Second World War, the most destructive and the most horrible of all wars in history.

It should be conceded that human beings do not always do what is best for them even when they know what is best. So one could maintain that the civilized nations of the world knew what was coming, but they could not or did not act. However, all the statements emanating from various capitals and the action which the nations took subsequently do not support such a contention.

Chapter VIII

THE PROPOSED ROAD TO ETERNAL PEACE

1. The Promise of the United Nations

"We, the peoples of the United Nations, determined to save succeeding generations from the scourge of war, which twice in our lifetime has brought untold sorrow to mankind. . . .

"Do hereby establish an international organization to be known as the United Nations."

Thus begins the charter of the United Nations which was worked out by some eight hundred delegates, representing fifty nations, after nine weeks of labor at San Francisco. Does the new charter give a greater promise of lasting peace than the old covenant of the League of Nations?

In some ways the charter has certain advantages over the covenant, but in other ways, it has certain drawbacks not found in the old document. I shall enumerate a few of the striking advantages and disadvantages of the new charter as compared with the old covenant.

The covenant of the League was not created by the spontaneous will to co-operate for the maintenance of peace by the various nations. It was a document which, according to Kenneth W. Colegrove, author of *American Senate and World Peace,* was imposed upon the nations by Woodrow Wilson and a few of his associates. The new charter is not a document handed down by the so-called Big Four to other nations with the dictatorial attitude "Take it or leave it." Although the Big Four laid the foundations of the new charter in their draft agreed upon at Dumbarton Oaks, the document as a whole is a product of the combined wisdom and the earnest desire for peace of the delegates of fifty nations, representing nearly three-quarters of the earth's population.

The original signatories of the old covenant were forty-two, including twenty-nine allied and associated nations and thirteen neutrals. The original signatories of the new document were fifty nations, all of whom had declared war on the Axis Powers. But one important difference in this respect is that the United States and Soviet Russia, both of whom were not in the League at the beginning, are now charter members of the new organization.

Both the covenant and the charter have provisions for the expulsion of member states, but the charter has no provision for the withdrawal of members from the organization, whereas the covenant has such a clause.

There seems to be no material difference in the composition and in the powers and functions of the two assemblies. The new assembly, like the old one, is largely a talking shop, with the Council serving as a work shop. The individual members of the new assembly, however, cannot sabotage the peace efforts of the whole world, as most important decisions are to be made by a two-thirds majority vote, not by unanimous vote as it was in the League assembly. But this difference is not as important as it appears on the surface because, as has been pointed out in the preceding chapter—"The Great Experiment"—what wrecked the League was not the unanimity rule, but the sabotage by the big powers, and this dangerous feature is by no means modified by the new charter.

The composition of the new council does not differ much from the old council. The original League council was to be composed of five permanent members and four nonpermanent members, but it started with four of each because of American nonparticipation. A few years later it had four permanent members and six nonpermanent members. By 1939 it had three permanent members—France, Great Britain and Soviet Russia—and eleven nonpermanent members. The new Security Council is composed of five permanent and six nonpermanent members.

The council of the League met from time to time as occasion required, and at least once a year at first, and later four times a year; the Security Council is to function continuously. For this purpose each member of the council is represented at all times at the seat of the organization.

In the council of the League all matters of procedure at meetings, including the appointment of committees to investigate particular matters, were decided by a majority vote, but most substantive decisions could be taken only by the unanimous vote of all its members, whether permanent or not. For instance, under Article 11, under which most of the disputes brought before the League were dealt with and decisions to make investigations taken, the unanimity rule was invariably interpreted to include even the votes of the parties to a dispute. Under Article 15, however, the League council could make a report with recommendations for the settlement of disputes submitted to it without the votes of the parties to the dispute.

Under the new voting formula, the Security Council shall make decisions on procedural matters by a vote of any seven of its eleven members; that is by a vote of any seven members, the Council can adopt or alter its rules of procedure; determine the method of selecting its president; organize itself in such a way as to be able to function continuously; select the times and places of its regular and special meetings; establish such bodies or agencies as it may deem necessary for the performance of its functions; invite a member of the organization not represented on the Council to participate in its discussions when that member's interests are specially affected; and invite any state when it is a party to a dispute being considered by the Council to participate in the discussion relating to that dispute. The Council likewise can discuss any subject affecting the peace and security of the world by a vote of any seven of its eleven members, and so no one member, permanent or nonpermanent, can veto a free discussion by the Council.

But a majority of seven members, including the concurring votes of the five permanent members, is required in any decision by the Council for dealing with a dispute either by peaceful means or by enforcement action, except that a party to a dispute must abstain from voting in the peaceful settlement stage. In other words, any permanent member can veto all decisions dealing with pacific settlement, including the decision to investigate and report, unless that member is a party to the dispute. Besides, any permanent member can veto all enforcement measures against any state, including itself. The nonpermanent members have no such veto power individually, but it has a similar veto power as a group because no decisions can be made by the Council without the concurring votes of at least two nonpermanent members.

The judicial organ of the United Nations is almost an exact duplicate of the Permanent Court of International Justice, with only a few insignificant modifications. The name of the court was changed from the Permanent Court of International Justice to the International Court of Justice. The new court will have fifteen full judges, instead of having eleven full judges and four deputy judges, as was the case in the old court. The new court, unlike the the old one, will be continuously in session except during vacations. But the most important feature of any court, the jurisdiction, is still optional, not obligatory, as it was under the old court.

The organization, powers and functions of the new Secretariat do not differ materially from the old. The Economic and Social Councils provided in the new charter do not seem to be very different from the numerous economic, financial, social, cultural, humanitarian bureaus, committees and commissions which were created under the old League. One important difference is that under the charter the Assembly, not the Council, is to direct and control the new agencies.

The Permanent Mandates Commission of the League consisted of ten members, the majority of whom where nationals of nonmandatory states. They were appointed by the Council and usually met once a year. It reviewed the annual reports submitted to it by the mandatory powers; it received petitions from responsible persons respecting the conduct of the mandates, and advised the Council on all matters relating to the observance of the mandates.

The Trusteeship Council is to consist of all members of the

United Nations administering trust territories, the permanent members of the Security Council not administering trust territories and as many other members elected by the Assembly until the number of the states not administering trust territories equals those which do. The Trusteeship Council shall have the power to make periodic visits to the trust territories at times agreed upon with the administering authority, in addition to the power to receive and examine the reports and petitions which the Mandates Commission had. The new organization, unlike the old one, will function under the direction of the Assembly, not of the Security Council.

On the subject of regional agreements, the old covenant stated specifically that nothing in it should be deemed to affect the validity of international engagements, "such as treaties of arbitration or regional understandings like the Monroe Doctrine for securing the maintenance of peace." The new charter definitely encourages the development of pacific settlement of local disputes through regional arrangements or agencies. "But no enforcement action shall be taken under regional arrangements or by regional agencies without the authorization of the Security Council," excepting the regional agreements, like the Franco-Russian pact, directed against renewal of aggressive policy by the enemy state, "until such time as the Organization may, on the request of the governments concerned, be charged with the responsibility for preventing further aggression by such a state."

The clauses concerning nonintervention in domestic issues, the registration and reconsideration of treaties and conventions, and the amendments of the constitution do not differ materially in the two documents.

The charter, however, shows a marked improvement over the covenant in that the covenant recognized the right of the League members to wage wars, while the charter closes this gap. Article 12 of the covenant stated, for example, that the members of the League agree not to resort to war "until three months after the award by the arbitrators or the judicial decision or the report by the Council," meaning that they might go to war after that period, if they liked. Furthermore, under Article 15 the League members reserved the right "to take such action as they shall consider necessary for the maintenance of right and justice," if the dispute submitted to the Council or to the Assembly failed to obtain a report for its settlement from the respective organs. But the charter reserves no such right to the members of the United Nations. On the contrary, the signatories specifically pledge themselves in the preamble of the charter not to use their armed forces "save in the common interest." Even the right of self-defense, which was frequently exercised by the aggressor nations as an excuse to conquer their neighbors, is explicitly limited by Article 51, which states: "Nothing in the present charter shall impair the inherent right of individual or collective self-defense if an armed attack occurs against a member of the United Nations, until the Security Council has taken the measures necessary to maintain international peace and security."

The charter shows another improvement over the covenant in that the methods of enforcing sanctions provided in the charter are much more concrete and definite than those in the covenant. It is a fact that the covenant provided for the automatic application of economic sanctions and also for the possible use of the armed forces of the member states to protect the covenant. But it had no detailed plans to enforce such sanctions. The charter, on the other hand, provides specifically for the working out of concrete military plans which would be previously arranged to meet all possible threats to the peace of the world. For the purpose of aiding the Security Council to execute such plans promptly and effectively, there shall be created a Military Staff Committee composed of the Chiefs of Staff of the permanent members of the Security Council or their representatives.

Much of the effectiveness of the new charter, however, is completely neutralized by the dangerous feature which makes it impossible for the members of the United Nations to restrain, by force if necessary, the big powers from violating the charter. This weakness nullifies all the strong points in the charter because the big powers more often have been the trouble-makers than the small states, and when the peace organization cannot cope with the chief disturbers of peace, it has little value as an instrument of peace.

For the purpose of clarifying the serious implications of this dangerous feature, let us see what the nations could have done with the Japanese aggression in Manchuria, if they had worked under the new charter instead of the covenant. In the peaceful settlement stage, Japan, though a permanent member of the Council, could not have vetoed the investigation of the Manchurian incident or the recommendations for the peaceful settlement of the dispute. In fact, she had no such veto power even under the old covenant. Had Japan refused to accept the reports, recommendations or decisions for peaceful settlement under the new charter and continued to pursue her aggressive policy by the force of arms, as she did under the covenant, the Security Council could not have halted her any better than the League Council because Japan, as a permanent member of the Council, could have vetoed all measures to invoke sanctions against her.

Under the covenant the League members could, at least if they chose, invoke sanctions against any recalcitrant member. But under the charter the members of the United Nations have lost this legal right to use sanctions against any of the permanent members of the Security Council. Technically speaking, therefore, the big powers can pursue their predatory policies with greater ease and comfort under the new charter than they could under the old covenant. For this reason there is a constant danger that some of the permanent members, who are no less aggressive and militaristic than the defeated Axis Powers, might be tempted to use this loophole as a means of perpetuating their aggressive designs.

It has been contended that this provision is immaterial because when force is used against a big power, it means a disastrous war, whether with or without the veto. But such a contention is dangerous nonsense, because when force is used in the defense of the principles of justice and law, it promotes peace, whereas, when it is used illegally, it perpetuates anarchy. Under the present charter the legal use of force by the United Nations against any of the permanent members of the Council is very difficult.

The members of the United Nations can, of course, use force against a permanent member of the Council over its veto, if they choose to do so. They, for instance, can declare war on the aggressor under Article 51, which permits them to take individual and collective action for self-defense until the Security Council can act. But in that case, they will have to violate one part of the Charter to save another part of it. When these things are all considered, one cannot help expressing the view that if the future world is to enjoy the blessings of peace, it will not be because of the constitutional superiority of the new document over the old.

2. The Future of the UN World Peace

If the new charter is not much superior to the old covenant, are the prospects for peace today any brighter than at the close of the First World War? Will the new experiment in international co-operation succeed where the last one failed? Or will the United Nations fail again where the League of Nations failed and lose the second chance to create international peace, the chance which was purchased at the cost of untold millions in lives and treasure?

Emery Reves declares in *The Anatomy of Peace* that the UN is not a step toward peace, but a step toward war, and "a step away from our goal." His reasons for entertaining such a view are that the UN is not a union, but a confederation of sovereign states foredoomed to failure. Overlooking the fact that most federations grew out of confederations, Reves joined the ranks of Clarence Streit, Ely Culbertson, Justice Owen Roberts and the isolationists in rejecting it and in damning it to eternity. But Reves feels that if we start right, that is, along the principles of union, it ought not take more than a dozen years "to bring to triumph the principles of universal law."

Pitirim A. Sorokin, Harvard's distinguished sociologist, told me bluntly that he does not expect to find a more durable peace following the Second World War than after the first one. He drew this conclusion from the assumption that the present-day sensate men with their sensate cultures and institutions are incapable of creating a lasting world peace. He anticipated, therefore, that all the futile attempts at creating peace and justice would be followed in two or three generations by a third world war, in which about three-quarters of all mankind would perish. Only by then will human beings have learned enough and changed enough morally and spiritually to co-operate with one another for the eradication of war.

Mortimer J. Adler, of the University of Chicago, does not expect to find a durable peace on earth within the next five hundred years. He fears that it might take at least as long as that for the civilized nations of the world to overcome the great obstacles on the path to peace—nationalism, patriotism, sovereignty, cultural and racial antagonisms—and to create a real workable federation of democracies for the perpetuation of just peace. If Adler were right, mankind would have to suffer about twenty world wars, figuring one war every twenty-five years, before humanity could hope to attain a durable peace.

Although they disagree on the period of time necessary for the consummation of a new order, many thinkers on international affairs seem to agree on one thing, and that is that men can and will overcome sooner or later their present international difficulties as they always have overcome similar perils. They succeeded in creating, though not without initial failures, the tribal organization, the city, state and national governments when they discovered that they could not live together without them. Now they find that they cannot survive in peace and security without an effective world organization which will banish international anarchy. There is no reason why they should not succeed in this new task on which the fate of all mankind depends. As a matter of fact, men cannot fail in this because the old world is being pushed into some sort of unity by the force of modern science and the struggle for survival in chaos.

At one time there were literally thousands of the so-called states on earth. But as no people could feel safe with hostile neighbors within a striking distance, all peoples sought to conquer and dominate their neighbors. In this mad scramble for security and survival, one state after another has been conquered or absorbed by more powerful ones. Now there are left only sixty-odd states which are divided into two rival spheres between Russia and the Western democracies. Unfortunately, both spheres remain within a striking distance of one another. As neither side can feel secure so long as both spheres remain with loaded guns across the alley, both would strive for unity either through peaceful means or forcible conquest until their final objectives are attained. Therefore, like it or not, human beings will have to live or die together under the same world authority, democratic or totalitarian.

Whether the civilized nations will voluntarily construct a democratic world federation through peaceful co-operation, or be forced to erect a world empire or republic under an iron rod, will largely depend on whether they have learned the never-to-be forgotten lesson that no nation, however powerful and however fortunate, can enjoy peace and security alone in the present state of international anarchy, protected by powerful armies and air forces, or by power politics or geographical position. If they have, they will probably overcome their hatred and prejudices and co-operate wholeheartedly even with their bitterest rivals, not excluding the devil, for the success of the new experiment. If they have the will and determination to act together for the preservation of peace and justice, they can accomplish their objectives under the new charter as well as they could under the old covenant. Or if they find the new instrument ineffective, they can easily change it into a workable organization by converting it into a world federation or by modifying the dangerous veto power retained by the Big Five. When they will have worked together harmoniously for a reasonable period of time, all the seemingly indissoluble problems will melt away in an atmosphere of friendship and all the apparently insurmountable obstacles to world peace, such as nationalism, sovereignty, economic rivalries, cultural and racial antipathies and the like, will be lost in the universal harmony of peace. We could then find a lasting peace established through voluntary co-operation in our generation rather than five centuries later.

But if the nations of the world, especially the powerful ones, still believe that they can enjoy the blessings of peace and prosperity in a world of international anarchy, protected by their armies and navies, power politics or favorable geographical positions, they can no more create world peace under the new charter than they could under the old covenant. Regardless of the nature of the new organization, regardless of what commitments they make for mutual co-operation, they will continue to race for armament, continue to play power politics, and continue to scramble for strategic areas and raw materials. Before long another world war will have come about, and the new war will be followed by another and still another until all the warring nations will have been conquered or destroyed by a super-dictator or a super-democratic commander. So either through peaceful co-operation or forcible conquest, the old world, as predicted by Kant and others, will continue to move slowly and yet surely toward a destined goal, a universal state. All that men can do, or should do, is to try to bring about this unification without unnecessary bloodshed.

Then, have the nations of the world learned enough of the value of mutual co-operation to forget their trifling differences and to construct a democratic world federation through peaceful means without risking another war, or wars?

Judging from the events following V-J Day, it does not appear that the civilized nations have learned much more from the last war than they have from other wars. They do not seem to have learned that in this day and age no nation, however big and strong, can enjoy peace and security without an effective world organization which will banish international chaos. Nor do they seem to realize that in this age of flying bombs neither territorial expansion, nor buffer states and spheres of influence, nor superiority in arms can give a better protection than the Great Wall, the Maginot Line or the Singapore Fortress. Or else, why should they continue to scramble for these things to the point of jeopardizing the chances for successful international co-operation?

Both the big and the small seem to believe that the removal of Hitler and Tojo forever eliminated the perils which once had threatened their very existence and, therefore, they could pick bones with their erstwhile allies. They do not seem to be aware that the spectre of a horrible Frankenstein monster is lurking over their shoulders with instruments of total destruction, while they are quarreling over the spoils of war. Or else, they would not have acted like a bunch of naughty little children fighting over a few pieces of spoiled candy, chewing gum, or broken toys without being aware of a big bad wolf stretching out its gory claws to snatch them all in a second or two.

The tragic developments in the post-war period, however, should not cause us to be unduly alarmed, for pending the establishment of a more efficient and workable world organization, it is natural that all nations should struggle separately for their own security, according to their old accustomed ways. It is natural for Soviet Russia to seek to strengthen her position in both Europe and Asia. It is natural for the United States to advance her claim over the Pacific islands and insist on retaining the atomic secrets for the time being. It is natural for the British to promote a Western bloc and to strengthen her defense against a possible Russian threat. It is natural for the French and the Dutch to strive to reconquer their rich colonies in southeastern Asia.

The period following the First World War was no less disconcerting than today. No sooner was peace pronounced than the Poles fought with the Lithuanians and the Ukranians. The Allied troops invaded Russia to put down the Bolsheviks. France invaded the Rhur, and Italy attacked Greece and seized Corfu. The Greeks burned Turkish Smyrna, and the Turks attacked the Armenian Republic and captured Kars and Alexandropol.

THE PROPOSED ROAD TO ETERNAL PEACE

There were revolts in Spanish Morocco, French Syria and British India. China was torn by civil war between rival factions as today. The Koreans arose with bare hands and cried for freedom from Japanese oppression only to be mowed down by machine guns. Above all, the greatest and the most powerful nation, the United States of America, on whose leadership the fate of all mankind depended, renounced her role in world affairs and crawled into her castle of isolation.

The League of Nations started its career under such a perilous situation, and yet, it gradually gained a world-wide support. At one time, it gave the promise of peace and security to all nations, and then it collapsed during the Manchurian Crisis due to no fault of its own. Who can foretell then what the UN will be like tomorrow?

The record of the UN, during its short span of existence, has demonstrated that it holds much greater promise of success than the League of Nations. It was organized more quickly than the League, and it has worked more efficiently than the League. Two years and four days elapsed between the Armistice of November 11, 1918, and the opening of the first assembly of the League on November 15, 1920. The United Nations Charter, on the other hand, was signed on June 26, 1945, when the war was still raging. It came into effect on October 24, when twenty-nine states, the last being Russia, ratified the Charter. The first assembly of the United Nations opened in London on January 10, 1946, or within half a year from the signing of the Charter.

Moreover, the League lost several more years in organizational matters, while the UN completed practically all such details at the first assembly. According to the first report of Tryvge Lie, Secretary General of the United Nations, the international Trusteeship Council is the sole principal organ of the United Nations which was not established at the first assembly. The speed with which the UN was organized was undoubtedly due to the benefits of the League's experiment. But one cannot deny that the willingness of the participating nations to make the new organization a success has played a very important part in speeding up the organizational setup.

Still more impressive than this is the way the Security Council has handled the delicate political questions which have been thrust on its lap when it was barely organized to function. When compared with the record of the League's Council, the achievement of the Security Council can be regarded a brilliant success. Even the Council of the League, it should be admitted, was moderately successful in settling the disputes between the small states, such as the Ashland dispute between Finland and Sweden and the boundary dispute between Albania and Jugoslavia. But when it came to the disputes between the big powers and the little or weak states, such as the Greco-Italian dispute and the Manchurian crisis, it proved to be a hopeless failure. The Security Council, on the other hand, though handicapped by the vicious veto, has shown its determination not to repeat the tragic failures of the League. Consider, for example, the way the Security Council handled the Iranian situation, which was the first major test case to come before that body.

On the surface, the Iranian issue does not seem very dissimilar to the Manchurian crisis. As Japan did in Manchuria, Russia appears to have sought economic concessions and political control in Azerbaijan by means which were contrary to the principles of the United Nations Charter. Iran appealed to the Security Council with the request to "investigate the situation and recommend appropriate terms of settlement." Just as the Japanese did during the Manchurian crisis, the Russians tried to block the consideration of the case by the Council. They did so on the ground that a direct negotiation for the settlement of the issue had not been exhausted. The Council, however, overruled the Russian objections and took up the question. After several days of bickering, the Council recommended that both parties continue their negotiations. At the same time, it reserved the right to request further information on the progress of negotiations.

Stung by the Iranian question, Andrie Vishinsky, the Soviet delegate, struck back at the British, although the British discouraged Iran at first from bringing her case before the UN. Vishinsky charged that the presence of the British troops in Greece and Indonesia constituted a danger to world peace; and that the Council, therefore, should take action in both countries. Ernest Bevin, the British Foreign Minister, declared that British forces were in Greece with the consent of the Greek Government and for the purpose of insuring a free election. He then demanded a clean bill for his country. At last Vishinsky agreed to withdraw his charges, and Bevin agreed to retract his demand for a clean bill.

No sooner was the Greek issue dropped than came the Indonesian question. Vishinsky now charged that the British and the Dutch intervention against the Indonesian people was contrary to the United Nations Charter and international law, and demanded an investigation by the Council, as the Indonesian situation might lead to another world war. The Soviet demand presented a heaven-sent opportunity for the Western democracies to show to the Russians how big and civilized they were by subjecting themselves to such an investigation. Instead, the British, supported by the Americans, flatly refused to allow an investigation, by branding the Soviet charge a "lie." The Russians then supported their charges with the facts reported in the press. Bevin then made probably the most disgraceful statement which could have been made by any statesman believing in the four freedoms. He said that newspapers have three functions: "to amuse, to entertain, and to misinform." Whereupon Vishinsky came to the defense of the freedom of the press, which cannot be found in his Soviet Union. When Bevin vigorously opposed the investigation by the Council on the ground that such a move would constitute an infringement on sovereignty, Vishinsky made the best speech against sovereignty which has yet been made. He declared:

"Can the United Nations exist? Can the UNO become an effective organ without certain limitations on national sovereignty? My answer is 'No!' There cannot be a United Nations unless each nation surrenders part of its sovereignty."

What a wonderful speech! But it could not prevent the Security Council from voting down the resolution calling for an investigation of the British and the Dutch action in Indonesia. Only Russia and Poland voted for it. It was a shameful defeat, not only for Russia, but for the United Nations. Nevertheless, Russia won a great moral victory over the Western democracies, for her stand against the Western colonial powers has caused millions of Asiatics to look upon Russia as a guardian of justice and to regard the Western democracies as imperialists and exploiters.

No sooner did the Russian attack on Western imperialism begin than the anti-British demonstrations came in Egypt, India, and other states in Asia. The representatives of Syria and Lebanon boldly appealed to the Security Council to recommend "total and simultaneous evacuation of British and French troops from the Levant." The American proposal recommending the withdrawal of the British and the French troops was vetoed by Vishinsky because he did not like the wording of the resolution. Nevertheless, the British and the French took steps to withdraw their troops before the end of the year.

Thus, all the issues which arose in connection with the Iranian dispute were thrashed out, but the Iranian question still remained unsolved. Had Russia withdrawn her forces from Iran by March 2, 1946, as she agreed to do by the Soviet-British-Iranian treaty of 1942, the issue might have been dropped. But Russia failed to recall her troops, although the British kept their agreement and moved out the last detachment of their troops before the dead line. (The American troops left Iran in January.) Instead, the Soviet Union announced on March 2 that some Soviet troops would leave Iran, but some would be kept "until the situation has been elucidated." The announcement created abroad the impression that Russia was as determined to stay in Azerbaijan as Japan was in Manchuria. Those who regarded the Iranian question as a major test for the UN were more determined than ever to uphold the principles of the United Nations Charter.

On March 20, the Soviet Government requested that the

meeting of the Security Council scheduled for March 25 be postponed until April 10 on the ground that direct negotiations with Iran were still under way. No action was taken on this request. The day before the scheduled meeting of the Council, the Soviet Union announced that Russian troops were being evacuated from Iran and that the evacuation would be completed within six weeks "if nothing unforeseen occurs."

The Security Council opened its session at Hunter College, New York, on March 25, as scheduled. Despite the Russian opposition, the Council placed the Iranian question on the agenda. Andrei A. Gromyko, the Russian representative, then moved to postpone the discussion of the question until April 10. When his request was voted down nine to two, he walked out of the Council meeting on March 27. The Council heard the Iranian side of the case without the Russian member and requested both parties to inform the Council by April 3 whether an agreement on the subject was reached.

The Soviet Union assured the Council on April 3 that her troops would be withdrawn from Iran unconditionally by May 6—evacuation had already begun on April 2. Being satisfied with the Soviet promise, the Council decided to postpone further consideration of the case until after May 6. A day later Russia and Iran jointly announced that they had concluded an agreement on all matters between them.

The Iranian issue would have died there and then but for Gromyko, who demanded on April 7 that the Iranian question be removed from the agenda. Two days later, the Iranian Government asked the Council to watch the activities of the Soviet Army in Iran until May 6. On April 15, the Teheran Government, presumably acting under Russian pressure, instructed its representative to withdraw the case from the Security Council. The request was voted down eight to three on the ground that the Council is not a mere registration agency, and, therefore, a situation which has been brought to its attention cannot be considered closed merely because a complaining state withdraws its complaint. So the Council decided to keep the question on the agenda until May 6, when it could ascertain whether Russia had completed the evacuation of Azerbaijan. Gromyko then declared that he would not participate in any future consideration of the Iranian issue by the Council.

The Iranian Government informed the Council on May 21, 1946, that the Soviet Union had completed the evacuation of her troops from Azerbaijan by May 6. The next day the Council, with the Russian member absent, voted to keep the issue on its agenda for an indefinite period. The following day, the Moscow radio reported that the Russian troops completed their evacuation on May 9. The Iranian Government instructed its delegate on May 29 not to make any more statements on the Soviet-Iranian dispute before the Council. Thus one aspect of the Iranian question appeared to be settled for the time being.

According to subsequent reports, Russia was promised an oil concession in northern Iran, subject to approval by the Iranian Parliament by October 24. Iran agreed to give Russia fifty-one per cent of the shares in a newly formed Russo-Iranian oil company for the first twenty-five years, and Russia agreed to supply machinery and technicians. After promising this oil concession, Iran was allowed to regain her sovereignty over Azerbaijan on the following terms agreed upon between the Iranian Government and the Azerbaijan rebel government: The Azerbaijan "National Parliament" was to be converted into a provincial council; the rebel army into a national army; seventy-five per cent of the local tax was to be reserved for the province and twenty-five per cent to be sent to Teheran; the central government agreed to build railways with local labor and to help establish a university; the government agreed further to pay for private lands which were confiscated by the communist regime for distribution to peasants and to approve the distribution of public lands to peasants; the government also promised to revise election laws so as to insure fair representation on a popular basis. Thus the price which Iran paid for regaining her sovereignty over Azerbaijan was great. But without the UN, Azerbaijan might have shared the fate of Manchuria under Japanese aggression.

As Tryvge Lie, Secretary General of the United Nations,

stated, the new organization has not succeeded in "capturing the imagination and in harnessing the enthusiasm of the peoples of the world" in the degree "that might have been hoped for." But when compared with the achievements of the League of Nations, the UN has done remarkably well during its short span of existence. Although the League, then ten years old, failed to survive the Manchurian test case, the UN which was barely organized, survived the Iranian dispute successfully with added prestige. So for the time being, one can share the optimism of Irving Talmadge, who stated in a recent issue of *Current History*:

"To the amazement of its nursemaid, the infant United Nations Organization has already learned to walk and talk—though it has still to cut its teeth. Robust in health, this bouncing baby has survived its growing pains, the successive attacks of Iranian 'measles' and Greco-Indonesian 'chicken pox.' Many rough hands have rocked its cradle, but the kid is tough and shows a tenacious will to live."

Historians will never agree as to what caused the League to fail and the UN to succeed in their first major test cases. It appears to me that the following three facts have made that difference. First, all nations, great and small, were solidly united against Russia, whereas during the Manchurian crisis they were not united against Japan. Second, Japan was in a position to risk a conflict with the League, if necessary, whereas Russia, having suffered incredible losses in the last war, was not prepared to carry out her designs in Iran at the cost of a major conflict with the powers. Third, the Russians desire international co-operation more than did the Japanese during the Manchurian crisis. The Japanese were willing to scrap the League, which they did not believe in, for the sake of attaining their immediate national objectives, whereas the Russians are wise enough not to go so far as to cause the complete breakdown of the collective system of security. Whatever the case, the civilized nations succeeded in pulling the infant organization through a major crisis.

The handling of the Iranian question has upheld my contention that if there is the willingness to work together for common security, even an imperfect organization can be made to function, whereas in the absence of the will to co-operate, even a perfect world union government will not work. Although it is too early to make a conclusive statement on the new world organization, it has already proved the fallacy of the prediction that the UN is foredoomed to failure.

If the civilized nations continue their fight for common security with the same spirit of co-operation as they did during the Iranian crisis, there will be no obstacle which the infant world organization cannot overcome. The much-criticized veto power of the Big Five will prove no obstacle when there is the will to work together, as even the Iroquois League of Five Nations functioned more than several centuries despite the veto retained by all the chiefs of the participating nations. The question of controlling the atomic bomb and other dangerous weapons of war will find a ready-made solution. The problems of economic reconstruction, of disarmament and of colonial empires will not remain long on the calendar of peace conferences or of the UN. Despite all its limitations, the new world organization will preserve peace among nations without ever facing the necessity of becoming a world state.

But if Russia or other states should refuse to work together and insist on going their way in search of their national security, it is doubtful if the UN, as it now stands, can survive the future crises. In fact, when we see how desperately the big powers struggle to promote their national security to the point of endangering the success of the collective system of security, and how dangerously they line up against each other throughout the entire world in their desperate search for a superior balance of power, we cannot help wondering if anything less than the dreaded atomic bomb can unite these rival powers under one authority for the enjoyment of peace. So, while doing everything to promote voluntary co-operation, it would be safe to proceed cautiously with the plans of making the UN strong enough to sail through the stormy seas of international turmoil.

One of the ways to improve the world organization is through the removal or modification of the veto power retained by the big states. As neither Russia nor the United States is prepared to abandon her veto power entirely, the total outlawry of the veto cannot be accomplished at this stage. But the problem can be solved in several ways to make it impossible for a single power to sabotage the progress of international co-operation. One way is to tackle the problem along the course mapped out by the Second Assembly of the UN, namely, to expand the scope of the procedural matters so wide as to narrow the field of substantial matters which require the unanimity of the Big Five. The other way is to ration the veto power as meat, clothes and sugar were rationed during the war. Each of the Big Five may be given limited points of veto—shall we say ten points each for the next five years. When they will have used up their points, no more shall be given until after the expiration of the time limit. Nor should any state be allowed to hoard its veto power. When the points are not used in the specified period, they should become useless.

The idea of rationing the veto seems to be a happy compromise between those who want to retain the power unrestricted and those who wish to outlaw it entirely. And yet, it can serve the purpose for the time being. When given a limited number of points, the powers will be obliged to economize their veto, as a poor man with only a few dollars in his pocket will economize his money. If the veto power is used sparingly, I do not think it will constitute a serious obstacle to the building of the UN as a bulwark of lasting peace.

Another practical way to make the UN an effective instrument of world peace is the adoption of the policy of settling all national and international issues in such a way as to give the maximum effect of enhancing the power and prestige of the world organization. As the ultimate solution of all problems are dependent on the success of this central organization, the settlement of no problem which will undermine the authority of the UN can be sound.

The American acquisition of her sole trusteeship of the Pacific islands cannot be considered sound because it will have the effect of weakening the authority of the International Trusteeship Council. The security of all nations, including that of the United States, would have been strengthened immeasurably had the American Government set a noble example for all nations by placing the islands under the International Trusteeship Council.

The American plan for financial aid to Greece and Turkey outside the UN cannot be considered a sound policy, not only because it has the effect of weakening the world security organization, but also because it causes Russia to be more desperate than before in her struggle against Western democracies. It seems that it would have produced a far more desirable effect on the whole world situation had the United States given the aid through the United Nations, or had she given the United Nations that much instead of giving it to Greece and Turkey. I think the British Government adopted a wise course when it decided to submit the Palestine question to the United Nations. Her example in this matter could be followed by others at good profit.

The Soviet refusal to accept an effective system of international inspection of fissionable material, her reckless use of the veto and her stubborn refusal to co-operate with other nations in the settlement of world problems are most stupid and shortsighted, for they arouse the fear and suspicion of all nations and threaten with destruction the very basis of international co-operation on which the future of the UN depends.

The Baruch atomic control plan is sound in so far as it insists on international ownership, control and inspection of all fissionable material, with penalties against the violators, who would have no veto power to protect them against such penalties. But the plan does not go far enough in enhancing the authority of the world organization. Therefore, even if it were adopted, it will not insure all peaceful nations against the bomb or other weapons of destruction.

As has been maintained previously (See Chapter V, Section 1 and 3), there are only two sure ways of controlling the bomb or similar weapons of war. One is through the invention of new weapons of destruction so powerful that the bomb would become useless. The other is through the making of a world organization just and powerful enough to leave neither the room nor the necessity to wage wars for whatever purposes. So, in the event that the civilized nations should fail to build a powerful machinery for collective security, regardless of what rules, regulations, treaties and conventions are made on the outlawry of the bomb, it will still be used unless more destructive weapons than the bomb are invented. Therefore, it is utterly foolish for Andrei Gromyko and his associates to demand the destruction of the bomb while refusing to co-operate for common security. All those who are really anxious to outlaw the bomb and other weapons of war should throw in all their moral and material powers behind the UN and fight for its success instead of wasting their time and energy in shouting for the control or the destruction of the bomb.

The Baruch plan places emphasis on the control of the bomb by making it difficult for the several states to manufacture it, but the plan fails to place emphasis on the reconstruction of a new world order in which the manufacture or the use of the bomb will be unnecessary. In other words, Baruch's method of safeguarding mankind against the bomb is negative, not positive. For instance, the plan calling for the destruction of the bomb after the establishment of a foolproof system of international control and inspection is not very different in principle from the old antiquated method of controlling weapons adopted at various disarmament conferences. And it will no more promote the cause of peace than did the destruction of a few old battleships, following the Washington Disarmament Conference, in 1921-22.

In this day and age when neither the fear of hell nor the love of God can unite men for a common destiny, the threat of the atom bomb will probably be the only means of uniting them under a universal authority. Instead of destroying the bomb, therefore, it should be placed at the disposal of the UN for the sole purpose of defending the Charter against those aggressors who would not listen to any other language than that which is spoken through an atomic tongue. The world will be safer from war with such a bomb behind the universal authority than without it. If there were no such bomb, one should be invented to enhance the authority of the world security organization.

Finally, as the solution of all world problems and the security of all mankind ultimately depend on the success of the UN or a similar world organization, what the United States and the Soviet Union must do is to put all their power and resources behind the world organization and drive forward uncompromisingly toward the single purpose of strengthening it. They must make it work by whatever means available. If they should fail to make it work by peaceful means, they must not falter; they must make it work by force, if necessary, as without such a powerful world organization no nation will enjoy peace and security anyway.

What other civilized nations must do is to combine all their energy and power, and support either America or Russia, whichever stands for international co-operation for common security, and oppose whichever pursues policies of isolation and non-co-operation. Nothing else should guide their future national and international policies.

It is unwise and unfair to oppose the Soviet Union just because she is a totalitarian state. It is foolish and stupid to back the United States blindly simply because she is a democratic state. Both should be judged by their acts and policies. When they pursue policies of co-operation for common security, all nations should line up behind them. When they practice policies of aggression and domination, all civilized peoples must unite against them, and force them to support the common cause. There may be some peril in adopting such a course, but in the end it alone will banish war and create peace among nations.

PART THREE

THE MAKING OF PEACE IN ASIA

Chapter IX

AMERICA AND RUSSIA IN ASIA

We have seen how the white man banished war among the primitive peoples. We have also seen how he has attempted, none too successfully, to create peace among modern nations in general. In this part, we will take Asia as a close-up of the world and concentrate our attention on his efforts to make peace in that part of the globe.

During the past several hundred years, during which the white man has dominated most of the world, including a large part of Asia, he has undoubtedly helped to banish many petty quarrels among the Asiatics, as well as among other peoples. He has done so by introducing his scientific means of communication and transportation, by introducing his superior technique of organization and of government, and above all, by forcing the natives to forget their petty differences and to stand together against his encroachment. But at the same time, he has caused the Asiatics to suffer numerous wars which he has fought on the Asiatic soil, either against the natives or against his own white rivals. Furthermore, he has helped the Asiatics wage bigger and better wars by rousing them against him or his rivals and by arming them with his superior weapons of war and engines of destruction. So his past contribution to the making of peace in Asia can be stated as follows: he has helped banish many petty wars and has helped create bigger and better wars.

Now we shall see what he can, or will, do in the building of peace and order in tomorrow's Asia.

In the wake of the Second World War, we find in Asia two of the mightiest powers on earth standing face to face. One represents the growing might of the Soviet Union and the other the fully matured power of the Western democracies. Between them lie no barriers, no distances, no buffer states, nothing but the rubble of the Japanese Empire, with its heaving mass of humanity seeking for freedom, and an immense and promising China, torn within and unable to form a solid wall of defense between the two rival powers.

When these two great powers were engaged in a bitter struggle for existence with the Axis Powers, they had little time to think of their future relations. "Let us defeat our enemies first," they thought and said to one another, "then we can solve our own problems later." But now that their common enemies are down, they suddenly find themselves face to face at the very end of the earth with nothing between them which can protect them against each other. Nor do they have any knowledge or assurance of what the other power will do next. So they naturally feel uneasy about one another, especially since both are giants armed with the most powerful weapons of destruction known to science.

It is not the first time that Russia and the Western democracies have met in the Far East. Their keen rivalry in the nineteenth century culminated in the Russo-Japanese War, in which America and Britain supported Japan. The new rendezvous in Asia is reminiscent of the old rivalry, which makes both sides feel all the more uncomfortable.

Even if both had the same ideologies and the same forms of government, they would have felt uneasy under similar circumstances, as democratic states can fight other democratic states and totalitarian powers can attack other totalitarian powers. But in this case one represents a capitalistic democracy and the other, totalitarian communism. It is no exaggeration to say that this fact alone can cause much uneasiness between them.

It is a fact that capitalism has travelled a long way from the state of *laissez faire* toward a Socialist millenium, and that Communism has moved closer to capitalism than ever before. The abandonment of the efforts to destroy the family, the church, and private property by the Russian Communists has narrowed the gulf between the two systems so much that one can jump over it without exerting much effort. Nevertheless, the feeling of antagonism still exists on both sides, a fact which makes the rendezvous all the more unpleasant.

Confronted with such an uncomfortable situation, they could have said to one another: "Do not feel uneasy with me. I have no sordid motives against you. What both of us want is the same—peace, security, and prosperity with liberty. Although our ideas and methods are somewhat different, we have fought side by side against the Axis Powers through these perilous years. With their destruction, our work has only begun. We still have to 'lick' the greatest enemy of all mankind, the ultimate breeder of all wars—the state of international anarchy. We can destroy this enemy, as we did the Axis Powers, if you and I work together for the creation of a world authority powerful enough to uphold the principles of justice between us. Unless we succeed in this fight against international anarchy, neither you nor I can enjoy the blessings of peace and security for which we have fought. So let us forget our differences and continue our fight against this most dangerous enemy which threatens all of us with total destruction."

Had they taken such an attitude toward one another, there is no reason why they could not have continued their wartime co-operation. Cultural and ideological differences did not prevent them from working together during the war when they saw the survival value of mutual co-operation. Despite the differences in ideas and methods, the Western democracies worked with Japan on various occasions. So they probably could have struggled together for their common security.

Unfortunately, however, both sides have hastened to strengthen their defense against each other. They have feverishly sought to fortify their positions against one another all the way from the Baltic Sea to Tokyo Bay for the primary purpose of insuring their security against each other.

One wonders who first started this separate search for security. The Russians, as a matter of course, blame the reactionary fascists of the capitalistic countries, and the Western democracies blame the Russians for starting it. Whoever began it first, the separate search for security against each other began officially with the most unfortunate speech delivered by Joseph Stalin on February 9, 1946. In that speech, Stalin declared that the fall of Hitler and Tojo did not mean peace for the Russian people. Communist Russia, he declared, cannot live in peace with the hostile capitalistic powers which were plotting to destroy her. After pointing out the danger threatening Russia with destruction, Stalin calmly told his comrades that they must introduce another series of Five-Year Plans to prepare for the coming struggle with the capitalistic powers. In March, Russia actually adopted another series of Five-Year Plans for the primary purpose of developing heavy industries to combat capitalistic states.

Whether the United States or the Soviet Union started the separate search for security, the great powers, by adopting this hasty and shortsighted course, have not only betrayed their mutual fear and distrust, but also have served notice to one another that their honeymoon is over, and that, henceforth, each should go its way and mind its own business. More than that, they have actually declared war on one another for mutual destruction. They have done so, not so much because of their hatred and jealousy, or because of their greed for profit and power, or because of their differences in ideas and methods, as because of their unconquerable fear that if they do not destroy the other power, it will destroy them.

It is a fact that both sides have vehemently denied that they seek to conquer and destroy each other. Both have assured and reassured that all they want is to safeguard their own security. No one can deny their honesty and sincerity. But the pity of it is that in a small world, without barriers and without a world government, the only way to insure one's security is either through mutual co-operation or through mutual destruction. With the abandonment of the first, the only available means of achieving security is the second. Consequently, both sides have reluctantly drifted into the road of rivalry and war for the ultimate control of the entire world.

In fairness to the democracies, it should be added that the democratic nations do not really seek for a complete political domination of the world. All that they would insist upon is that all states grant elemental political freedom and basic civil liberties to their peoples; that they open their portals wide to let others see that they are not planning for aggression on other countries; and that they co-operate with other states for the promotion of common security for all mankind through the UN or a similar world organization. When these minimum requirements are met, the democracies would prefer to let other nations run their own show. Rarely would they go beyond but for the fear that, if they do not establish their control, Russia might step in and establish her ironfisted rule. For the primary purpose of preventing Russia from expanding her system of absolute control, the democracies are obliged to compete for the ultimate domination of the entire world.

Alarming as it is, the present rivalry between the two power blocs is neither abnormal nor unnatural. All men of all ages and in all areas have sought to insure their security through conquest and domination whenever they have been threatened with danger. The ancient Egyptians, the Greeks, the Romans, the Chinese, the modern white men, and the modern Japanese all did, or tried to do, the same thing to insure their survival. They all have carried out their attacks on others in the name and for the sake of their own security—the security from attacks, the security from starvation, and the security from the wrath of the gods. Not even Hitler and Tojo carried out their program of ruthless conquest and domination without having the defense of their fatherland in their minds. And as the two rival power blocs are doing today, all have blamed the others as the aggressors and have classified themselves as champions of justice and right. However, what makes the present drive for domination different from others in history is that it is not confined to any specific areas, but it is carried out into the entire globe, a fact which is not difficult to explain.

The science of war has reached such a stage that neither mountains nor oceans can protect one power against another. As an attack can be launched against any state from any point in the world, no state can feel safe until it controls, directly or indirectly, the whole world and removes all possible threats to its security.

So far the race for control has been limited to this earth.

But when there arises a possibility of launching an attack from the moon or other planets, the rival powers undoubtedly will race for the control of those planets, for no nation can afford to remain smug and indifferent with the danger of total destruction hanging over its head like the sword of Damocles!

Before the discovery of the scientific means of communication and transportation, the Americans pursued a policy of isolation and tried to mind their own business. They could do so because the great oceans were big enough to insure their security. But the technological developments have wiped out that guarantee of security for all times. They cannot regain their security without scrapping all scientific inventions, or without creating a world organization powerful enough to protect all nations, large and small. As the scrapping of scientific discoveries is impossible, they naturally seek to insure their security through the creation of a United States of the World, composed of democratic republics.

The same is true of the Russians. They are just as human as the Americans and the British. They can no longer shut their eyes on what is going on outside their own country any more than can the Americans. They, too, feel that in this age of scientific warfare they must direct the course of events throughout the entire world in such a way as to remove all possible threats to their security. So they seek to attain their objectives through the creation of a world-wide union of the Soviet Socialist Republics.

But the more they strive to set up their forms of government, the more the Western democracies seek to prevent them from being established. Conversely, the more desperately the democracies struggle to spread their patterns of government, the more frantically the Russians try to sabotage such capitalistic ventures. So the race for security through the multiplication of their own forms of government has only precipitated rivalry, plunging all nations into a perilous situation.

Those whose thinking has been colored by Marxian ideologies are prone to think of this rivalry in the old terms of markets and raw materials. But the days when the powers scrambled for the mere control of gold, silver, oil, rubber, and other raw materials and markets are definitely over. Today the mere control of the trade routes, markets, and raw materials is only incidental. What the great rival powers want is nothing less than the political domination of the entire world, not for the purpose of satiating their sordid ambitions and desires for conquest and domination, but for the purpose of satisfying their ardent desire for peace and security in a world of chaos without an organized authority to preserve justice among nations.

Nor is this rivalry for the control of the world aimed at the mere propagation of their own ideologies, however dearly the civilized men evaluate them. They have sought to establish their own patterns of government over the entire world only because they believe, rightly or wrongly, that the multiplication of their own forms of government and of economy will strengthen their defense against each other.

Were it not for the fear of insecurity, the United States would not care whether dictatorship or democracy prevails in China, Korea, or Japan. Were it not for the fear of an attack by the capitalistic states, Russia would not care whether democracy or dictatorship prevails in Europe and Asia, or whether Harry Truman or John L. Lewis rules the United States. The Russians have not opposed the rule of Rumania by King Mihai when they found him not detrimental to their security. The Western democracies have tolerated Peron's dictatorship of Argentina when they found that it did not form an immediate threat to their security.

In other words, what has divided the great powers into two rival camps is not so much the difference between capitalism and communism, or that between democracy and dictatorship, as the policies which they have pursued to promote their national security independently. As a matter of fact, the pursuance of similar policies can split into hostile camps even the states with the same ideologies and structures. Had America and Britain pursued similar policies against each other, they would have been as widely split apart as the Soviet Union and the Western democracies.

More specifically, what has split the Western democracies and the Soviet Union into separate camps is not so much Russian Communism and her system of government as the Russian refusal to co-operate with other nations for the promotion of common security. If Russia were willing to co-operate with other nations in this matter, the democracies would have preferred to let Russia alone to enjoy or suffer her own forms of government and economy. But her failure to co-operate with other nations for common security and her desperate struggle to promote national security independently of other nations have aroused the fear and suspicion of the Western democracies and have caused them to stand together against Russia and her satellite states. So, if an open conflict ever results from such a hostile division of powers, it will have come, not so much from the differences of ideas and institutions, as from the pursuance of the policies of seeking national security independently. To put it in another way, the Third World War, if it ever comes, will have only one cause—the refusal of Russia to co-operate with the capitalistic states for common security.

Divided into rival spheres, both the United States and the Soviet Union have sought to win the Asiatics to their side. In this contest for the winning of Asia, both Uncle Sam and Uncle Joe have played the role of the old-fashioned missionaries. The former says: "Democracy is the way to peace, freedom, justice, and prosperity; communism is a road to oppression, poverty, slavery, and war." The latter says: "Communism is the way to peace, freedom, justice, and prosperity; capitalism is a road to exploitation, poverty, slavery, and war."

The natives are puzzled and bewildered. They do not know who is telling the truth or who is giving out false propaganda. But they recall their early experiences with the old-fashioned missionaries representing various denominations. One said: "My way is the only way to heaven; all other ways lead to hell." Another said: "My way is the only way to heaven; all other ways lead to hell." Before the natives had time to find out who was telling the truth, these missionaries started a holy war of their own and began killing each other to save their own souls. So the native rulers said to them: "We thought you came to uplift our people by teaching them your religion of love, charity, and justice. But now we see that you came to spread your bigotry and intolerance. If that is what you want, get out and fight in your own country." In that way the expulsion of the missionaries came in China, Japan, Korea, and other Asiatic countries.

Following their expulsion, the natives studied Christianity without prejudice. They found that there was nothing to quarrel over, as all the missionaries tried to sell the same spiritual vitamins in a different form. Some tried to sell it in pills; some in capsules; and some in liquid. So the Asiatics laughed at the stupidity and intolerance of the Christians and chuckled as did the Chinese laundryman in America, who could find no other difference between the denominations than a big wash, a little wash, and no wash at all.

To an outsider the difference between the professed aims of democracy and of communism does not appear much greater than the denominational differences, as both claim that they aim at the promotion of the welfare of the common man, as Christianity aims at the saving of the souls of the sinners. And the popular notion that Russia stands for reform and progress and therefore she backs the progressive and revolutionary parties in all countries, whereas America stands for the maintenance of a status quo and therefore she supports the conservative and reactionary elements everywhere is nothing more than manufactured propaganda of the most inexcusable sort.

It is a fact that the United States has often used the political and social organizations created by the reactionary Fascists and militarists as a means of executing democratic programs of reform and progress. But nowhere has she allied herself with the reactionary Fascists and warmongers for the avowed purpose of perpetuating their evil deeds. Nor has she ever sought to preserve all the pitiful conditions of wretched existence, all the feudalistic economy and land tenure, and all the political tyranny and economic despotism found in any of the so-called backward countries, as commonly charged by the charitable American journalists. On the contrary, everywhere she has gone, the United States has sought to introduce reform and progress. But where she differs from Russia in this respect is in the method of attaining the desired objectives. The United States seeks to accomplish her objectives through gradual process brought about by peaceful means. The Soviet Union seeks to achieve them through a direct and radical means brought about by forcible revolution. One seeks to attain its objectives with the support of the native leaders—leaders in business, politics, and education. The other works through the mass of the poor, dispossessed, and ignorant, who will swallow all the pills of propaganda without asking questions. One sets up a little democracy and exerts its influence through it, and the other creates a dictatorship and controls through its puppets.

While admitting that such differences are no small matter to laugh off, they do not seem to justify all the venom, bitterness, and hatred with which they denounce their erstwhile allies. If the democracies could tolerate Franco, of Spain; Peron, of Argentina; John L. Lewis and James C. Petrillo, of the United States, they should be able to tolerate Uncle Joe Stalin. If the Russians could work with Hitler's Germany and Tojo's Japan, they certainly can do business with the democracies. When all things are considered, the rivalry and intolerance between the two power blocs appear to be no more justifiable than were the hating and warring between the religious denominations over their petty religious differences.

One of these days the natives of Asia might say to both rival powers as their rulers said to the missionaries in the olden days: "We thought you came to help us out of poverty, ignorance, and misrule. But now we see that you came to wage war against each other. If that is what you want, get out and fight in your own countries." But the pity of it is that they are not in a position to say it now. They are caught in a tug of war and cannot extricate themselves because they are not equipped to assert their rights. Being pulled and pushed in both ways, they do not know which way to turn. Some turn to the right; some turn to the left. As a result, a widening gulf is being built in their political and social structure. Confronted with this intolerable situation, the native resentment is growing against both rival blocs. But neither the Soviet Union nor the Western democracies are willing to leave because they do not want their rivals to step in and dominate Asia.

What will happen if the big powers continue their present policies? Will they find a peaceful solution of Asiatic problems? Will they create a peaceful or warlike Asia? Will they build a democratic or communistic Asia? Will totalitarian Russia crowd the Western democracies out of Asia? Or will the Western democracies drive the Russian bear into the frozen arctic and liberate Asia's millions from its claws? Will the Asiatics side with Russia or the Western democracies in this contest for a superior balance of power which is being carried out on their own doorsteps? Or will they rise against both rival powers and assert their freedom and independence? These are some of the questions which will be discussed briefly in the following pages.

Chapter X

THE REMAKING OF MODERN JAPAN

Since V-J Day the United States has carried out in earnest her avowed policy of winning Japan for the cause of peace and freedom. She has sought to transform a militaristic totalitarian state into a peaceful democracy through the destruction of its military machine, Shintoism, emperor worship, the Zaibatsu monopoly, and through the introduction of democratic principles of government and economy. It seems as if the United States has transformed in a short time an aggressive military empire into a promised land of peace and democracy. But few students of world affairs realize that none of these measures which the American Government has adopted will permanently remove the menace of Japan for the simple reason that none of them really strikes at the root of all militaristic cultures and institutions, be they Japanese or German.

Men develop militaristic ideas and institutions such as belligerent gods, militant nationalism, martial concepts of values, autocratic governments, and absolute states because these are necessary for survival in the state of international anarchy without an organized authority to preserve justice among nations.

The modern white man has created a militant and materialistic civilization. He has developed science and inventions, and has increased a thousandfold his power of construction and destruction. He has built giant planes and ships, and has invented the atomic bomb and poison gas. He has done all these without developing to the same extent his moral and spiritual values of life, his kindness, love, sympathy, and compassion for his fellowmen. As a result, his boasted materialistic civilization is being threatened with total destruction.

Paradoxical though it may sound, what the modern white man has done is precisely what all men of all ages and in all countries have done, or have tried to do, when they have been forced to struggle for survival in a world of anarchy without an organized instrument of preserving justice and peace.

Many students of international affairs have maintained that modern dictators have sought for world domination, not so much for security or survival, as for the honor and glory to satiate their sense of vanity and pride. But one must realize that such abominable and unprofitable acts of conquest and domination appear honorable and glorious because they are useful for survival as free peoples in a world of chaos. For instance, the unsavory idea of racial superiority, which has been the chief source of inspiration for conquest, is a very valuable asset for survival in an anarchic world, because if you do not believe that your own people, your own ideas and cultures are superior to those of others, you will not fight for your own group. If you do not stand up for your own, you will not survive the impact of external attack.

The modern Japanese built a powerful military empire because they had realized that no people could exist free and independent without acquiring military power in a world of international anarchy. Having built a powerful military machine, they started conquering and dominating their neighbors, because in the state of chaos, conquest and domination mean security, protection and survival with honor and glory.

It is a fact that even before the opening of the islands to the modern world, the Japanese dreamed of conquering China. At the close of the sixteenth century Hideyoshi actually invaded Korea because he had been refused a passage for his troops through that peninsula. After seven years of a disastrous war the invaders were driven back. This ill-fated war for conquest, together with a brief but unpleasant contact with the western powers, Spain and Portugal, made the Japanese thorough-going isolationists in the true "Nyean" sense of the word. All they wanted was to be left alone to mind their own business.

For two hundred and twenty-five years they pursued a policy of water-tight isolation. No foreigners were allowed to visit the islands. Nor were the natives allowed to go abroad. The only contact the Japanese had with the outside world was through a handful of Dutch and Chinese merchants in Deshima, Nagasaki. The Dutch were allowed to bring in a single ship a year and the Chinese were allowed twenty junks annually. Then came Commodore Perry.

The age in which the veil of Japan was lifted was one of imperialism and war. It was the time when England, France and Czarist Russia were competing for commerce and trade, power and prestige in Eastern Asia. It was the time when France was launching her policy of conquest and expansion in Indo-China; when England was forcing her trade, including that of opium, upon China; and when Russia was moving southward in search of ice-free ports and strategic areas to prevent the British from bottling her up in the frozen north. Both England and Russia actually occupied a few Japanese islands with the intention of using them as their stepping stones. Indeed, there was a grave danger that these imperialistic powers would partition the islands among themselves. Had Japan been slow in adopting Western science of war and destruction, she would have been reduced to an insignificant European dependency. All that is necessary to prove the soundness of this statement is to point to the fate of other Asiatic states from the Suez Canal to the Korea Strait.

The islanders, however, quickly realized that without mastering modern science of war they could not hope to escape the fate of slavery which had befallen many an unarmed nation. So they rushed to the building of an empire with powerful military and naval forces. They succeeded in erecting such an empire in no time only because the Western nations, including the United States, Great Britain, Germany and others willingly extended their moral and material aid and lent them their naval and military secrets, their commercial and industrial knowledge and technique, their precious capital, raw materials and trained experts. They did all these and more, not so much from their charitable motives, as from their vain hope that some day Japan might be helpful in their struggle for profits and power against each other.

Having hurriedly mastered the Western science of war, the

Japanese began the role of a conqueror. They did so primarily because if they did not conquer, they would have been conquered by Russia or her rivals. But most of the lands which they wished to control were claimed by the European powers for their domination and exploitation. So they tactfully played one rival power against the other. With the aid of England and the United States, they checked the Czarist expansion in Eastern Asia. With the co-operation of the Allied and Associated Powers, they eliminated Germany from the Western Pacific. With the teamwork of Nazi Germany and Fascist Italy, they launched a general onslaught on the Western democracies and almost succeeded in erecting a mighty empire, larger, richer and more populated than any known in the world. Then they met their doom.

Such being the case, Japanese militarism and imperialism, like similar ideas in other countries, were born of international anarchy, and therefore, cannot be destroyed completely without demolishing their ultimate source. All attempts at building a lasting peace in the Pacific without banishing the state of anarchy, therefore, will be very much like trying to combat mosquitoes without draining the swamps which breed them. As the swatting of a few individual mosquitoes will not improve the general health situation, so the removal of Tojo and Hirohito, or the mere destruction of their militaristic cultures and institutions, will not insure the peace of the Pacific because in the continued state of international anarchy millions of new Tojos and Zaibatsus will arise to replace those who have perished. Therefore, all the loose talk of preventing Japan from ever rising again through the removal of Tojo and Hirohito or through the destruction of Shintoism or Zaibatsu amounts to little more than a barbershop peace planning.

Let us see how Japan could arise again despite all the precautionary measures now being adopted, in the event that the same old state of international anarchy continues to exist on earth.

In the world of chaos, without the collective means of preserving justice and law, both the democracies and the totalitarian states must struggle separately for their own national security and prosperity. This means the continued race for armament, the scramble for spheres of influence and for the balance of power between the Russian bloc on the one hand and the American bloc on the other. Each bloc will strive to gain a superior balance of power so as to insure the safety of its own group.

In this contest for a superior balance of power, Japan, as well as other Asiatic nations, will be wooed and cajoled. They would be showered with compliments and sympathies; they would be encouraged and prayed to arm themselves with the most destructive weapons of war, be it atomic bombs or something more deadly, so that they could help tip the balance of power in one way or the other. Japan would be up again in no time and the world would be no safer than it was yesterday.

Incredible as it may sound, this was the way Japan was helped to arm for world domination. This was also the way Germany was enabled to rearm between the two World Wars. Therefore, the same situation will develop so long as the same old system of rival power politics continues to rule the world, and this cursed old system of rival power politics and all its accompanying evils will continue to plague mankind so long as the present state of international anarchy continues to prevail.

So should the civilized nations, flushed with power and victory, fail to co-operate for the creation of order out of chaos in the realm of international affairs, they will have defeated the Axis only to help its members rise again tomorrow; they will have disarmed them and dismembered them only to help them rearm and reconstruct for the repetition of their ghastly past. And the dawn beyond the Pacific which we have hailed with the great hope will prove only a fake dawn, leading to greater darkness and despair.

We have been assured and reassured by those who formulate the present policies in the Orient that a democratic Japan will be a peaceful state and therefore will not wage wars for conquest as the old empire has. But we must not forget that democratic Athens sought the domination of the ancient Hellenic world.

Democratic Great Britain and her dominions have secured control, mostly by war, over one-fifth of the entire land surface of the globe. Democratic United States of America has invented the atomic bomb and has outfought the totalitarian states in every war.

Furthermore, it is doubtful if democracy could be successfully transplanted into Japan without abating the present rivalry between the United States and Russia. In the continued state of tension, each side will seek to win Japan and both sides will try to prevent the other from winning her. The American attempt to convert militaristic Japan into a democratic republic will be countered by the Russian attempt to win the Japanese for the cause of Russian Communism. Torn between two rival powers, Japan will prove a fertile soil for subversive revolutionary movements. In such a state of unrest and turmoil, Russian Communism rather than American democracy might gain the upper hand.

The Russians have already opened their propaganda barrage against MacArthur's rule. They branded it as reactionary and fascistic, and scorned its failure to promote the welfare of the working people of Japan. Even a child can see why the Communists are spreading this kind of propaganda—to prevent America from winning Japan for the cause of democracy.

Furthermore, there is a rumor that the Russians are training and indoctrinating some half million Japanese prisoners of war, and that, if and when the proper time comes, these men would serve as a vanguard of the Japanese army to "liberate" Japan from "American imperialism." This rumor is based on the fact that Russia has not sent back to Japan all Japanese soldiers captured in Manchuria at the close of the war. True or false, the Russians will not give up Japan without a struggle.

Besides, nothing can breed dictatorship as well as war or threats of wars, either internal or international. Without removing the threats of turmoil in the world, therefore, democracy in tomorrow's Japan might not fare any better than before.

The opening of Japan by Commodore Perry did not result in the ascent of democracy in that country, not only because democracy was a foreign idea to the islanders, but because of the state of turmoil prevailing throughout the world. Had Japan been introduced to a world of peace and harmony, democracy might have triumphed under the leadership of the gallant fighters for democracy, Itagaki and Ozaki. But unfortunately, she was thrown into a whirlpool of international chaos and the constant danger to national security enabled the militarists to crush the democrats and to establish ironfisted dictatorship.

In the ultimate analysis, there are only two ways to prevent Japan, or any other aggressor nation, from becoming again a menace to world peace. One is the total annihilation of the Japanese people and the other is international co-operation through a central world organization for the maintenance of the principles of justice and fairness.

The adoption of the first method is both impossible and useless. It is impossible because the Christian conscience would not tolerate the execution of such a barbaric policy in our twentieth century of civilization and enlightenment. It is useless because even if every Japanese is drowned in the ocean or blasted into shreds by the atomic bombs, other peoples will probably do the same things that she could have done—the militarization, conquest and domination—in the event that they have to struggle for survival in a state of international anarchy.

I do not mean to belittle what is being done in Japan today. But I do wish to point out that nothing less than the total banishment of international anarchy by the concerted efforts of the United Nations will remove permanently the menace of Japan and Germany to world peace. Assuming that my contention is sound, what is most important to insure future peace is not the mere temporary disarmament or dismemberment of the enemy states, but it is the promotion of international co-operation for the establishment of an effective world organization to uphold the principles of justice and fair play.

Chapter XI

SOVIET-AMERICAN RIVALRY IN KOREA

International rivalry in Korea has already created two great wars in modern Asiatic history: the Sino-Japanese War and the Russo-Japanese War. The present rivalry between the United States and the Soviet Union appears to be making another conflict which might imperil the whole world.

Although Korea is a small and mountainous country of 85,000 square miles with a population of 25,000,000, its strategic importance is invaluable. It serves as a stepping stone into rich, undeveloped Manchuria and Siberia, as well as a bridge between the continent and Japan and the Western Hemisphere. Because of its strategic importance, it has often been called the Balkan Peninsula of Eastern Asia, or a danger zone in Far Eastern international politics.

The Sino-Japanese War of 1894-5 was the natural outcome of the rivalry between the two countries in Korea. The Japanese felt that Korea, if controlled by a hostile power, would be like a dagger pointed at the heart of their country. They naturally proposed that the peninsula be reformed and modernized under their guidance so that Korea could have a progressive government friendly toward Japan. In other words, what the Japanese tried to do in Korea a half century ago was not materially different from what the American and the Russian governments are trying to do in the same country today.

The Chinese mandarins believed that the Japanese domination of Korea might endanger the security of their own empire. They, therefore, sought to block the Japanese attempts at dominating the country by supporting the pro-Chinese conservative elements in the peninsula. It did not take long before this policy of rivalry led the two countries into a war which resulted in Japanese victory.

No sooner was China driven from the country than Russia

stepped in. The rivalry between Russia and Japan converted the Hermit Kingdom into a veritable palace of intrigue. At one time the Japanese had a fair chance of establishing themselves in Korea. But their high-handed methods, including the murder of the queen who had opposed their reform measures, undermined their work and discredited the reformists associated with them. The king himself was so terrified by the assassination of the queen that he fled to the Russian legation where he ruled his kingdom for a year. The Russians by then had the whole country under their thumbs. The Japanese grew more desperate than ever before and prepared for another war, this time against Russia. They defeated the northern colossus in 1905 with the help of England and the United States.

With the elimination of both China and Russia, Japan had a free hand in Korea. It appears, however, that the Japanese were somewhat apprehensive of American intervention on behalf of Korea because the United States was bound by a treaty to use her good offices in case of trouble and to try to aid Korea if a third power treated her oppressively and unjustly. This apprehension was removed by concluding a secret understanding between Katsura, prime minister of Japan, and Taft, personal emissary of President Theodore Roosevelt. By this famous secret understanding, President Roosevelt assured Japan a free hand in Korea, in return for Japanese noninterference with American control of the Philippine Islands.

Having removed all possible dangers of external intervention, the Japanese began their policy of ruthless conquest and exploitation. They rounded up the Korean patriots and executed them or placed them behind bars. They forced the helpless Korean farmers to sell their good lands at a price fixed by their bayonets. They took over the ownership and control of commerce, industry, and finance. By the time their empire collapsed, they owned eighty per cent of the farming lands and eighty-five per cent of all industries. They gathered up Korean history books and made bonfires of them. They forced the Koreans to study a new history manufactured in Tokyo, and compelled the Korean children to study the Japanese language and to worship the Japanese emperor.

In spite of all these policies of ruthless destruction of everything indigenous, Korea refused to die. When Woodrow Wilson proclaimed his fourteen points, the Koreans rose like a man and cried for freedom, only to be mowed down by macine guns. Those who had escaped Japanese persecution gathered at Shanghai and set up a provisional government in 1919, with Syngman Rhee, a classmate of Woodrow Wilson, as its president. This government, however, gained no diplomatic support of the powers. Disappointed and discouraged, the Korean patriots all but abandoned their hope of regaining freedom.

On the eve of the Second World War, they revived their provisional government in Chungking. This exiled republican government enjoyed the *de facto* recognition of China and France and the moral and material support of Chiang Kai-shek's government. Following the attack on Pearl Harbor this government declared war on Japan and asked for material aid to carry on underground activities against the Japanese. Although practically all European exiled governments were given recognition and support, the Korean plea was ignored and unanswered. However, some 10,000 Korean troops and 50,000 partisan forces were claimed to have fought with Chinese troops and guerrilla bands in China, and 30,000 irregulars carried out underground activities in Korea. The provisional government itself was reported to have had an army of only 700 men who fought under a Chinese general. Some 400 men of this modest army received training under the United States Office of Strategic Services in Sian, but the war ended before they went into action.

Korea went through the war almost unscathed. Excepting a few naval bases, no cities and towns suffered bombing raids. Nevertheless, her people endured immeasurable hardship. The Japanese took all they could from the helpless Koreans to continue the war. They scraped the raw materials, foodstuff, and man power almost to the bottom. Furthermore, the Japanese increased their repressive measures against the Korean underground movements to such an extent that the people could hardly breathe without the fear of imprisonment and torture.

After all these years of oppression and deprivation came the collapse of the Japanese Empire. There was no other people in the world who welcomed V-J Day with greater joy than the Koreans. They celebrated the day of victory with hope and inspiration unparalleled in Korean history. It seemed as if all their suppressed hopes and emotions stored up during the years of slavery were pouring out simultaneously like an irresistible force of nature. But once more they were disappointed and disillusioned, for they found in the wake of their celebration that their country now had two alien masters instead of only one. In short, they found that they were confronted with a situation not dissimilar from that which preceded with Russo-Japanese War at the turn of this century.

The present partition of Korea into two hostile spheres is not due to any fault of Korea. It is almost entirely due to the rivalry between the Soviet Union and the United States. As neither Russia nor America could feel safe with Korea under the control of the other, they cut that unfortunate country in half, committing her to a national hara-kiri. The effect of this partition is most tragic, not only to Korea, but to the world as a whole, because it foments a discord which will tear up that country and jeopardize the peace of the entire world. This dangerous situation has been brought about by the powerful states without the knowledge or consent of the Korean people at home or abroad.

At the Cairo Conference, the heads of America, Britain and China agreed to grant Korea independence "in due course." At the Yalta Conference, the chiefs of America, Britain, and Russia decided to let Russia occupy the northern half of Korea and the United States the southern half. At the Moscow Conference, the foreign ministers of the "big three" decided to place Korea under a four-power trusteeship "for a period of up to five years." To carry out this agreement, they likewise made two other decisions at Moscow. First, they agreed to hold a joint Soviet-American military conference at Seoul for the purpose of co-ordinating the administrative and the economic functions between the two zones of occupation. Secondly, they decided to establish a joint Soviet-American Commission, which, after consulting with Korean leaders, was to recommend plans for the establishment of a provisional democratic Korean government. According to the recommendations submitted by this joint commission, the governments of America, Britain, China, and Russia were to establish a provisional government. After the creation of this provisional government, the Soviet-American Commission was to function as a guardian to help Korea achieve her full independence.

In accordance with the agreements made at Moscow, the delegates of the American and Russian occupation forces in Korea held a conference at Seoul. After long and tiresome negotiations, they closed the conference without a single agreement on any of the vital questions of exchanging raw materials, food, fuel, of unified currency, telephone and telegraphic communications, free circulation of news, the unification and co-ordination of the administration of the country.

The joint Soviet-American Commission met from March 20th to May 6th, 1946, with a view to preparing plans for the establishment of a Korean provisional government. After six weeks of futile discussion, the conference ended in a complete failure. The immediate cause of the breakdown was the Russian insistence that all Korean leaders opposed to the Moscow decision be barred from consultation in the creation of the provisional government and from the participation of its administration. As the Communists were the only Koreans not opposed to the Moscow decision (they had previously opposed it), the acceptance of the Russian demand would have meant a complete Communist domination of Korea and the total exclusion of all democratic Korean leaders friendly to the United States from the creation or from the administration of the provisional government. When the Americans refused to accept their demands, the Russians withdrew from the conference. Thus the deadlock in both conferences was the result of the keen rivalry between the Soviet Union and the United States rather than internal differences among the Koreans, who are helpless under the joint occupation of their country by two of the world's greatest powers.

It is a fact that the Koreans have been badly divided among themselves. When the Americans came, they were confronted with some sixty-odd so-called political parties, each claiming to represent a large segment of the population. In reality, the so-called parties meant nothing more than sixty-odd persons claiming to be leaders of different groups of people. The situation, however, has been made much worse because all these divergent factions are now divided into two hostile groups: the rightists, blessed by the American forces, and the leftists, backed by the Russian authorities.

In fairness to the United States, it should be stated that in both conferences it was the Soviet Union which refused to consider the American proposal for the abolition of the dividing line and the unification of the country's administration. It appears that the Russians turned down the American proposals because the abolition of the dividing line might hamper their efforts to create a communist state in north Korea. After the two unsuccessful conferences, the American authorities decided in July, 1946, to create a legislative for their zone of occupation. Composed of partly elected and partly appointed members, the new legislature will assist the administration of south Korea for the duration of the American military government. The unilateral adoption of this course by the American authorities seems to betray the complete failure of the two powers to reconcile their conflicting policies in that unfortunate country.

Colonel General Terenty Shtykov, chief of the Soviet delegation to the joint Soviet-American Commission held at Seoul in the spring of 1946, sounded the keynote of his country's policy in Korea when he declared that Russia is keenly interested in seeing Korea become "a true democratic and independent country, friendly to the Soviet Union, so that in the future it will not become a base for an attack on the Soviet Union." So Russia wants a "democratic" Korea, a brand of communistic republic, nourished by Russia, which will dance to the Russian tune, not the American swing.

On the other hand, General A. V. Arnold, first American Military Governor of Korea, sounded the keynote of the American policy when he stated that "it is our job to see that the Koreans get the American type of democracy and not communism." Thus what the United States wants in Korea is exactly what Russia wants, a friendly democratic state which could be relied on as a faithful ally in case of trouble in the Pacific.

As neither China nor Japan will be in a position to wage an aggressive war in the near future, when the United States thinks of trouble in the Pacific, she has Russia in mind. Similarly, when Russia thinks of an attack on her security, she has the Anglo-American combination in mind and nothing else. So, because of the Russian menace, the United States seeks to create a Korea friendly to her; and because of the fear of Anglo-American conspiracy, Russia seeks to set up a government in Korea friendly to her, not to her rivals. All the present major difficulties in Korea are the by-products of the interplay of these two rival forces.

Korea, torn between two rival powers, is symbolic of this sick old world, divided into two hostile camps. Put your finger on any troubled spot on earth. All the way from the Baltic Sea to Tokyo Bay, the same rival forces are at work behind the scenes. Therefore, the problem of Korea, like those of the Balkans, of Palestine, and of Iran, cannot be solved permanently without working out a basis of co-operation between Russia and the Western democracies.

It is anyone's guess what will happen if the present state of rivalry continues. The country might be won over by America or Russia. Or southern Korea might be converted into a little America and northern Korea into a little Russia. The north and the south might come to blows one of these days and throw the whole world into another catastrophe.

It appears at the present time that both the United States and the Soviet Union have about an even chance to win or lose Korea. That is one reason why the rivalry is all the more dangerous. America is as much admired as Russia is feared. Given a free choice, the Koreans will not hesitate to choose the United States as their friend and model. But the fear of Russia will have a considerable influence in preventing such a move. If the United States can rely on the support of the American-educated natives and the Christian Koreans, numbering close to a million, Russia can utilize some 600,000 Koreans who had left their fatherland under the Japanese pressure and made their homes in Siberia. The promise of American freedom and democracy is indeed tempting to many freedom-loving Koreans, but the promise of communism is equally attractive to the mass of poor people who constitute the overwhelming majority of the population. The United States has more benefits to offer in every way, but the Soviet Union, because of her geographical propinquity, can successfully challenge America's bid for leadership in that country.

At this moment, however, neither America nor Russia appears to be winning the Korean people, who resent both as conquerors rather than liberators. They have already staged many anti-Soviet-American demonstrations in protest against the continued occupation of their country and the repeated failure of the occupation authorities to adopt measures to create a free and united Korea. Although most of these demonstrations have taken place in the American zone, where the people can express their feelings, the resentment against the dictatorial rule of the Russian communists and their Soviet-sponsored Interim Committee is as intense as it was against the Japanese and their underdogs.

In spite of the bitter resentment of the natives, the Russians have created in north Korea a communist police state with all the efficiency and unscrupulousness with which they set up similar revolutionary governments in other countries. They have banished or gagged all those who do not support their ruthless methods of control, and they rule the country through the Korean puppets who are backed by Russian might and through the poor peasants who were given confiscated lands.

In south Korea, the Americans have not been nearly as successful as the Russians in north Korea primarily because of the communist intrigue and sabotage. No sooner did the Americans start building a democratic state in their zone than thousands of Korean communists came from the Russian zone. They resorted to fifth column tactics and created strikes and riots, resulting in bloodshed and turmoil. All reports coming from Korea show that the Russians have a good chance of expelling the Americans and of consolidating the whole peninsula under their hegemony.

Confronted with a similar situation in Greece, the American Government decided to grant financial aid to stem the tide of communist expansion. But in Korea where the situation is more critical than in Greece, no positive policy has yet been adopted to combat the communist drive for power.

While attending the Moscow Peace Conference in the spring of 1947, George Marshall again brought up the Korean question before the Russian Government. Should Russia again refuse to work together, the United States is expected to extend a similar financial aid to Korea for the purpose of preventing the communist domination of that country. The more the United States strives to check Russian expansion, the more desperately the communists will struggle for power. If the rivalry continues, it certainly will result in a gigantic conflict, not only in Korea, but throughout the entire world. Therefore, in the name and for the sake of the peace of the world, Korea must be freed from both America and Russia. This can be accomplished by adopting one of the several following courses.

The first is the immediate grant of complete independence. Hold a general election at once under the supervision of neutral observers as was done in Greece and turn the administration of the state over to the winning party or parties.

Those who have swallowed an overdose of Japanese propaganda for many years do not think that the Koreans are capable of self-rule at this time. But the Koreans believe that they can manage their own affairs. The proof of the pudding is in the eating. Why not let them try their ability and skill? If they succeed, it is well and good. If they fail, new measures may be adopted.

Contrary to the popular impression that she has always been a dependency under China or Japan, Korea's role in Eastern Asia has been next in importance to that of China. Until the dawn of modern history, Korea served as a bridge of civilization between China and Japan. But she did not exist merely as a transmitter of continental cultures. In many things her contribution was even superior to that of China. Take, for instance, the art of writing and printing. Although the Chinese were the first to use the movable wooden and clay types, the Koreans were the first to use the movable metal types, a half century before Gutenberg's invention.

Instead of stopping with the Chinese ideographs, the Koreans invented an alphabet which is so simple that any person of normal intelligence can master it in two weeks and can read any book printed in that alphabet. As a result, Korea has the highest percentage of literacy east of the Suez Canal, excepting Japan. Over sixty per cent of her population is considered literate. The next highest degree of literacy is found in the Philippine Islands where fifty per cent of the population can read and write. So, if literacy is one means of proving the preparedness for self-rule, Korea is as well prepared for independence as any state in Asia.

Although Korea has suffered serfdom under Japan for nearly half a century, she used to be one of the most powerful states in eastern Asia. In fact, the Koreans were about the only people, excepting the Americans, who defeated the islanders. It is true that they did not overrun Japan, but they repelled formidable Japanese armies which invaded and ravaged the peninsula for seven years at the close of the sixteenth century. The factors which brought about the Japanese defeat are declared to be the death of Hideyoshi, the ruler of Japan, the aid of China, and the domination of the Korea Strait by the Korean navy.

According to the scattered historical references on that war, the naval vessels which Admiral Yi Shun-sin devised and built were called "tortoise" ships because they resembled the shape of a tortoise. They were covered with iron-spiked plates to prevent boarding by the enemy. The sides were shielded by iron plates to protect the rowers and the archers who shot fire arrows to burn the enemy ships. They were also equipped with powerful horns to ram the enemy vessels. Using a fleet of these strange ships, the Koreans wiped out the Japanese fleet in two successful campaigns. On land warfare they were reported to have used fire bombs, known as "flying thunderbolt," a counterpart of modern hand grenade.

In the middle of the nineteenth century, both China and Japan were obliged to open their portals to Western commerce and trade, but Korea successfully withstood all attempts at breaking her isolation. Both France and the United States tried to open Korea by employing the same methods with which Commodore Perry broke the isolation of Japan. Both attempts failed to accomplish their objectives, and Korea remained a "Hermit Kingdom." Finally, the Japanese opened that country by using Perry's method and subsequently annexed it. But even forty years of slavery under Japan have not dented the pride of the formerly free and independent people.

They believe that if there is any nation which deserves freedom and independence, that is Korea. They point out that even the Japanese, who had looked down on the Koreans like the scum of the earth, came to recognize their merits so much that at one time five out of thirteen Korean provincial governors, as well as all the vice-governors of the remaining eight provinces, were Koreans. They do not think that they can transform their country into a promised land of democracy without mistakes. But they are confident that, given a fair chance without external interference, they can do well enough to shame those who have thrown their country into the present mess.

In spite of their claims, if the Western powers still believe that the Koreans are incapable of ruling themselves, they should place their country for a brief period of time under a real international trusteeship in place of the so-called four-power trusteeship agreed upon at Moscow. The four-power trusteeship as envisaged at Moscow is really a joint Soviet-American trusteeship with China and Great Britain only as spectators, and this two-power trusteeship will not lesson the rivalry between the two countries. Furthermore, Korea, torn by the rival states, will have no more chance to achieve her real freedom than under Japanese domination.

Therefore, if neither immediate independence nor a real international trusteeship is established, it would be better for the United States and the Soviet Union to invite the Japanese back to rule Korea. This would be most unfair and unjust to a nation which has suffered Japanese oppression and exploitation for forty painful years. But it would be no more unjust and unfair than the continuation of the present policy of cutting an innocent country into two hostile camps under two rival masters. And yet it can at least abate the rivalry between America and Russia, which, if allowed to degenerate into a feud, might blow the whole world to pieces.

Chapter XII

THE MAKING OF UNITED CHINA

Since the days of John Hay many students and statesmen have often repeated the statement that "Whoever understands China holds the key to future world politics for the next five hundred years." But it should be said today that whoever understands how far the big powers will go toward international co-operation can foretell the future of China and the future of all Asia for the next thousand years.

If the powerful states work together, they can create peace in China as well as in other countries with the wave of the wand. If they work at cross purposes, even a closely united China will split into hostile camps like Korea. Furthermore, if the great powers, by working together harmoniously, create a peaceful political atmosphere, the Chinese as well as other Asiatic peoples will develop peaceful cultures and civilizations. But if they are divided into hostile camps, more than a billion Asiatics, with their potential powers and undeveloped resources, will probably attempt to emulate pre-war Japan.

First, let us see how the solution of the present Chinese problems depends on the unity of the powerful nations. After disposing of this question, we shall see how the character of future China will depend on the harmony of the great powers.

The present crisis in China is more than a local fight between the Nationalists and the Communists: it is as much a struggle between Russia and the Western democracies as it is among the Chinese themselves. The Chinese puzzle, therefore, cannot be solved permanently without working out a basis of co-operation between the United States and the Soviet Union.

In the days when the Pacific Ocean was really an ocean instead of being a mere pond as it now is, all that the United States desired in the Far East was a fair chance to carry on commerce and trade on an equal footing with other powers.

She advocated the policies of the open door and the territorial integrity of China for the purpose of preserving equal opportunity for commerce and trade. That phase of the American foreign policy is definitely over.

Today the United States is not merely interested in commerce and trade with China. Her primary objective in the Far East is to create a strong, united, and democratic China, which can defend her borders against future Russian encroachment and which can be counted as a friendly ally in case of trouble in the Pacific. For this reason, she has done what she could to help the Chinese build a united democratic state.

Similarly, the Russians are no longer interested in securing commercial and industrial concessions alone. They are definitely interested in seeing that China is controlled by a party friendly to them so that no power can use that country as a basis of attack on the Soviet Union. Right or wrong, they do not think that China united under the American leadership will be a friendly ally of the Soviet Union. So they feel as uneasy over the American activities in China as the Americans might feel over the Russian activities in Mexico. It is very natural, therefore, for them to adopt counter measures to neutralize the American influence and to strengthen their position in the Far East. This is the main reason why the American attempts at unifying China have met with little success.

China, like other border states between Russia and the Western democracies, is a political arena of the rival power blocs. The shadows of the contesting powers are behind every move which she makes. The very pulse of Chinese politics beats to a tune played by London, Moscow and Washington. When they play in harmony, the tension in China eases up a little. When they strike a discordant note, the situation takes a turn for the worse. A brief examination of the recent events in that country will show how sound or unsound this contention is.

When America and Russia did not work together in the Far East, the United States supported the Nationalists to fight the Japanese, but the Soviet Union pursued a policy of neutrality benevolent to Japan. The pursuance of such a policy by Russia enabled the Japanese to withdraw their troops from the Siberian

THE MAKING OF UNITED CHINA

border in the summer of 1944 and to deliver crushing blows on the Nationalist forces and also to seize all the important American air bases in China, the basis from which American planes blasted Japanese shipping and the Japanese home blasts. The tragic military reverses suffered by the American and the Chinese forces in the fall of 1944 created a serious political crisis in China.

But early in 1945, the United States and Great Britain purchased Russian co-operation at the Yalta Conference by promising to give everything that Russia had asked for in the Far East. Subsequently, Russia denounced her nonaggression pact with Japan and declared war on that country. She likewise adopted the American policy in China, the policy of recognizing and aiding the Nationalist Government as the sole government of China.

No sooner had Russia announced this policy through the conclusion of the new Sino-Russian treaty than the Communists and Nationalists opened interparty peace talks at Chungking in the summer of 1945. After six weeks of continuous negotiations in an atmosphere of friendship and cordiality, both parties thrashed out all their major differences in principles. As a matter of fact, there were few irreconcilable differences because both parties wanted approximately the same principles for their country's unification and development. Although many thorny issues still remained unsolved, it seemed as though China at long last would regain her unity, lost nearly a century ago. Then something went wrong. The "big three" struck a discordant note at the Foreign Ministers Conference at London. No sooner had this happened than the Chinese were up in arms against each other.

The "big three" again played in harmony at the Moscow Conference in December, 1945. It immediately cleared the darkening shadows over the Chinese political sky. As a result, George Marshall, who had just arrived in China as peacemaker, succeeded in persauding the Nationalists and Communists to make an armed truce and to reopen a peace parley in which not only the two rival party leaders but those of other groups were invited to participate. Following a frank exchange of views in the presence of the American moderator, they settled most of the problems which hitherto had eluded all attempts at solution.

One of these questions was the disposition of the Communist army. The Nationalists contended that so long as the Communists retained their army, there could be no national unity. They demanded, therefore, that, as a first step toward unity, the Reds must place their army under the central government's control, or disband it entirely. The Communists felt that if they gave up their army, the reactionary elements of the Kuomintang might launch a blood purge against them. So they contended that the Nationalist government of Chiang Kai-shek first must be reformed, or else they would not give up their army. This deadlock was broken by the adoption of Marshall's formula.

The formula provided for the creation of a national army of sixty divisions, ten of which were to be Communists. This national army was to be placed under the direction of a non-political ministry of defense. Generalissimo Chiang, as the present commander-in-chief, was given the power to appoint or relieve all officers. But when he should remove a Communist commander, he was pledged to replace him with a candidate nominated by the senior Communist member of the coalition government which was to be formed.

Another difficult problem was the Communist demand for, and the Nationalist refusal of, the Communist governorship in four northern provinces and vice-governorship in two other provinces. While no satisfactory solution of this problem was found, it was agreed to maintain a status quo until a final settlement could be made by the reorganized central government. Thus it appeared that this thorny problem of local government in the Communist-dominated areas would be solved by the eventual grant of local autonomy to all provinces.

The third most troublesome question concerned the make-up of the National Assembly which was to be held in May, 1946, for the purpose of adopting a constitution for the republic. The Nationalists insisted on packing the assembly with their own men, half of whom had been chosen before 1937, and some of these men had collaborated with the Japanese or had since died. The Communists and other minority parties demanded a new election of the delegates and a liberal representation of their own men. The new understanding was that the Nationalists were to have a large majority of the 2,050 delegates, but no constitutional provisions were to be adopted without the votes of a three-fourths majority.

There was a satisfactory agreement on the principles of the constitution to be adopted. The new document was to combine the elements of the American and the British systems and of the constitution of the French Third Republic. It provided for a bicameral system of legislature with a popularly elected legislative Yuan and an upper house, or Control Yuan, whose members were to be elected by the provincial assemblies. There was to be a Judicial Yuan and an Executive Yuan which was to be responsible to the legislature. There was to be a national president with limited powers, a large degree of local autonomy to the several provinces, and a bill of rights granting political freedom and civil liberties to the people.

Six months after the adoption of the constitution a national election was to be held. From then on China was to be a fullpledged democracy of the people, by the people and for the people. In the interim period a coalition government was to replace the one-party dictatorship of the Kuomintang. In the State Council, which was to be the supreme organ of the coalition government, the Nationalists were to supply twenty out of forty council members, the Communists ten, and other parties ten.

Promising as these plans were, their success, as General Marshall stated, was dependent "in a large measure on actions of other nations." Had the United States and the Soviet Union continued to work together, the situation in China might have been different. But unfortunately, they were so divided over the questions of Greece, Indonesia, and Iran that they began to work at cross-purposes in China. No sooner had this happened than armed clashes between the Nationalists and the Communists took place in Manchuria.

To a casual observer, conflict in Manchuria appears to be only a clash between the Nationalists and Communists in China. The Nationalist troops proceeded to take over Manchuria from the Russians who were evacuating. There was nothing wrong in this Nationalist drive. The Russian Government had agreed to transfer the control of Manchuria to the Nationalists, not to the Communists. The truce concluded in January, 1946, provided for the cessation of hostilities and the end of troop movements in all parts of China, but it made a specific exception by giving the Nationalists the right to move troops into Manchuria "for the purpose of restoring Chinese sovereignty." But the Communists, who had slipped into Manchuria during the period of Russian occupation, tried to prevent the government troops from occupying the territory which was being evacuated by the Russians. The result was the renewed clash of arms.

The responsibility for starting the trouble did not lie entirely on the Communists and their supporters alone. The reactionary elements in the Nationalist Party, who have never believed in co-operating with the Communists, moved once more to block the unification of the two parties. Using the Russian rape of Manchuria and the Communist activities under Russian protection as an excuse, they quickly moved to scrap the basis of interparty co-operation which was worked out under the aegis of General Marshall. Such moves on the part of the Nationalist reactionaries did not help promote unity between the rival parties.

Without outside interference, the Nationalists, with American support, could have taken Manchuria in the spring of 1946. Had they taken that vast territory, with its rich resources and powerful industries and arsenals, they would have grown so powerful that they could have unified the whole country either through peaceful means or through war. But they failed to do so under circumstances which are well-known to all students of Far Eastern affairs.

The Nationalists moved their crack troops, the cream of their army trained by the American officers, equipped with American weapons of war (this was done to fight Japan) and transported on the American transports. When they arrived at the Manchurian ports of Dairen and Port Arthur, the Russians refused to allow them to land. But the Russians agreed to let the Americans land the Chinese troops at Yingkow, a minor port in Manchuria. When the American ships arrived, the Russians had pulled out of Yingkow and had turned it over to the Chinese Communists. The Chinese Communists, of course, refused to allow the landing of the Nationalist troops. So Vice Admiral Daniel E. Barbey was obliged to withdraw with the American transports loaded with the Nationalist troops. Now the Russians agreed to permit the landing of the airborne Nationalist troops at Changchun. When the Nationalist transport planes arrived, they found the city completely surrounded by the Chinese Communists, and they had to turn back.

Finally, the Nationalists were forced to fight their way into Manchuria through the snow and ice-packed land route held by the Communists. Now the Russian Army would not allow the Nationalists to use the Manchurian railways for transporting their armed forces. In a country larger than Germany and France combined, when they could not transport their men and materials through the railways and had to fight into Manchuria against the stubborn Communist resistance, one can imagine the difficulties which the Nationalists encountered.

It is likewise well-known that the Russian Army postponed its withdrawal from Manchuria from December, 1945, to the end of April, 1946. It is a fact that the Russians delayed their withdrawal on several occasions at the request of the Nationalists. The Nationalists had asked the Russians to remain in Manchuria until they could get into Manchuria and take over that territory. They did so for the purpose of preventing the Chinese Communists from seizing Manchuria before their arrival. But the Russians made it impossible for the Nationalists to move into Manchuria, so they could ask for further postponement. Clever these Russians!

This delayed Russian evacuation of Manchuria gave the Chinese Communists ample time to strengthen their position in Manchuria and resist the Nationalist entry into that territory. When the Russian Army finally evacuated, they took with them all the valuable industrial equipment, leaving behind only shells and shambles. Furthermore, the Russian Army carried out its withdrawal with clock-like precision, matched with the advance of the Chinese Communists. As a result, most of the evacuated territory fell into the Communists, not the Nationalists. Above all, the Russians allowed the Chinese Communists, deliberately or inadvertently, to arm themselves with Japanese war equipment. Consequently, the Chinese Communists grew so powerful that they could successfully frustrate all Nationalist attempts at unifying China.

When the situation in Manchuria was taking a turn for the worse, General Marshall, who had been in Washington to secure material aid to implement his unity program, hurried back to China in the middle of April. He found that the Communists, thanks to the Russian co-operation, had strengthened their position in Manchuria so greatly that they made new demands as a price for the resumption of truce, demands which the Nationalists refused to accept. When the Nationalists scored a military victory over the Communists, they also made new demands on the Communists. Despite these constantly shifting demands made according to the fluctuating fortunes of the civil war, Marshall succeeded in negotiating the agreements on the cessation of hostilities in Manchuria and in north China, on the relative strength and disposition of the Nationalist and Communist armed forces in Manchuria, and on the repair and the reopening of the railways. But he encountered insurmountable difficulties on the question of reorganization and the deployment of the rival armies in north and central China.

The Communists agreed to withdraw from parts of Hopei, Shansi, Shantung Provinces and the Yangtze Valley into specified pockets, but they refused to comply with the Nationalist demand for their complete withdrawal from northern Kiangsu and southern Jehol. Furthermore, they demanded that all areas evacuated by them should not be occupied by the Nationalist forces and that the Communist Peace Preservation Militia

THE MAKING OF UNITED CHINA

and their local governments should be left unmolested until an over-all political settlement for the entire country could be worked out. The Nationalists stubbornly refused to accept these demands.

Confronted with an unbreakable deadlock, the Communists launched a sweeping military offensive in Shantung on the very day, June 7, when the ill-fated fifteen-day truce was announced. The Nationalists accepted the Communist challenge and launched counterattacks. The truce was extended eight more days, making a total of twenty-three days, all of which were used by both sides to prepare for a large scale civil war.

As the situation was growing worse, Generalissimo Chiang Kai-shek announced on August 14, the first anniversary of Japan's surrender, a set of new proposals in which he promised:

(1) To end the period of political tutelage and institute a constitutional government without delay, and to open the National Constituent Assembly on November 12 for the purpose of adopting a new constitution.

(2) To abide by and execute the agreements reached by the political consultation conference early in 1946.

(3) To enlarge the government's political basis by including members of all parties and nonpartisans.

(4) To abide by the truce agreement of January 10 and demand that the Communists withdraw from areas where they threaten peace and obstruct communications.

(5) To continue to use political means to settle political differences, but only if the Communists give assurance and evidence that they will carry out the truce agreement, restore communications, integrate the Communist army into the National army, and respect the decisions of the Executive Headquarters which was created for the purpose of carrying out the truce agreement (this body was composed of the representatives of the government, the Communists and the American peace envoys).

The Communist reply to this proposal was a call for a full-scale civil war on all fronts. Marshall then prevailed on the Generalissimo to invite the Communists to participate in the reorganization of the government. But the Communists refused to participate until Chiang issued an unconditional cease-fire order for the entire country. The Generalissimo, however, would not issue such an order until the Communists withdrew their troops from certain specified areas. Now Marshall and Stuart suggested that if the Communists participated in the coalition government, they would try to persuade Chiang to issue a new truce. The Communists again refused to participate in the coalition government unless they and the Democratic League, which usually votes with them, were granted fourteen out of forty seats in the State Council, the supreme organ of the coalition government. The Nationalists were willing to grant them twelve seats, but not fourteen. Neither the Communists nor the Nationalists would yield on this point. It was due to the fact that all major decisions in the State Council were to be adopted by a two-thirds majority. With fourteen seats the Communists could veto all the measures which they disliked, but with twelve they could not, and therefore, they would not participate without the veto power. The Nationalists were willing to let the Communists participate in the coalition government, but they did not want to give the Reds the veto power with which they could sabotage all their program for reconstruction.

In the meantime, civil war raged far and wide. City after city fell to the Nationalist troops. The Communist stronghold of Kalgan itself was about to fall to the Nationalists. Here Marshall and Stuart proposed a ten-day truce, which could have been extended. The acceptance of the truce would have meant a great Nationalist concession. But the Communists rejected the truce on the ground that it would only have given the Nationalists a breathing spell to bring in their reinforcement for the final drive on Kalgan. A few days after the rejection of the proposed truce, Kalgan fell to the Nationalists.

In the middle of October, the liberals of the Nationalist party and the leaders of the third parties, all of whom were sympathetic with the Communists, persuaded Generalissimo Chiang to issue a new eight-point proposal. One of the points called for the maintenance of military and political status quo as existed at that time. Another provided for the proclamation of a nationwide cease-fire order to be issued when the Communists named their delegates to the Constituent Assembly scheduled for November 12, Dr. Sun Yat-sen's birthday. The Communists made a counterproposal calling for the maintenance of the military and political status quo as existed in January, 1946. The Nationalists rejected the proposal because its acceptance would have wiped out all their hard-won military gains.

Four days before the opening of the constituent assembly, Chiang issued an order to all his forces to cease hostilities "except as may be necessary to defend their present position." When he did so, he hoped the Communists would participate in the assembly. He even postponed the opening of the assembly three days at the request of the third parties. But the Communists persisted in the boycott. So the Nationalists went ahead with the adoption of the constitution without the Communists.

At times the Nationalists were more irreconcilable than the Communists. But since the Communists had strengthened their position with Russian support, they grew much more uncompromising than the Nationalists. Invited by the Nationalists to participate in the interim coalition government, the Communists refused to participate unless they were given the right to veto on all important measures brought before the State Council. Invited to join the national assembly to draft a democratic constitution, they insisted first on the postponement of the assembly and later demanded its total dissolution. Asked to reopen negotiations in January, 1947, they demanded the scrapping of the new constitution which was adopted in December, 1946, and insisted on the withdrawal of the government troops to the positions held in January, 1946. The Communists were so adverse to making a fair compromise that General Marshall found it impossible even to get them to sit down at a conference table with government representatives.

Undoubtedly, the Communists are counting on the collapse of the Nationalist government, brought about by the economic and financial collapse, accelerated by the Communistic guerrilla action against the long lines of rail communications. That may explain their unwillingness to compromise, as George Marshall believes. But Wellington Koo, the Chinese Ambassador to the United States, declared in his address before the Cleveland Council on World Affairs that the Chinese Communists, "owing allegiance to the Communist headquarters abroad," are perhaps themselves not free to work together with the Nationalists without the approval of their superiors abroad.

When the statement of Ambassador Koo is taken out of its diplomatic formality and is put in plain and honest language, it is tantamount to saying that the Russian Communists have prevented the unification of China by encouraging the Chinese Communists to hold out against the Nationalists instead of making a compromise with them. This contention of the Nationalist government is countered by China's Communist diplomat, Chou En-lai, who blamed the failure of the peace negotiations on Marshall's partiality to Chiang's government.

The Communist charge against American partiality and the Nationalist accusation of Russian intrigue in Chinese affairs have by no means freed the extremists and the reactionaries from their share of responsibility for the failure of Marshall's peace mission. But few can deny that the rivalry between the United States and the Soviet Union is as mighty a saboteur of peace as the deep-seated hatred and jealousy, fear and suspicion between the Chinese rival factions.

When America and Russia worked together, and jointly brought their pressure to bear upon the Communists and the Nationalists simultaneously, even the reactionaries and the extremists could not torpedo the peacemaking. For instance, in the summer of 1945 and again early in 1946, when the two great countries worked together, both rival factions were more than willing to bury their hatchets and make peace on the basis of fair compromise. Only when the two giants are divided into hostile camps, the reactionaries and the extremists grow irreconcilable toward each other and wreck all plans of making peace.

It is not difficult to explain why the division between the United States and the Soviet Union has such a baneful effect on the Chinese political situation. In the first place, the mere division between the two powers gives both factions in China the prospects of obtaining outside aid to defeat their enemies. Whenever there is a possibility of getting outside aid, both sides grow more irreconcilable than when there was no such possibility. Secondly, when America and Russia are divided into rival camps, both powers are afraid of each other, and both seek to win China and to prevent the other from winning her. The natural result of such a policy is the frustration of all attempts at unifying China by either party and the inevitable partition of that country into rival camps.

It is undoubtedly this division between the two power-blocs which encourages the opposing factions, not only in China, but also in other countries, including Palestine, Iran, India, Burma, Indonesia, French Indo-China, and Korea to be irreconcilable and uncompromising toward each other. It is true that these peoples fought long before the emergence of America and Russia in their countries. They will probably keep on fighting long after the departure of the Americans and the Russians from their countries. But the fact is that today they are, in large measure, obtaining the nourishment to feed their grudges against each other from the gulf between the two power blocs. The problems of these countries, therefore, cannot be solved satisfactorily without working out a basis of co-operation between Russia and the Western democracies.

In view of the recent development of affairs in China, I take the liberty of quoting a paragraph from my article published in *Current History,* September, 1946, when Marshall was still endeavoring to make peace between the Nationalists and the Communists. I wrote:

"If the United States and the Soviet Union are united on a common policy, they can make peace in China by merely telling the Chinese factions in plain and honest language that neither power will give them support, moral or material, until they stop fighting each other. With the loss of the prospects of outside support, even the uncompromising Communists will gladly make a compromise with the Nationalists as they did in the summer of 1945 when the prospect of Russian aid was gone. But with America and Russia divided into hostile spheres, neither George Marshall nor John Leighton Stuart can be expected to make a permanent peace in China or anywhere else. Unless the relations between the two great countries improve, all that a statesman can do in China, or anywhere else, will be a temporary truce, not a permanent peace. Assuming the soundness of this contention, one wonders if George Marshall did not go to the wrong country to make peace. He should have gone to Russia rather than China."

When the situation was growing hopeless, Marshall at last admitted his failure. He abandoned the warring factions to their fate and returned to the United States in January, 1947, and became the Secretary of State. It appeared for some time that Marshall would have a better chance to solve the Chinese puzzle at Moscow where he had an opportunity to talk with the Russian leaders. Fortunately, the Russians were willing to discuss the Chinese question. In fact, they brought up the question for discussion. Marshall was willing to review the whole situation, if the Chinese were invited to participate. The Chinese Government refused to participate in any discussion touching on China's internal affairs. As a result, the golden opportunity to solve the Chinese question was lost, to the sorrow of millions.

It should be admitted that the discord among the big powers is not the only factor which has created strife in China. The appalling conditions of living, the abject poverty, the primitive state of agriculture and industry, the lack of transportation and communication, the impoverished system of education, the corruption and inefficiency in government, and above all, the keen rivalry and the deep-seated fear and suspicion between the Nationalists and the Communists—all these are sufficient to ferment endless strife in the land which has long been noted for peace and tranquillity. But no one can deny that the rivalry among the powerful Western states has had the tragic effect of dividing not only China but the whole world into two hostile spheres. As matters stand today, in the absence of unity and harmony among the big powers, regardless of how desperately the Chinese struggle for unity, their country will split like Korea. There is no country which is strong enough to retain unity when the two giants pull from opposite directions.

Some old China hands doubt that China with her teeming millions of uneducated and inexperienced people can achieve democracy in our times even if the big powers work harmoniously and give her a united support. But to my mind, there is little doubt that in a favorable international political atmosphere, democracy will have as much chance to succeed in China as elsewhere, because the Chinese are fundamentally a democratic people. However, with the world torn into hostile camps by international rivalry and war, democracy will have no more chance of success in China than in Japan and other totalitarian countries. The flower of democracy can bloom in a peaceful climate, but it withers away when war comes like frost.

The answers to other problems such as industrial development and educational and social reforms will be likewise found in this great question of unity or disunity among the big powers. In a peaceful international atmosphere, China will have no difficulty in developing her industry for the benefit of her poverty-stricken millions. In the continued state of international tension, she will have little opportunity or capital to exploit her resources for the good of mankind. And the long dreamed of opportunities for fabulous commerce and trade with China will have to wait for an indefinite future.

Now let us see how the success or failure of the big powers co-operating for the maintenance of peace and justice on earth will determine the future patterns of Chinese culture and civilization.

We have already seen how political atmosphere affects the cultural patterns of the people. We have also seen how the old

Chinese, as well as other peoples, built a peaceful civilization in the absence of danger, but how they all took to the sword whenever they were threatened with danger and insecurity. Other things being equal, the modern Chinese probably will follow the same behaviour patterns, namely, if the powerful Western nations succeed in creating a peaceful atmosphere throughout the world, the Chinese and other Asiatics will develop peaceful cultures and civilizations. But if they should convert the whole world into hostile camps, the Chinese, like all other peoples, would attempt to create a militaristic state with militaristic cultures and institutions, however distasteful they may be, for the failure to do so in a world of anarchy may mean their enslavement or total annihilation.

Years of tragic experiences with the Huns, the Mongols, the Manchus and the Japanese, to name just a few of the invaders of China, have taught the modern Chinese the unforgettable lesson that in a chaotic world they must arm or be enslaved and annihilated. As a matter of fact, since China was thrown into the modern world of chaos created by the powerful aggressor nations, the Chinese reverence for scholarship as well as their contempt for soldiery have undergone a considerable change. If the present trend continues, it will not be very long before the peaceful Chinese will worship soldiers rather than scholars.

Japan is a small and poor country. Wealth resources and her population were very small when compared with those of China. But when the Japanese developed a powerful military empire with a mighty army and navy, they could disturb the peace of the entire world and cause the mighty western empires in Asia to crumble like a house of cards. So if the Chinese and other Asiatics with their immeasurable man power and resources should develop a military power in proportion to what Japan built, the world might witness a spectacular demonstration of power not yet found in modern history, provided, of course, that the white man in the meantime does not blow the whole world to pieces.

If the future of China and the solution of the present problems depend on the success or failure of the Soviet-American co-operation, the present policies pursued independently by the several big powers cannot and will not solve the Chinese question now or in the future. On the contrary such policies, lacking unanimity between the big powers, will only complicate the already complex Chinese situation because when one power pursues a policy with the view of strengthening its position, others take countermeasures to precipitate rivalry leading to international conflicts.

The policy of unilateral withdrawal from China would be even worse than that of aiding the Nationalists singlehanded because it might result in the complete domination of China by a Russian-supported Communist regime. With China within the Russian orbit, the United States might feel unsafe in the Pacific. So if the primary object of America is to achieve her national security, as undoubtedly it is, neither a unilateral intervention nor a singlehanded withdrawal will meet the requirements.

On the other hand, any joint action, either a joint intervention or a joint nonintervention, can achieve the desired result, namely, unity in China and security for all parties. Therefore, the only sound policy for peace and security in the Far East is a united policy carried out through the UN, or through a regional instrument specially created for the purpose of co-ordinating the rival policies of the big powers in the Pacific region. Where no basis of united action could be found, a unilateral policy may be pursued, but only with the understanding that it is a step toward international rivalry and war.

Chapter XIII

THE FUTURE OF THE WHITE MAN'S BURDEN

The colonial areas with their rich, undeveloped resources have often been a source of international rivalry. Therefore the problem of removing this fertile source of international friction has been one of the paramount tasks of Western statesmen.

At the close of the First World War, they made a feeble attempt to lessen this source of international conflict by creating a mandate system. Under this system, the mandatory powers were to take over the colonial possessions of the defeated states on behalf of the League of Nations and to apply the principle that the well-being and the development of the subject peoples form a sacred trust of civilization. Had the mandatory system been developed according to the spirit which inspired its creation, it might have helped solve some of the colonial problems without unnecessary bloodshed. But the system was abused from the very beginning as an instrument of exploitation in the name of high-sounding idealism. Benefiting by the failure of the mandatory system, the Charter of the United Nations provided for the creation of an international Trusteeship Council, which is to be far superior to the Mandates Commission of the League of Nations.

The Trusteeship Council as envisaged in the Charter is to serve as a guardian of the colonial peoples who are still considered unfit for self-government. It is to see that the colonial powers live up to their pledge to accept as a sacred trust the obligation to promote the well-being of their subject peoples; to respect the principle of equal rights and self-determination of all peoples; and to insure equal treatment in economic and commercial matters for all members of the United Nations and their nationals. If the Trusteeship Council grows strong enough to assert its authority, it might help solve most of the colonial problems peacefully, to the satisfaction of all concerned. But as the Council itself has barely been set up, no one can tell how long it will take before this arm of the UN will grow powerful enough to be the guardian of the subject peoples. In the meantime, the agitation for freedom by the colonial peoples and the rivalry for the control of the dependent areas between the Western powers are endangering the peace of the entire world.

The present surge of nationalism among the submerged millions in Asia has its roots in man's natural desire for freedom from alien control. The late Manuel Quezon, the first president of the Philippine Commonwealth, sounded the keynote of the sentiment of all subject peoples when he said: "We would rather be governed like a hell and do it ourselves than like heaven and have it done for us."

Excepting the United States in the Philippine Islands, none of the colonial powers has yet satisfied the native aspiration for freedom and democracy. On the contrary, most colonial governments have put down the movement for independence with ruthless policies of oppression. But these repressive measures have only kindled the native desire for freedom because the heathen have learned the value of the forbidden fruit as well as the Christians. Finally, when the colonial powers have promised eventual freedom, their subject peoples have taken it as a sign of weakness and have cried for independence louder and oftener than before. Besides, the subject peoples have learned the value of the white man's promise. They think it is as good as a weatherman's promise.

"You help us win this war"; said the white men during the First World War, "we will give you freedom when the war is over." They helped—they had to help—their masters win the fight. The war ended but no freedom came. They waited and waited until the Second World War broke out. The white men again said: "You help us win this war; we will give you freedom when the war is over." The war ended. The British, the Dutch, and the French returned to stifle freedom with the backing of the Japanese troops and the American lend-lease materials.

Furthermore, the colonial powers which have ruled their rich colonies from a century to three centuries have done little to promote the welfare of their subject peoples. In spite of the fabulous wealth and resources which the imperialistic powers have exploited year after year, the natives still suffer misery, poverty, famine, and starvation. As centuries of white rule have failed to save them from disease, ignorance, poverty, and slavery, the subject peoples have lost all their hope of attaining better and finer conditions of existence under the white man's domination.

In spite of all the shortcomings and failures of the colonial rule, the Asiatics might have continued to look upon the British, the Dutch, and the French as their overlords, had the Western nations defended their colonies successfully against the Japanese invasion. But they failed to do so. It is no exaggeration that this failure forever sealed the fate of their empires in Asia.

The subject peoples who have placed their faith in their ruling powers for protection are bitterly disappointed and disillusioned. They have come to doubt the ability of the white man to protect them against similar future attacks. They wonder why they should continue their servitude to the nations which have exploited them, robbed them, oppressed them, disarmed them, and made them helpless, and have failed even to protect them against other robber nations. So by failing to guard their possessions against attacks, the Western nations lost the only valid excuse they had for controlling their colonies—to protect them against hostile powers.

Worse still, the colonial powers lost their "face" by their pitiful defeat at the hands of the little Japanese. The subject peoples who have always feared or revered the white man as a sort of superman have lost all their respect for their erstwhile masters. Whenever they think of their rulers, they will always remember the incredible sights which they have witnessed with their eyes; that is, the amazing spectacle of the mighty Western empires collapsing like a house of cards and the pitiful plight of the superior men who were kicked and whipped and driven like sheep by the contemptible Japanese. So long as they remember these, they will never again look up to their erstwhile masters and take orders on bended knees as they once did.

Finally, the complete inability of the Western nations to set their own houses in order and their utter helplessness in preventing incessant wars among themselves have made most subject peoples believe that the white men have forfeited not only their privilege to rule over other races, but their inherent right to rule over their own peoples. This may explain why, following every catastrophic world war, the movement for freedom from European control has been intensified with added vigor.

Perhaps one can understand the nationalist movement for independence by the subject peoples better if one examines the nature of the colonial rule in the several colonies. Let us take the case of French Indo-China, a rich rice and rubber producing empire of 281,000 square miles, with a population of 23,000,000.

France conquered this territory in the middle of the nineteenth century under the pretext of protecting Christian missionaries. For nearly a century the French ruled and exploited the country with such efficiency and thoroughness as to cause the Japanese colonial rulers to look upon them with envy.

In the last World War Japan could have taken the territory easily from France with the aid of the natives, had the French resisted the Japanese invasion. But the Vichy Government made the French colonial administration a willing tool in the Japanese hands and removed the necessity for Japan to seize the colony by force. When the French and the Japanese exploited together the native resources to continue their war on China and the Western democracies, the native patriots under the leadership of the Viet Nam Nationalist Party carried out their fight for freedom against both the French and the Japanese. In consequence, they suffered incredible forms of torture and massacre.

Early in 1944, the Japanese betrayed the French, lest the French might betray them, and set up their direct rule through a native puppet emperor. After the collapse of Japan, the Nationalists dethroned the emperor and proclaimed a republic.

Then came the French with the open backing of the British and the tacit approval of the American Government.

Harold R. Isaacs, Far Eastern correspondent of *Newsweek,* describes how he witnessed the incredible manner in which the French gained a foothold in their lost empire with the support of the British and the Japanese forces, and how they wreaked vengeance on the natives who had fought and bled for freedom and democracy all these years. According to Isaacs' accounts, the returning French tortured the natives to exact confessions, and punished and maltreated them just to show how strong France was, so that they could regain French prestige which had been flattened out by the Japanese. It is such injustice and cruelties which pour oil on the flames of nationalism.

The Dutch probably have done better in their Dutch East Indies than the French. They have not oppressed or tried to "Dutchify" the natives to the extent that the French have. After 350 years of Dutch rule, eighty-five per cent of the people still remain Moslem. This fact alone indicates how tolerant the Dutch rule has been when compared with other colonial rule. Perhaps no other colonial people have enjoyed or suffered a more liberal and benevolent alien administration than the seventy-five million Indonesians scattered in a 735,000 square-mile empire.

In some respects the Dutch have been even more liberal than the British, who are regarded the world's most experienced colonial administrators. For instance, in India any person who has a drop of native blood is classified as colored, a sign of inferiority. In the Dutch East Indies any one who has a drop of white blood is considered white, and, therefore, he is entitled to all the rights and privileges of the chosen race. Besides, while the British mix with the natives as well as oil does with water, many Dutch intermarried with the natives and brought up a large segment of hybrid population whose loyalty to the Dutch rule was unquestioned. When the Japanese were heading for the south in the last war, most students of colonial affairs believed that the Dutch, with the loyal support of the gratified natives, could hold out against the invaders at least six months.

But many of the ungrateful heathen joined with the invaders against their benevolent masters. That explains why the Dutch empire collapsed with a dramatic suddenness before the Japanese.

The reasons for the native resentment against the Dutch are not different from those in other subject countries. While the Dutch have been liberal in many ways, they have done little to promote the welfare of their subject people. In spite of the fabulous wealth and resources in the islands, the natives have suffered filth, poverty, and ignorance. While the Dutch have reaped annually over one hundred million dollars in profits, 350 years of their rule have left ninety-two per cent of the native population illiterate.

Nor have they given the natives much voice in their colonial government. They ruled the empire through a governor general who was a dictator in every sense of the word. In the Volksraad, a people's advisory council of sixty members included thirty Indonesians. This representation in the Volksraad, however, only kindled the native interest in the movement for freedom, which was suppressed ruthlessly.

Following an open demonstration against the Dutch rule in 1926, twenty-six native leaders were executed, 4,500 were thrown into prison, and 1,360 were doomed to Tanah Merah, the world's most terror-ridden concentration camp in the jungle area of Dutch New Guinea. Scores perished there, and the survivors were liberated by the Japanese in 1942.

When the Japanese came to "liberate" the Indonesians from the Dutch oppression, some of the Indonesian nationalists collaborated with the invaders. But when Japan collapsed, the Nationalists proclaimed the Indonesian Republic. Soekarno, the first premier of the republic, frankly stated why he worked with the Japanese: "The Japanese tried to use the Indonesians for their own purpose and let us prepare for our independence under false promises. But we turned the tables on them. We prepared for the hour of liberty and then took the matter into our own hands. And no power on earth can take it from us."

But the Dutch and the British, who had been fighting for

freedom and democracy, came to Indonesia to stifle them with the help of the Japanese forces and the American lend-lease materials. They tried to re-establish by force the defunct Dutch empire. This naturally led to armed conflict with the Indonesian nationalists.

According to the first-hand reports of Major E. Crocket, head of the American military mission in Java, which were published in *Harper's,* the conduct of the returning Dutch was similar to that of the French in Indo-China. They were so brutal and provocative that Crocket thinks the Dutch deliberately provoked the natives into making trouble to cause the British to send in more troops for the purpose of helping them regain their lost prestige.

The story of the British rule in Burma, India, and Malaya is too well known to require additional comments. It suffices to state that the Indians and the Burmese say the British rule is as selfish, cruel, and unbearable as those of the French and the Japanese; it is only more subtle, cunning, and crafty than those of other colonial powers. From the British point of view, of course, there is no more benevolent and charitable colonial power on earth than the British Empire.

Whether the British rule is beneficial or not, the colonial peoples of the British Empire cry as loudly for their independence as any other subject people in the world. Perhaps it may be due to the fact that they are freer than others to demand freedom. Or it may be due to the fact that the liberal share of freedom granted by the British sharpened their appetite for more freedom. Whatever the case may be, they will not cease to struggle for their independence until they get it.

However dynamic, nationalism alone will not be able to tip the white man's burden from his willing shoulders in the foreseeable future. But it can, and probably will, do it with the aid of the rivalry between Russia and the Western democracies.

International rivalry has always been a potent factor in overthrowing colonial empires. Were it not for the rivalry among the European powers, the nationalists in the two Americas might not have been so successful in achieving their independence from the British, French, and Spanish empires. Were it not for the same international rivalry, the colonial empires of Germany, Spain, and Czarist Russia in Eastern Asia and the southwestern Pacific would not have collapsed. But the keen rivalry among the colonial empires, resulting in incessant fratricidal wars, has so weakened the ruling powers that the nationalists in the subject territories have been able to overthrow their oppressors with the aid of one or more of the rival powers.

There probably has never been a time when international rivalry was keener than it is today when the whole world is divided into two rival spheres between Russia and the Western democracies. The present rivalry is more intense and more dangerous than that found in the history of the past because it is not merely for the control of gold, silver, the markets and the raw materials, but for the very survival of mankind torn into hostile camps.

In her struggle for a superior balance of power to insure her security, Russia has already gained a considerable influence among the subject peoples with her definite stand for their freedom from European domination. There is hardly a subject country where Russia is not looked upon as a protector and liberator. From the land of the Arabs to the defunct empire of the rising sun, every country has some political faction which looks to Moscow for support in attaining freedom. The nationalist parties in French Indo-China, the Dutch East Indies, Burma, and Malaya, all have communist leaders directing their people's fight for freedom with the moral, if not material, support from Moscow. This communist inroad into the colonial areas is going to be definitely more dangerous for the maintenance of the colonial empires than the Japanese invasion which came and went.

Hitherto, all colonial powers have allied themselves with a handful of arrogant and wealthy natives who have supported the alien rule for the protection which they have received against their poor, helpless fellow countrymen. Because of this alliance with the vested interest, the colonial powers have been able to rule their countless subjects with a handful of colonial troops. But now the Communists are shaking the very foundations of this source of the colonial power by rousing the mass of the dispossessed, who have been exploited and maltreated jointly by the alien powers and the native exploiters.

To prevent Russia from winning the colonial peoples and to prevent the subject peoples from turning toward Russia, the colonial powers have belatedly adopted measures to win the good will and co-operation of the people whom they have mercilessly exploited and oppressed for many centuries. The bait which they now use to catch the support of the submerged peoples is the promise of eventual freedom within their own commonwealth, whatever that may mean. The Dutch have offered it to the Indonesians. The French have offered it to the Indo-Chinese. The British labor government has gone further by offering the Indians freedom either inside or outside the British Commonwealth.

The question now is: Can they win the co-operation of their resentful and discontented peoples with such a bait? It seems that the degree of support which they will get will largely depend on how honestly and faithfully they will execute this kind of plan. If they use it just as another subterfuge to exploit the people, as they did the mandatory system, they will be fortunate to get back their hook and line. If they carry it out honestly and faithfully for the freedom and welfare of their colonial peoples, there is no reason why they cannot win the good will and co-operation of these people.

The Filipinos used to resent American rule. They cried out against American imperialism and exploitation as vehemently as any other colonial people. But they ceased to be enemies and became a faithful ally of America when they were definitely convinced that the United States intended to give them their independence. One will not be surprised to see the same miracle take place in the other colonies where the resentment against the ruling powers has been growing in intensity.

Win or lose, the road to liquidation appears to be the only course open for the colonial powers to take because their refusal to liberate their colonial peoples will drive them into the arms of the Russian Communists, who will be obliged to play the role of a liberator and cause the expulsion of the colonial powers by forcible means. Thus the old imperialists are faced with the alternative of either walking out of their colonies through the front door with their hats on and with the magnanimous gesture that they are moving out for the cause of freedom, or being thrown out through the window without their shirts or pants.

Under the circumstances, the best way to solve the colonial problems in the interest of peace appears to be that which was used by the builders of the United States. As is well known to all students of history, the statesmen of early America prevented the rivalry among the several states by placing the unorganized territories under the control of their federal government, instead of leaving them to the several states. In due time, when people moved in and the territories were organized into states, they were admitted into the union on an equal footing with the other states. Looking backward, the way that the territorial question was handled appears to be one of the wisest acts of statesmanship demonstrated by the builders of America.

If the civilized nations of the world are really interested in promoting peace and justice, as they undoubtedly are, they should not fail to profit by the American experiment. They should immediately place all the dependent areas under the direct supervision of the Trusteeship Council and make an honest attempt to promote the welfare of the colonial peoples. The failure to adopt such a course will inevitably lead them into conflict, not only with the subject peoples fighting for freedom, but with the rival colonial powers themselves.

Chapter XIV

A SOLUTION FOR ASIA

The foregoing brief survey of the problems of peace in Asia reveals that none of them can be solved permanently without a basis of co-operation between Russia and the Western democracies. Japan cannot be kept disarmed permanently without abating the Soviet-American rivalry in the Far East. Korea cannot be made into a peaceful democratic state without harmony between the Soviet Union and the Western democracies. China cannot be made into a united democratic republic without the Soviet-American co-operation. Nor can the problems of the Asiatic colonies be settled peacefully without harmony between the two spheres. To put it bluntly, the problems of Asia cannot be solved independently of other problems of the world.

Furthermore, in the absence of unity and co-operation, neither the Soviet Union nor the Western democracies can find peace and security in the Pacific, or anywhere else for that matter. It is due to the fact that the absence of co-operation for mutual security means a separate struggle for national security. The separate search for national security in this small world without barriers inevitably means international rivalry, the race for armaments, the race for the control of territories, and above all, it means the mutual destruction of the rival powers through war and conquest, if necessary.

Thus, the peace and security of Asia as well as the rest of the world depend on the unity and harmony between the two power blocs; and the task of working out some basis of co-operation between the two spheres has become the world's most urgent task: With these two power orbits united, there is no problem in Asia or elsewhere which cannot be solved; with the two spheres divided into hostile camps, no question of importance can be solved peacefully.

Many students and statesmen have proposed various plans for promoting unity and co-operation between Russia and the Western democracies. Some believe that the rivalry between the two power blocs can be arrested and a program of co-operation for mutual security can be launched through the conclusion of a triple alliance or a quadruple alliance between Russia and the Western democracies. The consummation of such an alliance will undoubtedly help bridge the chasm between the two hostile spheres. But it is doubtful if these rival powers with their feeling of distrust and suspicion can make such an alliance in good faith. Their repeated failures to work together for post-war reconstruction make one wonder how well the big powers can co-operate without the other nations. Even if a triple alliance were concluded, one wonders if it would last, as most such agreements in history have died a premature death. The fate of the entire world, therefore, cannot, and should not, be abandoned to this undependable combination of big powers, some of whom still seem to have an undying faith in their ability to defend themselves separately.

Some other students propose the formation of new blocs, the Asiatic bloc, the European bloc, and so forth, to checkmate the two rival blocs. But the pursuance of such a course will not make the world any safer. Besides, it is doubtful that the formation of such blocs can keep the giants with wings apart.

Of late, we have heard many speeches by Henry Wallace. His idea of promoting one world is sound, but his method to create such a world is unsound. For instance, he advises the British people and other peoples, by inference, to remain neutral between the United States and the Soviet Union. The pursuance of such a policy of neutrality will not hasten the creation of one world. He should have advised them to side with either state which pursues a policy of international co-operation for common security, while opposing either power pursuing the policy of non-co-operation and isolation.

Wallace further wonders why the great rival powers cannot solve their problems peacefully and live side by side as good friends by letting Russia mind her own business in her sphere and by letting the Western democracies mind theirs in their sphere. But it does not seem possible that such a policy can be carried out; or that it will lessen rivalry, even if it is carried out.

The world has grown so small that no state lies outside the defense zone of others. Russia lies within the first line of defense of the United States and vice versa, because an attack can be launched against either country from the territory of the other. Consequently, neither Russia nor America can let the other mind her own business until both sides are convinced that there is no risk in so doing. When there is no such assurance, neither side can afford to let the other mind its own business, lest one side or the other might use this freedom to mind its own business as a cloak to hide its preparation for world domination.

If the earth were cut into two separate parts like a melon and kept apart by millions of miles in limitless space, it might be possible for each sphere to mind its own business. But even then, if there is a remote possibility of collision, one part will try to blow the other to pieces. Only when the world is sufficiently organized like the United States to insure the security of all nations can the several states be free to mind their own business and to enjoy or suffer their own cultures and institutions without external interference. Therefore, all the nations wishing to preserve their own ideals and institutions, instead of shunning international co-operation, should co-operate wholeheartedly for the strengthening of a world organization.

The cure of a disease lies in the right diagnosis of the disease. The cure of this world's trouble lies in the correct diagnosis of the trouble.

We have seen in the beginning of this part what has brought about the present tension between Russia and the Western democracies. We have seen that what has divided the great powers into two hostile camps is not so much the difference between capitalism and communism, or that between democracy and dictatorship, as the policies of promoting national security independently. We have seen further that they have started their separate search for security when they were suddenly brought face to face without barriers, without distances, without buffer

A SOLUTION FOR ASIA

states, and above all, without a world government strong enough to protect them against each other. Assuming the soundness of this analysis, what is most urgently needed is not the scrapping of communism or capitalism, or the destruction of Russia or the Western democracies, but it is the abandonment of the separate search for national security which only increases the danger of insecurity, and the adoption of a program of co-operative search for common security, which is the only way pointing to permanent security for all nations. Unfortunately, however, the great powers, notably Russia, refuse to work together for common destiny and insist on continuing their separate search for security.

Wallace could have rendered a great service for the peace of the entire world by telling his Russian friends what they ought to be told in a friendly way. Such a speech could easily have been his best speech and the most valuable one. Since he has failed to do so, I write part of that speech in the hope that he will give it to his Russian friends someday. The best speech which Wallace has failed to give should be something like the following:

"You know as well as we do that in this small world you and we must work together and live, or work against each other and perish. Our people and government cherish no hatred against you, and we are most anxious to co-operate with you for the common security of all mankind. But you shun international co-operation and recoil into your shell of isolation like a clam. When you refuse to work with us, we are suspicious of you and we are afraid of you, not so much because you are communists and totalitarians as because you refuse to work with us. When you refuse to co-operate with us for common security, we fear that you don't like us and that you are plotting to weaken us and destroy us. Our people, therefore, are backing the democratic peoples everywhere who will work with us for the primary purpose of promoting our security.

"Don't resent our policy of aiding the Greeks, the Turks, the Chinese, the Koreans, and all other peoples who are fighting for freedom. You can cause the change of our policies in no time merely by co-operating with us for common security. Don't blame us for refusing to destroy the atom bomb. You can cause its destruction anytime by submitting to a foolproof system of international inspection and by co-operating with us for common security. We don't want to manufacture these deadly weapons of war any more than you do, but we are forced to keep on producing because you refuse to work with us for common security.

"We are a peaceful people. We don't want war any more than you do. We don't want to destroy your communism, or your system of government, although we don't like it. We don't believe in wasting our wealth and in sacrificing our sons and daughters for the purpose of imposing our system of government and economy on other peoples. All we want is that you co-operate with us for common security because neither you nor we can survive in peace and security without working together for the common destiny of all mankind.

"If you should continue your policy of non-co-operation and isolation, it will create such fear and suspicion in the hearts of our people that we will increase our aid to all democratic peoples fighting for freedom; we will step up the production of the atom bomb; we will even be forced to blast out your iron curtain and force you to co-operate with us for common security, even if such an attempt should result in our destruction. If we should ever come to blows with each other, don't blame us, for your refusal to work together for common security will be the sole cause of such a conflict."

Should Russia continue her policy of non-co-operation and of separate search for security, there are only one or two things which the other nations could try to do. One is to erect an impenetrable barrier between Russia and themselves so that neither side can endanger the survival of the other. It would be wonderful if such a barrier could be erected. But it cannot be done without destroying all science and inventions. So there is only one thing which can, and should, be done—that is to strengthen the new world organization with all available means until it grows powerful enough to protect all nations, large and small. When peaceful means should fail to make the new world organization a just and powerful instrument of international peace, the nations should not falter; they should crush all opposition, overcome all obstacles, and make it work by force, if necessary.

While recognizing the right of all peoples to have their own forms of government and to preserve their own sacred ideals and institutions, no nation should be allowed to boycott international co-operation for the maintenance of justice. Should any state refuse to support such collective movements because of the differences in ideas and institutions, it should be overthrown and its ideas and institutions should be destroyed by peaceful means, if possible, by force, if necessary. If war comes as a result, let it come. Without a strong world authority no nation will enjoy peace and security anyway. If a war must be fought, the sooner the better because it would be less destructive if it came sooner than if it came later. But force must be used only as the last resort, after all peaceful means of strengthening the UN will have failed to accomplish their objectives.

Most students of human relations seem to doubt that the nations of the world, which are so filled with hatred and jealousy, fear and suspicion, will ever succeed in uniting for peace voluntarily under the UN. They may be right, but then they may be wrong. It is hoped that they are wrong.

From time immemorial the fear of hell has probably sent more souls to heaven than the love of God. Science has destroyed one hell, but it has created a new one, a real one, in the atom bomb. So the threat of total destruction by the atom bomb rather than the love of humanity might cause modern nations to forget their petty differences and to co-operate for their common security through the UN or a similar world organization. However, if they should fail to do so within the next ten or fifteen years, they should, and probably will, be forced to do so through war, not in the distant future, but probably in our generation. The fear of total destruction in an atomic war is so great that the powerful states will not hesitate to force their rivals to co-operate for common security, or to conquer and destroy them completely, lest the failure to do so might spell their own annihilation. In other words, if the great Western nations should fail, as they probably will, to unite the world with education, philosophy and religion, and with political and economic theories and plans, they will unite mankind, dead or alive, with the atom bomb.

It is difficult to foresee what the outcome will be if all peaceful means of uniting the nations should fail, and if a disastrous conflict should take place between the two great power blocs. At present the Western democracies have a superiority in technological development, and they probably will retain such superiority for a long time despite Russia's frantic efforts to outstrip the capitalistic countries. But such technological superiority alone may not necessarily insure the winning of the war.

Atomic scientists have been telling us that the next war will be won by the party which strikes first. If that be true, the United States will lose the next war, for she does not believe in striking first. Unless she changes her traditional belief, which is held sacred, she will not strike first; she will wait until the enemy strikes. Then, unlike in 1941, it will be too late. She will have neither the energy nor the means of winning the war.

Furthermore, there are other factors than technological superiority which will help determine the outcome of such a conflict. Let us examine briefly some of these assets and liabilities of both power blocs.

Russia controls, directly or indirectly, some 10,000,000 square miles of territory with a total population of about 400,000,000. The Western democracies have in their sphere nearly 30,000,000 square miles of land with a total population of nearly 1,500,-000,000. But the area which Russia controls is contiguous, whereas the areas which the Western democracies control are scattered over the entire globe. Furthermore, most of the area and population within the Russian sphere is largely Russian. Nearly half the total population and four-fifths of the area which Russia controls is Russian. However, a large part of the area and the population within the sphere of the Western democracies is not within the circle of their home base. If China and the colonial possessions are taken out, the area and the population within the sphere of the Western powers would not be much greater than those of Russia in her sphere.

The fact that Russia is a communist state and the Western democracies are capitalistic states does not seem to give many advantages or disadvantages. Both Russian communism and Western capitalism have retreated so far from their primitive state of existence that most advantages and disadvantages formerly attributed to the two systems have disappeared.

But communism, which has been largely discarded by its own mother, Russia, has a tremendous export value. Nowhere can it find a more ready market than in Asia, where live countless millions of impoverished peasants. All that is necessary to sell it to the poor peasants is to explain to them that they are poor despite the hard labor which they have contributed year after year because what they produce with the toil of their hands goes to the landlords and the tax collectors.

Fortunately for the Communists, they do not have to explain at this moment that when the old landlords and the tax collectors are gone, a new landlord and a new tax collector representing the omnipotent state will take away from the peasants not only the fruits of their labor, but also their very right to exist as free men. Nor do the Communists have to explain to the peasants that they are poor because there are too many of them crowded into too small an area available for cultivation, and that even if all the lands were equally divided among them they would still be poor. When the whole truth is explained, communism may not sell well. But at the present time it sells literally like a hot cake. It is this communism sold to the poor peasants which constitutes one of the chief sources of Russian power in Asia today.

As all men love freedom and dislike restraints, democracy has a decided advantage over totalitarianism. No state founded on the power of compulsion alone can last, for no man will continue to be loyal to such a state. So the denial of political freedom and civil liberties to the Russian people, who have fought for their fatherland so bravely and so unselfishly, constitutes the greatest weakness of Russia in this battle for world supremacy. It is true that Russia offers to her people some compensation for the deprivation of civil liberties and political freedom, such as cultural autonomy, security of employment, religious tolerance, the sanctity of the family, and private ownership of consumable goods, if they can find them. But the Russian people are far from being satisfied with the lot mapped out for them by their state. The fact that Russia has 15,000,000 political prisoners sentenced to concentration camps and hard labor, or ten times more than the combined total for the rest of the world, seems to indicate the magnitude of discontent in the Soviet Union. When the Russian people are disloyal to their own system, the conquest of the entire world will not save it.

As is well known, the pattern of government which Russia creates in other lands in the name of freedom and democracy is the same totalitarian setup found in Russia. It is based on one party dictatorship, and that party is composed of the poor peasants who were given confiscated lands, and are under the absolute control of Russian puppets and Quislings. For some time these poor peasants, who form an overwhelming majority of Asiatic population, will be loyal to the communist puppets and take orders from Moscow without a murmur or protest. But as all men love freedom, such instruments of oppression and terrorism cannot perpetuate themselves in other lands any better than they can in Russia. So Russia's chief weakness seems to lie in her political system. Of course, she may change her course in time to save herself, but that is another story.

On the moral issues which might have an important bearing in determining the outcome of the contest for supremacy both spheres are about equal in their assets and liabilities. One of the chief moral weaknesses on both sides is their failure to practice at home what they seek to impose on others abroad. Russia fights for the freedom of other people, although she denies it to her people. She fights for the liberation of Asia's submerged millions, while she keeps her own people in chains. America denies equality to her own minorities and fights for the equality of other nations. Britain, France, and the Netherlands fight for the freedom of all peoples except their colonial peoples, whom they wish to protect and civilize. They attack the Soviet Union for adopting policies of expansion, while they themselves pursue a similar course. Conversely, Russia attacks the capitalistic states for carrying out imperialistic expansion, while she seeks to outdo those whom she attacks. Believe it or not, the pursuance of such inconsistent policies has caused the great powers to lose most of their credit as leaders of the civilized world.

The greatest moral asset of the European democracies is their professed claim to be the guardians of freedom for all mankind. But unless they can show, not only in beautiful words, but also in concrete acts, that they stand for the freedom of their colonial peoples as well as for themselves, they will not have even the pretense that they are the defenders of freedom and democracy. With the total loss of this valuable asset, they will lose their right, moral and legal, to criticize Russia, or even Germany and Japan, for the policies of conquest and domination. They will likewise lose the co-operation of countless millions of Asiatics and their rich colonial possessions to boot. Worst of all, these resentful natives will join hands with the enemies of these colonial empires wherever they can find them and will seek to settle an old score with their erstwhile masters.

On the other hand, if the European democracies honestly and sincerely work for the freedom of their colonial peoples as the United States has done in the Philippine Islands, they could gain, at the cost of losing their political control, the good will and friendship of a billion Asiatics, which will be the most valuable ally that any nation can hope to have in peace as well as in war. The present British offer of freedom to India, either in or outside the British Commonwealth, appears to be a right step toward the winning of Asiatic friendship and co-operation.

The greatest moral asset of the United States, the pivot of Western democracies, is her willingness to uphold the cause of freedom for all peoples and her repudiation of the policies of conquest and domination of other countries. Because of this, the United States of America is probably the least feared and most trusted big power on the face of the globe. What she has done in the Philippine Islands, in China, and in other parts of the world has been a source of inspiration for all Asiatic peoples. Much of this great American asset, however, has been cancelled, not only by the failure to assert her leadership in world affairs, but by the ineradicable race prejudice, which is America's greatest liability for her assumption of the moral and spiritual leadership of the world.

The repeal of the Chinese Exclusion law during the war, and the extension of the immigration quota and of the right of naturalization to the Indians and the Filipinos in July, 1946, have slightly improved American prestige in this respect, but by no means have they entirely removed the stain from the stars and stripes. In the first place, the repeal does not apply to all Asiatics. In the second place, the law has not removed or modified any of the racial discrimination against the Orientals and other minorities in the United States.

Just recently, a Chinese professor, teaching at the University of California at Los Angeles, purchased a house in the Westwood district. He was forced to move out because his refined white neighbours scattered garbage on his lawn, threw stones through his windows, and threatened to evict him by force, if necessary. And every time such an incident as this takes place against the Orientals or other minority groups, the American asset as a leader of Wetsern democracies dips like mercury before cold air.

The greatest moral asset of Russia is her determined stand against a racial discrimination, and her greatest liability is her policy of domination, which is not different from those pursued by other imperialistic powers.

In a country where all kinds of nationalities and races mingle, there is no discrimination based on racial differences, although there are discriminations based on other standards. This is very significant because a billion Asiatics who have enjoyed or suffered some form of European domination for several centuries are very sensitive about such matters. In the absence of racial discrimination, most Asiatics would more likely look to the Russians as their big brothers than they would to those who discriminate against them. As a matter of fact, Russia is already wresting the moral leadership of the submerged Asiatic millions from the United States. When her representatives to the UN decried the British, Dutch, and French colonial policies in their Asiatic possessions, a thing which the United States could not or did not do, millions of Asiatics began to look to Moscow rather than to Washington for guidance and leadership.

But Russia will not enjoy long the support of all or even most Asiatics unless she modifies or completely liquidates her policies of domination. In the event that the Russian Bear shows its naked teeth and indiscriminately preys on the helpless ones, the Orientals will rise against Russia just as they did against Japan. Besides, the public sentiment of the world will be so aroused against Russia that a new war of liberation against her aggression cannot be ruled out, a war in which the Russian bear itself might be driven into the valley of death where all aggressors have perished.

On the other hand, if Russia adopts a moderate course similar to America's good neighbor policy, she could win not only a billion Asiatics, but also millions of other peoples in America and Europe to her side. Her position then would be so impregnable, both morally and materially, that there could be nothing, not even the atomic bomb, to fear because no nation would be so foolish as to strike such a country.

Thus both sides have advantages and disadvantages in the contest for a superior balance of power to insure their survival in security. It is difficult to foretell whether the Western democracies or the Soviet Union, or some other powers will inherit the earth. But one thing seems to be clear; that is that the present rivalry among the big powers, if left to take its natural course, will inevitably result in another global war, unless one side grows so overwhelmingly powerful and the other so hopelessly weak that the latter could not dare to challenge the power of the former.

If the worst should come and the civilized world were again thrown into a titanic struggle, both the victors and the vanquished might be so completely crushed and exhausted that it would take them centuries to recover, if they ever recovered at all. At a fraction of the cost and at a fraction of the sacrifices which might be demanded of them by the next war, the civilized nations can create a warless millennium in which they shall literally beat their swords into ploughshares. But will they?